The Project & Programme Support Office Handbook

Volume 1 Foundation

The Project & Programme Support Office Handbook

Volume 1 Foundation

David E Marsh

MBA, DMS, FMS, MBCS

Project Manager Today
PUBLICATIONS

Project Manager Today

PUBLICATIONS

First published 2000 by Project Manager Today,
Unit 12 Moor Place Farm, Plough Lane, Bramshill, Hants, RG27 0RF UK www.projectnet.co.uk

ISBN for complete set of 2 volumes: 1-900391-07-4
ISBN for this volume: 1-900391-05-8

British Library CIP data
Marsh, David, 1947-
The project and programme support office handbook
Vol. 1: Foundation David E Marsh
1. Industrial project management - handbooks, manuals, etc
2. Office management - handbooks, manuals, etc
I. Title
658.4'04
ISBN 1-900391-05-8

Printed and bound in Great Britain by Intype London Ltd

For my father Leslie Marsh

Foreword

I am delighted that David Marsh has brought together his wealth of experience in these two volumes so that organisations have a ready source of reference to all aspects of creating, implementing or using a Project or Programme Office.

As businesses and organisations increasingly adopt project based structures, they realise that effective project management needs an infrastructure to support it. We have seen the rapid growth and adoption of PRINCE2 and with it the development of qualifications in that method. There has also been an explosion in the provision for training and qualifications in project management. However, while many people have implemented project and programme offices successfully, there is little guidance readily available to steer them towards success.

With the launch of an ISEB qualification in Project and Programme Support and the publication of these two volumes which mirror the syllabus, anyone thinking of starting a PSO or looking for help will find it here.

David Marsh comes from an engineering and IT background. Although many of the examples given in these two volumes come from the world of IT, their application is universal. David has seen at first hand the problems and solutions adopted by many different organisations developing both 'virtual' and 'real' PSOs.

Now anyone can share his experiences and the world of projects will be all the richer his contribution.

Ken Lane
Editor
Project Manager Today

Contents

Chapter One

The need for the PSO and what it provides

1. The raison d'etre for the PSO

Unless an organisation only ever executes one programme or a very small number of projects there is a vital need to establish some form of programme and/or, project support office (PSO). This need increases not only with the number of programmes and projects the organisation undertakes, but also with the importance the organisation places upon them.

All programmes and projects are transient by nature. They are defined, commissioned, executed and closed – they do not form a continuous process. Without a PSO the organisation will be forced to develop a supporting infrastructure for each new programme and project and, very importantly, the lessons learnt will not be passed on.

In addition, without some central focus point, monitoring and control can become a logistical and actual nightmare.

The PSO provides the organisation with a focus and the means to:

- **maintain, update and extend the scope of the programme and project support infrastructure;**
- **support the planning of the programme and projects;**
- **support the monitoring and control of the programmes and projects;**
- **ensure the programme and projects have the required technical and business integrity;**
- **provide a repository for the experience and knowledge gained;**

- **audit the use of the programme and project support infrastructure.**

A PSO can be implemented either as a physical entity or a logical entity, or a combination of the two. The physical entity usually entails the establishment of a team of staff allocated to the office. A logical implementation requires no staff to carry out the functions as they are generally executed by the systems, procedures and processes themselves.

However, logical implementations must have a custodian and be supervised. It is essential to establish a process, or a person, to ensure that this monitoring and control takes place and to be the focus for the definition and implementation of any necessary updating.

2. What Should a Programme and or Project Support Office Provide?

This obviously depends on the organisation and the scope of the programmes and projects it undertakes.

Having implemented a PSO, the functionality and support provided can be extended to assist the programme and project management processes. In some organisations this has meant PSOs become an essential part of the process, for example organising contracts or purchases. In extreme situations PSOs create and manage the programme or project themselves.

This extension of PSO functionality into these added value areas is largely dependent upon the environment in which the organisation operates. In relatively stable environments, PSOs are likely to assume their traditional role of support to the programme and project management process. However, in a more volatile environment they are likely to be agents of change.

However, it is possible to define certain functions which nearly all PSOs support, across organisations. These are listed below in terms of both Project and Programme Support Offices. Although, it is worth stressing again that the functions PSOs provide may vary considerably.

3. Project Support Offices

The typical functions are as follows:

3.1 The Definition and Planning of the Project

Most projects do not exist in isolation. They are very likely to be part of a programme or portfolio of projects. The PSO can assist the organisation in defining each of the component projects. In particular, assisting in the identification and establishment of any links that exist between projects and the nature and content of such interfaces.

The support provided by the PSO to the project planning process often overlaps with that of programme support; they are both involved in the development of projects plans, though from different perspectives. These overlaps are usually addressed by the organisation using the same basic information, but applied in two ways. For example, organisations will use an extremely "broad brush" approach to programme planning, while project planning tends to be more detailed. What is important is that these processes interlink and use a consistent approach.

3.2 The Quantification of the Costs and Benefits of the Project

The initial quantification of the costs and benefits of an individual project may have been carried out as part of the definition of the programme that contains it. This high level analysis produces a degree of accuracy suitable for the programme definition process, but will not be precise enough for individual projects. Therefore it is common practice to update and refine the initial coarse analysis into a detailed and more accurate assessment.

This process can be carried out by the project's development team – however it is unusual for such a team to possess all the skills needed to prepare the analysis. In addition, the need for a consistent approach and the use of standard accounting and other conventions (including impartiality) often means this analysis is better prepared by the PSO or another independent team.

3.3 Assessment and Management of Risk

As at the programme level, there is an element of risk in all projects.
There is a wide range of approaches available for identifying and managing such risks. The PSO can ensure that this process is:

- carried out;
- consistent;
- regularly updated;
- reflecting experience gained and/or lessons learnt;
- facilitated.

As with the support provided to the quantification process, the PSO must ensure that it has the information required for this process and the skills to ensure that it has been correctly applied. The unique position of the PSO in being able to see across all the projects also ensures that any new risks, avoidance and containment strategies that are developed can be applied to other projects as appropriate.

3.4 The Monitoring and Control Process

Once the project has been initiated the relevant project board must ensure that it regularly monitors the progress made and, if necessary, instigate control action. The PSO can serve both the individual projects and the programme by carrying out this function. It can also help to identify where any actual or potential bottlenecks occur.

To ensure that this support is efficient and effective, it is essential that the function is integrated with the planning process and the collection of "actuals", so that the collection of information and its collation into progress reports can be made with ease and accuracy.

The monitoring and control process can be further supported by the production of "what if" analyses of the eventual project outcome. Efficient and effective monitoring requires this function to be planned and modelled before the systems that are to provide the information are developed and implemented.

3.5 The Supply of Experience and Knowledge – Knowledge Management

Typically the PSO supplies the organisation with information on experiences and knowledge gained from previous projects for current projects. This can at its simplest be advice and, at the other extreme, coaching. The PSO may have staff or other resources which it supplies to projects to form either the project management team and/or specialists to assist the projects work.

Adopting this type of PSO enables a level of consistency across projects which is otherwise difficult to attain. Indeed if such a centralised function is supported by an effective and efficient infrastructure of procedures, systems and standards, it is possible to have project management team members involved in simultaneous projects. This strategy has enabled some organisations to dramatically reduce the number of project managers they require.

3.6 Supporting the Project Management Process and Procedures

Under this heading can be found a wide variety of activities. Rather than list them all, it is better to consider what support may be required. Typically this includes:

- **updating and maintaining project management documents;**
- **project accounting;**

- resource contract administration;
- capital goods acquisition;
- liaison with external suppliers;
- contract and other negotiations;
- work plans and timesheets;
- progress reports;
- standards definition;
- quality control review administration & organisation;
- administration;
- filing;
- configuration management.

Before the project is commissioned, it must be decided which of these are delegated to the PSO and which should be carried out by specialist departments, the project manager or the project development team. The need to plan and co-ordinate the development of a supporting infrastructure for projects is often overlooked. All too often PSO's end up with a disjointed collection of functions rather than an integrated infrastructure. This occurs because the functions were not developed and implemented as part of an overall plan, and were simply taken onboard because it seemed a logical thing to do at the time!

3.7 Capturing Experience and Knowledge
The final function and, for many organisations, the main reason for a PSO, is the capturing of information about the experiences and knowledge gained from previous projects. The widespread use of structured approaches to project management and system development has assisted this by providing a framework for the collection of experience and knowledge. The PSO helps frameworks by providing data on:

- skills used on previous projects;
- skills available in the organisation;
- project or system development methods that work and those that do not;
- development metrics;
- common faults found at quality control reviews;
- example products.

This information must be collected and collated so that it can be "recycled" for the good of future programmes and projects.

3.8 Providing Specialist Skills

As stated earlier, the staffing of a PSO can be on a logical rather than a physical basis. The logical basis is where the project support infrastructure holds all the information and support tools required to assist the project manager to complete his tasks. However that infrastructure will need to be maintained and updated. The skills and experience needed to carry out this maintenance and updating may be located in a number of places in the organisation – including the project managers who use the infrastructure.

If it is decided to establish a physical PSO then the organisation will need to allocate staff to this function who have the following skills and experience:

- **project management;**
- **quality management;**
- **configuration management;**
- **planning and control;**
- **risk analysis;**
- **consultancy support;**
- **information administration and management.**

3.9 The Project Support Infrastructure

One of the key roles of the PSO is to maintain and update the project support infrastructure (or even build it.)

This infrastructure usually contains the following:

- **the agreed procedures and standards to be used by the project manager;**
- **example documents from previous projects;**
- **metrics and other resource usage information from previous projects;**
- **the resource and other asset registers for the organisation;**
- **software and other tools to assist with all the project management processes.**

4. Programme Support Offices

The typical functions that a Programme Support Office undertakes or supports are as follows:

4.1 The Definition of the Programme Contents
– Strategic and Business Planning Support

The responsibility for identifying the need for, and content of, the programme rests with the organisation' s strategic and business planning function. This is initially assisted by the programme director(s) and, later, by the remainder of the individual programme executive or board – the business change, technical, or design manager and the programme manager.

The PSO can support this process by gathering, analysing and presenting information to help identify business areas the programme is to address and its goals. This support role can be purely administrative or it can include the gathering and analysis of inter-organisation or departmental information to provide benchmarks and targets for the programme. Such support is vital to ensure that any decisions made and goals set are based on fact rather than supposition.

4.2 The Quantification of the Costs and Benefits of the Programme

Once the direction and content of the business strategy and the supporting programmes has been decided, it is vital to quantify their benefits and costs. There are a number of such quantifications required. These include:

- **the benefits planned to be realised;**
- **the resources required to implement the programme/s;**
- **the availability of resources, at the right time, and in the required quantity/quality.**

To support these processes the PSO will require access to data held by a number of the organisation's departments. For the PSO to obtain access to the appropriate level of accurate and up-to-date information can involve considerable changes in working practices and procedures. Experience has shown that a failure to appreciate this and firstly to model the information requirements prior to installing an information gathering process and support system, can result in either an over bureaucratic system or one that operates with inaccurate information.

4.3 Assessment and Management of Risk

When embarking on deliberate programmes of change the number of, and level of, risks increase dramatically. There are a wide range of approaches to identify and manage such risks. The PSO can help ensure that this process is:

- **carried out;**
- **consistent;.**
- **regularly updated;**
- **reflecting experience gained and/or lessons learnt;**
- **facilitated.**

As with the support provided to the quantification process the PSO must ensure that it has the information required to support this process fully and the skills to see that it has been correctly applied.

4.4 The Identification and Initiation of the Component Projects

The PSO can provide a range of support services to the programme manager(s) in the identification and initiation of the constituent programmes and projects. The services and information systems which are needed to enable it to perform these functions can be free-standing, or interlinked with those used for project support. This information typically includes:

- **project or system development methods and metrics;**
- **resource and asset availability;**
- **planning and control standards and systems;**
- **project risk assessment information.**

The major support provided by the PSO is the research and production of "position" and other papers and the initiation of the constituent projects.

4.5 The Programme Monitoring and Control Process

Once the programme(s) have been established the organisation must ensure that it regularly monitors the progress made and, if necessary, instigates control action. The PSO can serve both the programme(s) and individual projects by carrying out this function. It can also identify where any actual or potential bottlenecks occur. In order for this support to be efficient and effective, it is essential that this function is also planned and modeled *before* it is installed, enabling ease and accuracy in the collection and collation of the progress reports.

4.6 Capturing Experience and Knowledge Gained

It is very likely that having carried out one programme the organisation will commission others. It is vital that the lessons learnt and the experience gained is captured for use on these subsequent programme(s). The information collected may be about the opportunities and, or, the problems encountered in executing the programme and the constituent projects. It is also important for the PSO to collect and analyse the difference between what was planned and what actually occured. Allowances can be made for this in future, or counter-measures employed to contain it.

4.7 Providing Specialist Skills

As stated previously, the PSO can operate on a logical basis rather than physical one. In the logical PSO the programme support infrastructure may hold all the information and support tools required to assist the programme manager(s). The skills and experience needed to carry out the maintenance and updating of this logical PSO infrastructure can be located in a number of places in the organisation.

A physical PSO requires the organisation to allocate staff to it, either on a full or part-time basis, who have the following skills and experience:

- business analysis;
- financial analysis;
- information and other technology specialists;
- planning and control;
- strategic and business risk analysis and management;
- programme and project management;
- information administration and management.

4.8 The Programme Support Infrastructure

One of the key roles of the PSO is to build, maintain and update the programme support infrastructure.
Typically this infrastructure contains the following:

- the agreed procedures and standards to be used by the programme manager;
- example documents from previous projects and programmes;
- metrics and other resource usage information from previous projects;
- the resource and other asset registers for the organisation;

- **software and other tools to assist with all the programme management processes.**

5. Establishing the Costs and Benefits of a PSO

It is vital that the organisation has an accurate and agreed definition of the programme or project support office's terms of reference and also the business case for its establishment and operation. Without this, the true purpose of the PSO will not be understood and the organisation will not obtain the added value benefits. Also, without these definitions it is very likely that there will be confusion about the role of the PSO, often leaving it to decline into an administration support unit. This section examines how the organisation should define the reasons for the PSO and its business case.

5.1 Establish the Reason for the PSO

Why does the organisation need such an investment? Define the terms of reference before constructing a business case to justify the investment. This definition must identify the functions that the PSO is to supply or support and the scope (extent or use) of the services it provides.

See example: **The terms of reference for a PSO** *(at the end of this chapter)*

The reasons for establishing a PSO can be classified into two categories:

- **direct financial;**
- **qualitative and indirect financial.**

5.1.1 Direct Financial

The direct financial benefits are those that typically reduce the effort needed by the programme and project manager, an expensive resource, to carry out the programme and project management processes.

Ideally, the person who prepares the business case should carry out a quantification, or work measurement survey, to identify how much effort is spent at present on such activities, and then estimate what reduction in effort and cost will be achieved by the use of a PSO.

To give a guide, experience has shown that without a PSO a programme or project manager spends between seven and 17 % of his or her time on the operation of project and programme management processes. This percentage can be reduced by over 50% if the PSO provides support to all the major infrastructure functions such as planning, monitoring and control.

5.1.2 Qualitative and Indirect Financial

In this category are those PSOs that are installed primarily to achieve better control of programme and project management processes and to ensure that the organisation benefits from the experience or knowledge gained from other programmes and projects.

There are some quantifiable benefits but they tend to be intangible or indirect. The business case is based on cost avoidance examples rather than direct savings.

Example of cost avoidance are:

- **reduction in effort putting right repeated mistakes;**
- **reduction in effort in developing standards.**

5.2 Developing the Business Case – Costs of the PSO

A common mistake made when developing an analysis of the costs is not to look widely enough into the organisation to identify and assess them. The following checklist helps ensure that this does not happen and provides a start point for the analyst.

5.2.1 The Cost of Services Provided by the PSO

The collection of the data/information to be provided:

- **define the data/ information that will be required;**
- **calculate the cost of the collection and cleaning of the data;**
- **estimate/calculate the cost of the storage of the data.**

The cost of the PSO infrastructure:

- **define the contents of the programme or project support infrastructure to be provided;**
- **estimate/calculate the cost of the development and installation of that infrastructure;**
- **identify and define the cost of maintaining the infrastructure.**

The cost of non-use – define the costs that organisation will incur in:

- – having the PSO staff research and identify the support needed for the programmes and projects of the future;
- – preparing the infrastructure to support the programmes and projects of the future.

5.3 Developing the Business Case – Benefits

As with costs it is all too easy not to look widely enough into the organisation when assessing the benefits. The following checklist has been used to ensure that this does not happen and to provide a start point for the benefits calculation.

5.3.1 The Benefits provided by the PSO

Knowledge Capture:
- – what will be the reduction in effort required by programme and project managers to develop programme and project management process documents (e.g. project plans and reports)?

Central Focus
- – what are the benefits from having either a central audit or policing function?
- – what are the benefits of having spare resources to assist with programme or projects if required (e.g. in the event of absence due to unforeseen circumstances etc.)?

Added Value
- – what is the worth to the organisation of having the experience of one programme or project being available to others?

Centre of Excellence
- – what is the benefit to the organisation of not re-relearning from or repeating previous errors and mistakes?
- – what is the benefit of shortening the learning curve of new programme and project managers?

See example: **Typical business case for a PSO** *(at the end of this chapter)*

5.4 Other Considerations

The PSO can also assume the role of the auditor of, or consultant to, the individual programme and project managers. If this role is incorporated into the business case then a benefit equal to the cost of procuring this service from other sources should be included.

In developing the business case it is also worth considering whether the PSO should operate a recharge mechanism to those parts of the organisation that are using its services.

If it is decided to operate on a recharge basis then the justification of the PSO becomes both simpler and more complicated. It becomes simpler because the justification for its existence is made by the people who use it – ie, they will not use it if it does not provide value for money. However, it becomes more complicated because the PSO has to be "sold" to the organisation and those who will use its services. Also the cost benefit analysis can become more complex.

6. Summary

The need for an organisation to implement and install a PSO largely depends on its own environment, as do the functions to be provided.

What is critical is that:

- **the needs of the organisation for these services are defined;**
- **they are implemented in an integrated framework to obtain the maximum benefit from the investment in programmes and projects, and capture and retain the experience and knowledge acquired for future reference.**

Example   Terms of Reference for a PSO

Background and Purpose of the PSO
The XXX project support office (PSO) has been implemented to provide support to XXX in the definition, monitoring and control of its portfolio of projects and business as usual activities.

The PSO is to install and maintain the infrastructure of information and other supporting systems needed to provide value added services to the organisation.

Objectives of the PSO
The XXX PSO is to design, implement and maintain the infrastructure provided for the support of the portfolio of projects undertaken by the organisation.

The measures of success to be applied are:

1.   The infrastructure is viewed as providing value added services to :
              The senior management team.
              The sales team.
              The XXX line and resource managers.
              The XXX project managers.

2.   The infrastructure is actively used and promoted by its users.

3.   The infrastructure is maintained and updated to ensure that year on year it's perceived worth is increased.

Scope of the PSO
The scope of the PSO activities are defined as:

The implementation and support of processes, and information systems needed to support the XXX management strategic and tactical planning process. The implementation and support of processes and information systems to support the presales and sales activities of XXX.

The design, development and implementation of a project support infrastructure consisting of:

      Project management methods and supporting standards and templates.
      Project or system development methods and supporting template plans and deliverable library.
      Estimating guidelines.
      Training and support for project managers.

Constraints
The PSO is to provide the above services within the following budget of £xxx per annum and using XXX full time staff at grade XXX.

All extensions to the coverage and contents of the infrastructure must be cost justified in the form of a business case submitted to and approved by XXX senior management.

Reporting
In respect of line management the XXX PSO will report to Mr. xxxxx the head of xxxx.

In respect of the support required by and provided to the senior management the XXX PSO will report to Mr. xxxxxx.

In respect of the support required by and provided to the sales team the XXX PSO will report to Mr. xxxxxx.

In respect of the support required by and provided to the project managers the XXX PSO will report to Mr. xxxxxx.

EXAMPLE   PSO BUSINESS CASE

Introduction
The following document describes the business case for the development and operation of the proposed programme and project office (PPO) for XXXX. This document has been developed in conjunction with the proposed terms of reference for the PPO attached as annex one.

The Aim of the PPO
The PPO will perform the following major functions:

1. Support the masterplan committee in ensuring that XXX has a portfolio of programmes and projects that will enable it to meet its strategic goals and targets.
2. Support the masterplan committee in monitoring and controlling the agreed portfolio.
3. Supporting programme and project managers in using the organisation's programme and project support infrastructure.
4. Act as the custodians of the programme and project support infrastructure.

Options Examined
The options examined in this business case for developing and operating this service are:

- In house build and operation of the PPO.

- Outsourcing the development or the PPO, leaving its operation in house.

- Outsourcing both development and operation of the PPO.

The Development of the PPO
The development of the PPO will involve the following activities.

1. Establish a project board and user liaison group for the PPO project.
2. Establish the masterplan committee.
3. Establish a programme and project lifecycle that interfaces with the organisations business planning, budgeting, manpower planning and other related processes.
4. Researching the current portfolio of programmes and projects – developing the masterplan and linking it to the existing business strategy, goals and targets.
5. Develop and establish programme and project reporting process
6. Development of programme and project management methods
7. Develop programme and project management support Infrastructure
8. Develop project and system development methods and associated templates.
9. Develop remainder of the project support infrastructure
10. Develop programe and project management handbook.
11. Develop and provide training in the new processes.

Estimates of Effort for the Development

Development	Man Days
1. Establish a project board and user liaison group for the PPO project.	10
2. Establish the masterplan committee.	10
3. Establish a programme and project lifecycle that interfaces with the organisations business planning, budgeting, manpower planning and other related processes.	40
4. Researching the current portfolio of programmes and projects - developing the masterplan and linking it to the existing business strategy, goals and targets.	40
5. Develop and establish programme and project reporting process	20
6. Development of programme and project management methods	30
7. Develop programme and project management support infrastructure	35
8. Develop project and system development methods and associated templates.	70
9. Develop remainder of the project support infrastructure	100
10. Develop programe and project management handbook.	40
11. Develop and provide training in the new processes.	50
Contingency 12.5%	**55**
Total Developer Man Days	500
Total User Days (1,2,3,4,5,7,8,9,11)	500

Operation of the PPO
Once the development has been completed the PPO will provide the following services.

1. Maintenance of the masterplan, including progress reports.
2. Support of the masterplan committee.
3. Research work for the masterplan committee.
4. Provision of information to other business departments.
5. Provision of coaching to programe and project managers.
6. Assistance with planning and using other parts of the programme and project support infrastructure.
7. Maintenance and updating of the programme and project management infrastructure.

Operation	Man Days
1. Maintenance of the masterplan, including progress reports.	200
2. Support of the masterplan committee.	100
3. Research work for the masterplan committee.	100
4. Provision of information to other business departments.	50
5. Provision of coaching to programe and project managers.	100
6. Assistance with planning and using other parts of the programme and project support infrastructure.	100
7. Maintenance and updating of the programme and project management infrastructure.	50
Contingency 12.5%	100
Total Man Days	800

Benefits

Quantitative 1	Current	Future	Saving	Direct Financial Benefit
Increase in number of projects managed by each project manager.	Each manager looks after 1 project.	Each manager looks after 2 projects 1 large and one small.	Elimination of recruitment of 3 project managers	3 x £60,000
Reduce number of programmes and projects	Current portfolio is 150	Estimated to be £100	Reduction in number of contractors required	10 x £100,000
Elimination of unnecessary programmes or projects	Currently £3 million expenditure	Reduced by 10%	10% of £3 million	300,000
				£980,000
Quantitative 2	**Current**	**Future**	**Saving**	**In Direct Financial Benefit**
Reduction in effort in correcting repeated mistakes.	Currently approx. 1000 man days per year	Reduced to 250	750 Man days	750 x £200
Time spent by staff developing standards.	Currently 75 man days per year	Eliminated	75 man days	75 x £200
Reduction in external audit requirements.	Currently 40 days per year	Time spent on each reduced	10 man days	10 x £1000
Reduction in the time new project managers take to "bed in".	Currently 6 weeks	Operational (with coaching after one week)	25 man days x 1.5	25 x 1.5 x £300
				£186,250

Cost Profiles –   External Developer £700 per day, External Operation £500 per day, Internal Developer £300 per day, Internal Operation £ 250 per day, Users £200 per day

Cost Benefit Analysis

Option One	Year 0	Year 1	Year 2	Year 3
Costs				
Development	275,000			
Operation	100,000	200,000	200,000	200,000
Total Costs	375,000	200,000	200,000	200,000
Benefits		1,136,250	1,136,250	1,136,250
Net Cash Flow	(375,000)	936,250	936,250	936,250
Discount Factor	1	.909	.826	.751
Net Present Value (NPV)	(375,000)	851,051	773,342	703,123
Cum NPV	(375,000)	476,051	1,249,393	1,952,516

Option Two	Year 0	Year 1	Year 2	Year 3
Costs				
Development	475,000			
Operation	100,000	200,000	200,000	200,000
Total Costs	575,000	200,000	200,000	200,000
Benefits		1,136,250	1,136,250	1,136,250
Net Cash Flow	(575,000)	936,250	936,250	936,250
Discount Factor	1	.909	.826	.751
Net Present Value (NPV)	(575,000)	851,051	773,342	703,123
Cum NPV	(575,000)	276,051	1,049,393	1,752,516

Option Three	Year 0	Year 1	Year 2	Year 3
Costs				
Development	475,000			
Operation	200,000	400,000	400,000	400,000
Total Costs	675,000	400,000	400,000	400,000
Benefits		1,136,250	1,136,250	1,136,250
Net Cash Flow	(675,000)	736,250	736,250	736,250
Discount Factor	1	.909	.826	.751
Net Present Value (NPV)	(675,000)	669,251	608,142	552,923
Cum NPV	(675,000)	(5749)	602,393	1,155,316

Risk and Sensitivity Analysis
The major risks to this project are:

1. Delayed implementation (up to 6 months).
2. Only achieving 50% of the benefits.
3. Internal development and operation costing up to 25% more.

Effect of Risks on the Cost Benefit Analysis

Baseline	Approx. Cum Year 3
Option One Cum NPV	1,952,516
Option Two Cum NPV	1,752,516
Option Three Cum NPV	1,155,316
Risk One	
Option One Cum NPV	1,852,516
Option Two Cum NPV	1,652,516
Option Three Cum NPV	1,055,316
Risk Two	
Option One Cum NPV	248,141
Option Two Cum NPV	48141
Option Three Cum NPV	(549059)
Risk Three	
Option One Cum NPV	1,709,516
Option Two Cum NPV	1,577,516
Option Three Cum NPV	1,155,316

As a result of the evaluation of the impact of the risks – Option three has been eliminated, Option one provides the highest benefit even if development and operation costs are increased by 25%. Option two however is very close to Option one .

Recommendation
The recommended option is a combination of one and two – in that the development activity is supported extensively with external consultants and internal staff operate the PPO.

Chapter Two

Programme and Project Organisation Structures

1. Introduction

A crucial aspect of a programme or project management method is the organisation structure. It is an indispensable interface between the organisation and the programme or project team. A specific organisation structure ensures that the organisation retains ownership of the programme or project throughout its execution, ensuring it retains a business rather than a technical focus.

Failure to build a satisfactory interface will result in the programme or project becoming the property of the developers rather than the organisation. This, of course, means it is unlikely to be viewed as a success by the organisation.

This chapter looks in detail at these structures – what they seek to achieve, what they consist of, and how they are tailored to fit a particular programme or project.

2. Why Programme and Project Management Need an Organisation Structure

Organisations commission programmes and projects to achieve business benefits. However this crucial fact is often forgotten during the execution of the development activities. The organisation structure ensures that:

- **the organisation retains control;**
- **the organisation understands its responsibilities for the programme or project;**
- **the programme or project manager receives direction from the "right" person;**
- **the organisation knows who to contact about the programme or project;**

- **the programme or project manager knows who to contact;**
- **management of the programme or project is efficient.**

Underpinning all such organisation structures is the rule that the management of a programme or project must address three main issues:

- **why investment in the programme or project is needed**
- **what the programme or project is to deliver or achieve**
- **how the programme or project is delivered.**

The first two are clearly the responsibility of senior management, the last is for the programme or project manager. Without a formal structure with defined roles, these responsibilities can be switched with dire consequences for the programme or project.

Diagram 1 **The Responsibility Pyramid**

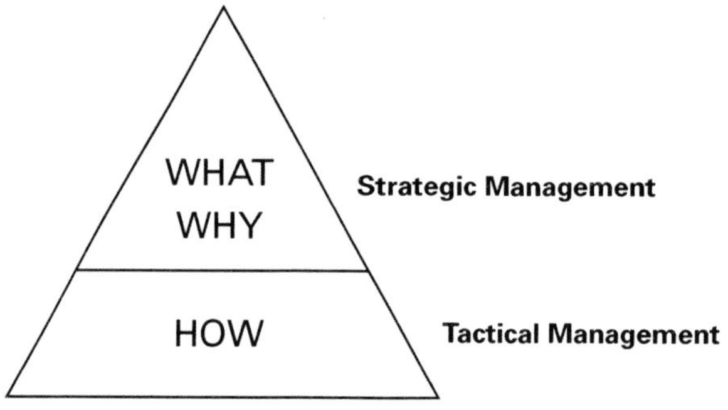

The Programme/Project Responsibility Pyramid

Another major problem that the organisation structure addresses is the "rule of nine." Unless there is an organisation structure, with defined responsibilities, the programme or project manager will often require at least nine meetings with other managers to get a decision.

3. The Typical Programme Organisation Structure

A number of programme and project management methods recommend organisation structures. This section looks at what these typically are and what they are designed to achieve.

Programmes are commissioned to achieve large-scale change(s) – or they control a large amount of investment. Therefore the level of management involved in deciding the what and why of the programme, is the most senior in the organisation. A programme organisation structure must link the decision making in the programme to the organisation's strategic decision making process. To open this channel effectively, a senior manager – usually a member of the organisation's board – becomes the programme director or sponsor.

Diagram 2 **Programme Organisation Structure**

```
┌─────────────────────────────────────────┐
│        Strategic Management              │
└─────────────────────────────────────────┘
                    │
                    ▼
┌─────────────────────────────────────────┐
│      Programme Executive Board           │
├──────────────┬──────────────┬───────────┤
│  Programme   │ Business     │  Design    │
│  Director    │ Change       │  Authority │
│              │ Manager      │            │
└──────────────┴──────────────┴───────────┘
                    │
                    ▼
        ┌─────────────────────────┐
        │   Programme Manager      │
        └─────────────────────────┘
```

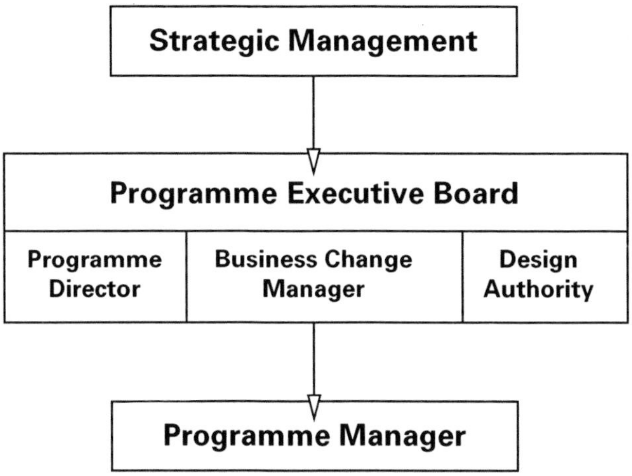

3.1 The Programme Director or Sponsor

This role requires a person who can achieve the following:

- **full delegated authority for all decisions that affect the programme;**

- **recruit a programme team with the right skills and knowledge;**

- **motivate and involve end users and suppliers;**

- **allow adequate contingency or tolerance to reflect the scale of the changes undertaken;**

- **apply continued focus on the long term – the programme vision and the benefits it should provide.**

The programme director or sponsor's role is challenging and requires a special set of abilities and skills. It must be a senior management appointment, with the power to resolve issues quickly and effectively.

3.2 The Programme Executive or Board

The programme director will need assistance in managing the programme and its delivery from a number of other senior managers in the organisation. This assistance is obtained effectively from a programme executive or board, which can provide the following:

- **management of the changes that need to take place for the programme to succeed;**
- **management of the delivery of the defined business benefits (business integrity);**
- **efficient co-ordination of the projects within the portfolio;**
- **successful introduction of the new business systems and architectures (technical integrity).**

The strategy the organisation uses to acheive this assistance varies considerably. In a classical implementation the programme board usually groups these roles into four areas with the following titles:

- **programme director or sponsor: responsible for the programme;**
- **programme manager: responsible for the co-ordination of the overall programme and the constituent projects;**
- **business change manager/s: responsible for the business integrity of the programme and management of changes and realisation of benefits;**
- **design authority: responsible for the technical integrity of the programme.**

The final part of the structure is the PSO (Programme or Project Support Office). Its role is to provide support to the whole of the programme organisation structure. The nature of this support is specific to each organisation and programme.

Like all organisation structures, many people can be allocated to, or share, one role. Or a person can have more than one role. In addition, it may be necessary to create other groups to assist in the delivery of the functions – the formation of a programme liaison group is common.

The Serious Fraud Office (SFO) undertook a major programme to redesign and implement the investigation of large-scale fraud cases. The programme involved the complete re-engineering of the collection of evidence and a move to team investigation of the evidence. In addition new methods of preparing and presenting this evidence to court were to be developed.

To investigate these cases the SFO uses a large number of specialist skills including lawyers, law clerks, accountants, forensic computer specialists, administration staff and the police.

To ensure that all these staff had an opportunity to be part of the programme, a user liaison group consisting of managers from all the departments affected by the changes, was formed. This group assisted the programme and the members of the board by providing a sounding board for the many changes that were required to complete the programme.

In some organisations the role of the programme board is allocated to other committees or functions. There may not be a formal programme executive or board in a physical sense – it can be a logical grouping with named individuals allocated to the various roles.

The tuning of these structures to reflect the specific needs of a programme must be made with care to ensure that nothing critical is omitted or overlooked.

4.   The Typical Project Organisation Structure

Projects are commissioned to develop or deliver specific deliverables. The project may be part of a portfolio either within a programme, or independently. They can be either small in size or affect all of the business. Thus the organisation structure must represent the appropriate level of management.

Diagram 3 **Programme/Project Organisation Structure**

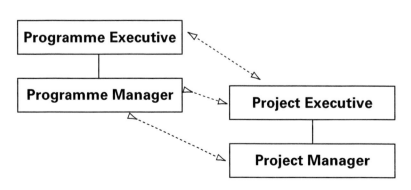

The project organisation structure must link the project's decision-making to that of a programme, or to the strategic decision-making process of the organisation.

To effectively open this channel a senior manager – usually a member of the programme executive/board or the organisation's board – is allocated as the executive member of the project board.

In some organisations there is also a project director or sponsor. This role equates to that in programme management of the programme director – the project director or sponsor sits on the project board as the executive member.

Exceptionally the project director or sponsor remains outside of the formal structure and has a role, which is more accurately named the project champion.

The project board is designed to ensure:

- **the changes that need to take place for the project to succeed are properly managed;**
- **the delivery of the defined business benefits (business integrity) is managed;**
- **the business systems affected by the changes brought by the project are successfully introduced (technical integrity);**
- **the activities within the project are efficiently co-ordinated.**

Therefore the roles typically adopted in the project board are:

- **Executive member: Responsible for ensuring the business integrity of the project (and possibly the link to any programme that contains the project);**
- **Senior user: Responsible for providing assistance to the project team in respect of ensuring the users are involved in the specification, development, testing and implementation of the deliverables (and as a consequence assisting the changes to occur)**
- **Senior supplier: Responsible for the provision of resources to the project and also the technical integrity of the deliverables.**

A further role that needs to be allocated is that of assurance. The term assurance is used to describe the processes of continual audit of the project management method and the execution of the project. The areas of the project where assurance is needed – e.g. cost, performance, user acceptance etc. – and the way that assurance is provided to the project board varies from project to project.

This assurance role can either be allocated to the members of the project board or to separate teams. The typical project organisation structure does not have the project manager as a member of the project board.

A number of methods also have defined roles for the project leaders or team managers. This member of the project management organisation structure is a scaled-down version of the project manager role.

5. Tuning the Organisation Structure to the Requirements of a Specific Programme or Project

It would be impossible to describe all the possible permutations and tuning of the organisation structures. Below are some of the most common tailorings.

5.1 Programme Organisation Structure

One of the major problems is the source of the funding for the programme.

CASE STUDY

In one part of the MOD the budgeting systems used meant that the programme director/sponsor did not have direct control over all the resources needed by the programme.

To accommodate this deficiency the organisation either had to modify its normal budgeting process to give the programme director the responsibility for the budget or incorporate the budget holder into the programme executive. This problem was solved by tailoring the structure as follows:

At the top level there was a programme board responsible for all programmes. A programme executive (a mini programme board) was formed consisting of the budget holders and departmental managers and the programme manager, to manage the programme on a daily basis.

CASE STUDY

In a financial organisation a large programme was commissioned to introduce a new series of products based on credit cards with microchips.

This programme affected numerous departments, so there was a plethora of managers who were candidates for the programme executive or board. To deal with the situation, the organisation formed a programme implementation committee with all these managers as members. Two of them were appointed to the programme board as the business change managers.

CASE STUDY

The Post Office was faced with a major communication and liaison problem between its many programmes.

This was tackled in two ways. Firstly, by having a common programme director for several programmes. Secondly, it allocated a programme consultant (who also dealt with all investigation and preparatory work needed by the programme director) to support up to four programme managers.

In these examples the organisation took the standard roles and, finding they did not fit either their programmes or the organisation structure, modified the standard organisation structure so that all the normal functionality was present in their non-standard organisation structure.

5.2 Project Organisation Structure

Similar tailoring is often required for the project organisation structure.

CASE STUDY

In one of the Inland Revenue's most important projects, the development resources were being supplied by an external organisation. To ensure that the two organisations worked together two project boards were established.

The "customer-only" project board made all the strategic decisions and a second, joint project board was responsible for the day-to-day management of the project.

CASE STUDY

The DTI had a project which affected users in 27 of its departments. To ensure that the project board was not swamped, a user liaison group was formed with its chairman assuming the role of senior user on the project board.

A German computer equipment manager had a severe shortage of experienced project managers. To tackle this the organisation upgraded the support provided by the PSO by using junior or trainee project managers to carry out a large number of the tasks typically performed by the project manager. This enabled one experienced project manager to supervise a number of projects simultaneously.

As with programme management – the structure will need to be modified to reflect the organisation and the projects themselves.

6. Summary

Both programme and project board members are always very busy outside of their programmes or projects. It is vital that they understand their role and if they delegate part of it, they must ensure that the tasks are performed with diligence and application. Both the programme and project boards are decision-making bodies and it is vital for the members to perform that function – not to be simply talking shops.

When tailoring the organisation structure *always* start with the basics, make sure that no roles or responsibilities are ever eliminated. When allocating a role to individuals it is vital that they fully understand and agree to their role – and that those elements of the role which they cannot perform are given to those who can.

Chapter Three

Programme and Project Planning

1. Introduction

One of the first skills that any programme or project manager is taught is how to develop a plan – this process is the truly creative part of their role. To the outsider the creation of the plan seems to be a "black art"; however it's only a series of processes, supported by techniques. Planning is 10% inspiration and 90% perspiration.

Vital to the success of a programme or project are its plans, which must contain enough information to assure the organisation's management that the objectives of the programme or project are achievable. The objectives of the planning process are to define what work will be undertaken; how the work will be executed; when it will be undertaken; who will perform each activity; and how much it will cost.

2. The Reason for Programme and Project Planning

Before any organisation embarks on investment in a programme or project, it needs to have proof that:

- **the person entrusted with the investment is competent;**
- **there is a reasonable chance it will deliver its objectives;**
- **the timescales and costs are within its means.**

The programme and or project plan is one of the major devices used by the organisation to ensure the above, as it describes:

- **the major deliverables;**
- **the activities needed to develop them;**
- **the resources needed to perform those activities;**
- **estimates of the necessary resource, ('the Ms' – minutes, manpower, money, materials etc).**

The organisation tests the logic and "correctness" of the plan by comparing it to its own knowledge. Without this confidence and assurance the organisation should hold back on the execution of the programme or project.

However, once the organisation is satisfied of the programme or project integrity, the practical use of the plans has to be explained. To mobilise the project team, individuals need to be told what is wanted, the quality standards against which it will be judged and the resources to be consumed – "the Ms."

The plan provides this information in a format that can be used by the team members without using a major data or information transformation exercise.

The plan, having defined what is being done by whom, when and at what cost, also provides the basis of the monitoring process which informs the programme and project control processes. Without such a plan the organisation can monitor what is being achieved, but cannot assess whether it needs any control action to keep the programme and project on target.

The preparation of the plan also provides the basis of the quality plan for the programme or project. It does this by:

- **describing which activities the end users and customers will be involved in;**
- **the deliverables and activities that will be used to capture and define their requirements;**
- **the deliverables and activities used to ensure the deliverables meet those requirements.**

The development through the programme or project of a new business system, or product, does not necessarily mean that it will be adopted by the end users or customers. The management of the change needed to complete this adoption process needs information such as who will be affected by the programme or project goals and its deliverables.

The programme or project plan helps this process by identifying when these changes will occur, and what deliverables will be provided so that the effect that they have on the organisation can be assessed.

3. The Various Levels of Plans

To explain why different levels of plans are needed, a useful analogy is that of a new computer. In a bad example, the handbook's chapters begin with a schematic wiring diagram for the whole computer and then goes on to discuss the function of every single component.

That's what a bad plan for the detailed execution of all the programmes and projects needed to deliver a business strategy would be like. What is required are various levels of plan. (The level refers to the amount of detail in the plan).

Continuing the concept of levels, the computer handbook should start with an overview of the whole computer, then move into more detail about each function (programme or project) and then even greater detail for each tranche or stage.

Diagram 4 **Levels of Plan**

INTEGRATED PROGRAMME
OR MASTERPLAN

PROGRAMME
PLAN

PROGRAMME
TRANCHE PLAN

PROJECT PLAN

STAGE PLANS

TEAM PLANS

INDIVIDUAL PLANS

Levels of Plan

This levelling approach not only makes the plans more understandable, it also eases the workload needed to up-date them.

This is referred to as the "rule of seven" – the amount of detail needed for each lower level plan is seven times that of the one above.

If the Integrated Programme or Masterplan has one level of detail, each supporting programme or project level plan will have seven times more detail, each tranche plan will have seven times more than that, and so on.

These levels of detail are expensive both to create and to keep up-to-date. Therefore it is vital that the plan only contains the level of detail which assures management and provides the required level of control. There is no point in providing the board of directors with a plan which describes every activity.

The following section looks at the levels of plans required, their typical contents, the techniques used to develop them and the measures adopted to assess their progress.

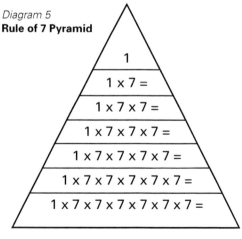

Diagram 5
Rule of 7 Pyramid

1

$1 \times 7 =$

$1 \times 7 \times 7 =$

$1 \times 7 \times 7 \times 7 =$

$1 \times 7 \times 7 \times 7 \times 7 =$

$1 \times 7 \times 7 \times 7 \times 7 \times 7 =$

$1 \times 7 \times 7 \times 7 \times 7 \times 7 \times 7 =$

Complexity of Plans

3.1 Business Strategy (Integrated Programme or Masterplan)

At this – the highest level of plans the requirement is for a plan which describes:

- **the major milestones or events to be achieved;**
- **the planned achievement of benefits;**
- **the major deliverables needed to fulfill the strategy;**
- **the expenditure of resources.**

This plan is focussed on the strategy not the programmes or projects.

See example document **1**: *A business strategy level plan.*

Often executive and senior management is presented with a plan which is only an amalgamation of the programmes, and is left to deduce how and where the elements of the strategy will be delivered. All that is needed for the executive and senior manager is a simple bar chart or table that contains details of what are the major achievement points and when they will be delivered. The audience does not usually need the detail of how this is being provided – that is a technical problem.

However, if more detail is required then the programme and project plan will need to be recast into a new "amalgam plan" showing how these achievement points will be delivered.

3.2 Programme Level

The programme level plan is used by the programme manager and the programme executive/board to manage and control the programme.

This is a similar plan to that used at the strategy level. At this level what is important is the achievement of the programme, not the individual components – the projects.

This plan therefore identifies:

- **the major milestones or events to be achieved;**
- **the planned achievement of benefits;**
- **the major deliverables needed to fulfill the programme;**
- **the expenditure of resources.**

See example document **2**: *A programme level plan.*

The programme plan is likely to be a bar chart or table highlighting the individual projects, the programme milestones and events. The reason that some of the technical components of the plan – projects – are visible at this level, is that the senior managers, responsible for the programme, are involved with decision making on the execution of the whole programme and the individual projects. At the strategic plan level they are not.

This plan is developed from the project plans to show the programme's achievements, deliverable points and how and where the projects contribute to those points.

3.3 Programme Tranche Level

The programme tranche plan is predominately used by the programme and project managers to manage a specific tranche of the programme. It is also the basis to report to the programme executive/board on the plan's progress.

Therefore this plan will contain a greater amount of detail than the programme plan. Typically it will contain all the programme milestones, the major deliverables in the programme and the interdependencies between the projects and the major project milestones – those monitored by the programme manager.

This plan is derived from an amalgamation of the project plans with the details from the programme plan superimposed on top. It is again likely to be a bar chart and a table. However it is also likely to have an accompanying resource usage spreadsheet attached.

*See example document **3**: A programme tranche plan.*

3.4 Project Level

The project plan is used by the project manager, the project board and the programme manager. It provides a total overview of the project from start to finish and is likely to be very approximate in terms of timescales and costs, particularly towards the start of the planned project lifecycle. It identifies the key products, the major resource requirements and costs, and stage boundaries.

Once accepted and approved for implementation the project level plan is baselined and retained for future comparison with actual progress.

Initially it does not contain a lot of detail of what will be performed at each stage – it acquires this level of detail with the incorporation of detailed stage plans as they are developed (just before each stage).

They typically consist of a bar chart, resource spreadsheet, and a table of the major milestones and deliverables.

*See example document **4**: A project plan.*

3.5 Stage Plan Level

The stage plan is used by the project manager and project leader/team managers to provide the information needed to manage and direct the project team. It is therefore a detailed plan and is used to manage the day-to-day work of the project. It contains all the same charts and documents as the project level plan but, in addition, will be supported by other technical documents such as the project network technique diagram.

This plan must also show any links that exist between itself and the project, programme tranche, programme and strategic plans.

See example document **5***: A stage plan.*

3.6 Team Plans

The team plan is not always required, as often the stage plan will provide sufficient detail for the project manager, with help from the project leader/team manager, to manage a stage. If the stage is particularly complex, or the team remote from the main project team, then a team plan is developed to show exactly what that team is expected to do. It can be just an extract from the stage plan – however usually these plans are needed because the stage plan does not have sufficient detail.

The contents of the team plan are similar to those of the stage plan except that a finer level of detail (granularity) will be given.

See example documents **6***: A team plan.*

3.7 Individual

The most detailed level of plan is the individual plan. This is a plan for a specific person, machine or other resource. It is developed from either the stage plan or the team plan and describes in detail what must be performed and when.

These individual plans are usually deployed where individuals operate in isolation, where the individual is a trainee, or unfamiliar with the task. They are typically a checklist, table or work sheet – occasionally a bar chart is used. These plans are used by the stage manager and the project leader/team manager to ensure that individuals have their details and as the basis of their monitoring activities.

See example documents **7***: An individual plan.*

4.   The Planning Process

This section describes the planning process. It can be used when defining plans at any of the previous levels. The basic steps are identical – what varies is the level of detail and the depth of application applied.

4.1 Define Major Products

The first step in the planning process is to define the major products also called outputs or deliverables. These are deduced by the use of a brainstorming workshop, reference to a previous programme or project, or from information contained in the project support infrastructure, particularly any project or system development methods. Sometimes a combination of these approaches is used.

To accompany each of these outputs a brief description is prepared. Next, break down each output into the components that will be needed to deliver them. This is then drawn as a hierarchical chart called an output or product breakdown structure. The same approach can be used with the work to be performed as the components of the structure diagram – this is called a work breakdown structure.

Diagram 6 **Work/Product Breakdown Structure**

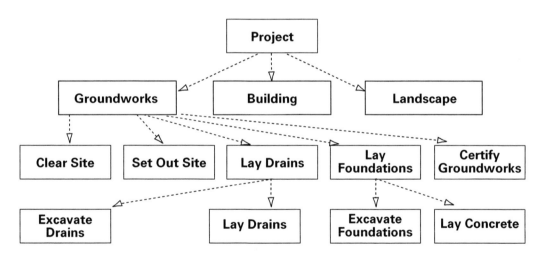

This structure diagram must also depict those 'outputs or products required to facilitate programme and project management (management products), and those required for quality management (quality products)'.

Once this list of outputs has been developed, the planning process defines each of them in a product or output description.

These descriptions are used to clarify and validate the structure by defining each of the outputs and their relationship with others in the structure. The format and content of these descriptions vary according to the type of programme or project management method used.

One such format used in the PRINCE project management method is as follows:

- **product title;**
- **purpose (what purpose the product fulfils, whether it is a means to an end or an end in itself);**
- **composition (the components of the product);**
- **derivation (the source(s) from which this product is derived – a design based on a specification, a product purchased from a supplier, or a product obtained from another section or team);**
- **format and presentation (a standard appearance to which the product must conform);**
- **allocated to (who has to produce the product);**
- **quality criteria (the specification, standards or other measurements against which the product will be inspected);**
- **type of quality check required;**
- **people or skills required for reviewing, testing and approving the product.**

*See example document **8**: A product description.*

Having completed these definitions it is normal to find "bits missing." The planning process then looks at the sequence of development of the outputs. This is achieved by the construction of an output or product flow diagram. This is a high-level dependency chart and is used to check that there are no missing outputs or products. It also identifies dependencies on any outputs or products that lie outside the scope of a particular plan.

Diagram 7 **Product Flow Diagram**

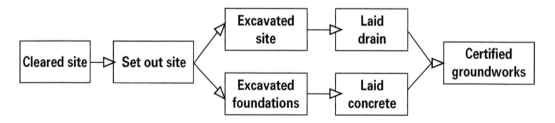

4.2 Identify Activities to Develop the Products

The next step is to identify the activities needed to realise the products. These are determined through consultation with the project leaders/team managers, from information contain in the project support infrastructure, or project or system development lifecycles.

4.3 Define the Sequence of Development

The planner then determines through a process of discussion and agreement with the project leaders/team managers the sequence that these activities will be performed. This is called the project network technique.

4.4 Develop the Programme or Project Network Chart

The project network technique is used to construct a logic chart showing the logical sequence in which each of these activities is performed. In simple programmes or projects the same process is used but instead of activities the chart is drawn using the outputs or products.

The logic of this chart is then checked with the project leader/team managers or any other manager with relevant experience. As before, these dependencies can come from information contained in the project support infrastructure, or any project or system development lifecycles.

See example document **9**: *A network diagram.*

4.5 Estimate the Duration and Effort Required

Next add to the network diagram an estimate of the resources required to complete each of the activities. This sounds relatively simple. However, do you use an estimate of the elapsed time – the number of days or hours in total needed to complete the task – or the pure work involved, making no allowance for delays caused by non-productive work?

The other consideration is how many people do you assume are working on the task simultaneously? This also affects the duration or elapsed time of each activity. Most organisations use the elapsed or duration approach and estimate the team size on the usual number allocated to such tasks. These estimates are then added to the network diagram.

This estimating can also be carried out during the initial stages of defining the outputs or products. These high-level estimates can either be used to build programme or project level plans or to validate development at the activity level.

The planning process then calculates the projected end dates or overall duration of the project, by performing what is known as the forward pass.

See example document **10**: *A forward pass network diagram.*

4.6 Develop Second Pass Programme or Project Network Chart

Having used the forward pass to identify the total duration of the programme or project the project network technique is then used for the second (or backward) pass. This second pass identifies the critical path – those activities which govern the overall duration of the project, and also the "float" or free time available to the other activities.

The data from this second pass is then analysed to see if any changes could be made to the dependencies or the structure of the products that would effect the critical path and, therefore, the duration of the programme or project.

See example document **11**: *A second or backward pass network diagram.*

4.7 Analyse the Resources Required and Minimise Them

Having ensured that the network represents the "best situation", analyse the resources required and either minimise or smooth them.

This step uses the information from the network and then rationalises the resources so that there are as few peaks and troughs as possible, and the resources are used in the most economical way.

This step sometimes changes the network where a more economical use of the resources can be made without adversely affecting the overall duration of the programme or project.

See example document **12**: *Resource smoothing.*

4.8 Identify Major and Minor Decision Points

Having now fully defined the plan the final step is to identify where the major and minor decision points occur. These decision points are used to decide where the programme or project will be divided into tranches or stages and where the intermediate review points should occur.

This step involves looking for the major points in the programme or project – either where a decision has to be taken which involves the expenditure of a lot of resources; the programme or project is committed to a defined course of action; or a product is produced which has considerable significance to the overall programme or project. The minor decision points are where a product of significance is achieved.

5 Deciding Milestones & Review Points

One of the key decisions is what will be used as the intermediate measurement points? These measurement points are usually referred to as milestones. This section looks at the possible measurement points that could be selected as milestone events.

5.1 Programme Milestones

When looking for potential events for programme milestones, all too often the programme manager selects those used to measure project progress. This is not wrong, but it does not support the concepts of programme management. More relevant are events such as:

- **benefits realised;**
- **cultural change achieved;**
- **cost or resource commitment;**
- **major interdependencies.**

The programme manager will need to identify which of these potential events is relevant to their programme.

5.1.1 Benefits realised

One of the most relevant events in any programme is where benefits are realised. These events can be triggered by a deliverable from a single project; however, it is more likely to be where a number of deliverables from a number of projects have joined together to realise the benefit.

5.1.2 Cultural change achieved

Some programmes are designed to achieve major shifts of changes in attitude or culture, therefore the programme manager may wish to use events which mark a change in attitude or culture. If it is decided to use these events as milestones it will be necessary to quantify and measure the attitude or cultural change. This sounds obvious but experience has shown that in a number of programmes, cultural change milestones have been set which only relate to the actions carried out by the programme and the projects, not to a change in culture.

5.1.3 Cost or resource commitment

Another event used as a measurement point is where significant cost or resources are committed to the programme. However, this is usually used with other measurement points, as it does not assess progress.

5.1.4 Major interdependencies

This event represents some of the most common milestones. Major interdependencies are where either deliverables produced in separate projects meet to form a significant output, or a deliverable from one project is passed to other projects to enable them to proceed. Many programme managers favour this type of milestone because it identifies and measures significant progress. A common expression among programme managers is "look after the interdependencies and the programme will keep on track!"

5.2 Project Milestones

The events commonly used as milestones for projects are:

- **major deliverables;**
- **technical development stages;**
- **standards.**

As with the programme management milestones, it is necessary to select a combination of these events to provide relevant measurement points.

5.2.1 Major deliverables

The strongest contenders for a project milestone is the delivery of the project's most important products. These are important because they indicate something to the customer, or user, as well as the development team. They measure achievement, not activity, and are therefore useful at project and programme level.

5.2.2 Technical development stage

The completion of a stage in the project or system development method is another event and can be used as a milestone. However, the problem with using this as a milestone is that, unless you have a small project, it can be a long time between the milestones and these events mean very little to the end users.

5.2.3 Standards

These are standard points in each project, which can be a combination of deliverables, development stages, or events that relate to the project lifecycle or expenditure of x% of the total budget.

6. Deciding Review Points

Decisions must also be made where review points occur. These points are where the programme or project board reviews the programme or project and, if necessary, control action is performed.

6.1 Programme review points

There are three types of reviews that must be included in the programme plans:

- **regular reviews (e.g. monthly);**
- **business process interfaces;**
- **islands of stability.**

Deciding review points is similar to milestones in that the programme manager must decide which events will be used to trigger the reviews.

6.1.1 Regular reviews

The first of the review points included in the programme plan are the regular reviews. These are assurance or confidence reviews, which are held throughout a tranche. They may be either a physical meeting or simply a report, which can result in a meeting if required. How often these reviews are performed, and whether it is time triggered or purely programme-event driven, will depend on the following factors:

- **how easy it is to get the programme board together at short notice;**
- **the overall timescale of the programme and its tranches;**
- **the risks associated with the programme;**
- **its size or costs.**

6.1.2 Business process interfaces

In addition to the regular reviews, it is essential to include interfaces between the programme and the organisation's other business processes. These are events such as the regular management and performance reviews; budgeting and planning; statutory (e.g. VAT or tax); or business-driven events (e.g. shareholder meetings).

6.1.3 Islands of stability

The most significant review points are those selected at the end of the tranche or the islands of stability. Events selected as potential end of tranche points are those that mark a significant delivery of a part of the programme; the attainment of a significant benefit; or where a major decision or commitment of resources occurs.

The programme manager must also take into consideration the overall timescale of the programme, and the rate of change in the external and internal environment which shaped the need for the programme.

6.2 Project review points

The most important review points for projects are:

- **regular reviews (e.g. weekly and monthly);**
- **major deliverables;**
- **technical development stages;**
- **standards.**

6.2.1 Regular (e.g. weekly and monthly)

Regular time intervals are good review points. Typical intervals are weekly and the end of the month. It could also be every four or six weeks, or tied to the organisations accounting periods. When deciding which of these to select it is important to remember:

- **each review has to be cost justified;**
- **it is important that the review corresponds with the organisations other management review processes;**
- **the review period corresponds with the activity rate on the project – i.e. if it is a very slow moving project then extend the timescale of the review points.**

6.2.2 Major deliverables

The planned or actual completion of a major deliverable is a suitable review point. These can be combined with time-based reviews – for example, weekly reports with an additional report when one of the major deliverables is completed. However, it is important that the project manager considers the impact that these irregular reports have on the visibility or perceived complexity/bureaucracy of the project. It is all too easy to create the impression that the project is nothing but "paperwork and reports".

6.2.3 Technical development stage

One of the strongest contenders for a review is the delivery, or end of a stage, in the technical development of the project. These points are usually described in the project or system development lifecycle and can be easily identified as they are those points where major decisions are made.

6.2.4 Standards

Another review point is based on the organisation's standards. For example if the organisation's projects involve considerable amounts of expenditure, review points are often defined as specific levels of spending.

These standards can also be designed to correspond with the other review points described in this section.

7. Summary

Planning is often considered as an art of some description, however the truth is that it is 10% inspiration and 90% perspiration. There are a number of techniques and tools that can be deployed to perform what many people consider as the most important task of the programme or project manager. It is important that this critical process is given sufficient time and intellectual effort. The outputs from the planning must be treated as working papers – it must not be assumed that they are also the only way that the programme or project manager describes what has to be done, when and by whom.

Experience has shown that it is not only vital to plan the activities to be performed by the programme or project team, it is equally important to plan review points which ensure that appropriate management monitoring and control processes operate.

Chapter Four

Resource, Deliverable and Task Categories

1. Introduction

The infrastructure which supports a PSO needs a categorisation of the various resources used in the programmes and projects. This is also required for the deliverables, products or tasks that the resources are used to develop or perform.

2. The Need for Categories

A category is a logical grouping of skills within a project or programme which are identified by a coding system. All levels of the planning process will need to be supported by codes and categories, particularly the detailed planning of the programmes and projects. These codes and categories are required at this level because the programme, project and line or resource managers use them as the starting point in the detailed planning processes – which identifies and selects the specific members of the organisation to be allocated to the deliverables, products or tasks.

The categories and codes also support other aspects of the PSO infrastructure, including information provided to strategic management. Therefore it is essential to develop categories and codes for resources and tasks which are meaningful to the managers who carry out strategic and tactical planning.

In addition the system supports the functions of trend analysis. Trend analysis is performed during the budgeting and business review processes and also in response to specific situations or requirements. The codes and categories are used to obtain a view of the current situation in comparison with other points in time.

Finally the use of codes and categories, particularly in the initial planning of a programme or project, forces the programme, project and line or resource managers to adopt the team concept rather than identifying individuals. The use of the code and category team approach provides the staff with a natural group .

3. Which Infrastructure Elements use Codes and Categories?

A number of the elements of the PSO infrastructure will not only use these codes and categories, but will depend on them in order to operate efficiently and effectively.

3.1 Strategic Planning of the Portfolio

When preparing reports to executive level management regarding the portfolio of programmes and projects, coding and categorisation of resources and tasks is vital. These reports summarise the existing and projected workload on the organisation and must provide the information in a format which helps quick analysis and decision making. The codes and categories required here are those for the human resources, the work being undertaken, and the use of financial resources.

3.2 Project or System Development Methods

The codes and categories are particularly important in the use of project or system development methods. Here they outline the skills required for each of the deliverables, products or tasks and to which work package and team they are allocated.

3.3 Template Plans

The codes and categories are pre-loaded into the template plan in the form of the resources needed for each of the deliverables, products or tasks. This enables the programme or project managers quickly to identify, in summary form, the resources required. Also when developing these plans into a more detailed view it indicates which line or resource manager needs to be contacted when converting generic resources into specific individuals.

3.4 Estimating Guidelines

The resource and task codes and categories are also used in the estimating guidelines provided in the infrastructure. They are used in the estimates of the required resources, manpower, skills and use of finance at each of the required three levels – whole project, stage or phase and deliverable, product or task.

3.5 Deliverable Library

The coding and categorisation of tasks is also vital to the deliverable library as it provides the basis of the grouping types or "families" of deliverables that the library uses to file or cross reference its contents. The cross-references and file groupings are used by the programme or project manager when looking for a deliverable that matches their requirements.

3.6 Deliverable/Staff Database

The deliverable/staff database keeps records of which members of staff have worked on what deliverables. The use of a code and category system enables the programme, project and line or resource manager to identify which members of what team have worked on a specific deliverable.

3.7 Deliverable Costing and Trend Analysis

Coding and categorisation also identifies what expenditure the organisation has incurred on them. This helps to identify any new trends or where method improvement projects should be directed. The same codes and categories can also be used in benchmarking the activities of the organisation.

4. The Codes and Categories

Before looking at how these codes and categories are identified and developed, this section examines the two most commonly used code and category structures.

4.1 Flat Structure of Codes and Categories

In a flat structure the codes and categories are held at only one level – i.e. no codes within codes. This structure is perfectly acceptable where only a small number of codes and categories are required and there is little need to use the coded and categorised information at different levels.

However, because this structure is easy to install, it is often implemented with little or no research. Consequently the number of codes and categories keep growing. In one company they grew from 20 to over 400 in the space of six months, resulting in confusion as to which code and category should be used and misallocation was extremely common.

Research has shown that the human brain can only typically handle 5 (+ or -2) pieces of information at one time. Therefore when confronted with a list of many codes and categories mistakes can easily occur.

4.2 Multi-Level Code Systems

Multi-level systems have codes and categories at the highest level, subdivided at a lower level and perhaps subdivided again.

This structure tends to be more successful because the design of the codes and categories require more research before they can be installed. Also the levels used in this type of structure means that they can be aligned to specific processes within the organisation.

When designing this type of structure it is worth remembering "the rule of six". This rule refers to having approximately six codes and categories at any one level, with these six

Diagram 8 **Example Resource Code System**

DEPARTMENT NAME	SKILL GROUP	SKILL LEVEL
Groundworks **(G)**	Excavation **(E)**	Expert **(P)**
Building **(B)**	Lay drains **(D)**	Intermediate **(M)**
Landscape **(L)**	Lay Foundations **(F)**	New **(N)**

Resource Code

G	Groundworks department
E	Excavation skills
P	Expert skill level

divided into six lower level codes and categories and so on. This approach obviously enables the selection of a more reliable and appropriate code or category.

The multi-level system must ensure that any categories used in the infrastructure match those used in other parts of the organisation. Particular care should be taken to ensure that they match any corporate planning systems – particularly in respect of financial expenditure and other budgetary considerations. Any resource codes and categories used in respect of staff must match with those used in the human resource departments.

Achieving these matches can be difficult and the temptation to "de-couple" them is great. Experience has shown that if this "island mentality" is used, then not only is the organisation failing to realise the full benefits of the codes and categories, it also instills an attitude that the programme and project functions are separate from the rest the organisation. When designing your codes and categories ensure they follow the organisation structure.

CASE STUDY

A Belgian organisation had the six top level activity codes representing the six major departments of the company, while at the next level the codes represented the major divisions in each department.

The third level had similar codes in each of the divisions for common activities such as operational management, sales support, after sales service, personnel management, research and development. This common category system allowed for cross organisation analysis of manpower, expenditure and work effort.

Another important consideration is the selection of the name given to each of the codes and categories. The names selected must be self-explanatory, the code or category should require little, or no, supplementary information in order for the user to locate and use the correct one.

The codes and categories need to be organisation specific, except when the code or category will be used to provide benchmark data to compare the organisation with others.

Diagram 9 **Multi Level Codes**

MAJOR FUNCTIONS	BUSINESS AREA	ACTIVITY
LEVEL 1	LEVEL 2	LEVEL 3
Operations (**O**)	Sales (**A**)	Budgetting (**B**)
Support (**S**)	Distribution (**D**)	Planning (**G**)
New business (**N**)	Development (**P**)	Research (**R**)
Management (**M**)	Customer service (**C**)	etc...
etc...	etc...	

5. How They Are Developed

The design and development of the codes and categories is best carried out as part of the overall design for the programme and project support infrastructure.

5.1 Develop the Codes and Categories as a Deliverable in the Project

To ensure that they are developed successfully, the PSO implementation project must define a deliverable description.

Diagram 10 **Checklist of Steps in Developing Codes and Categories**

● Develop codes and categories as a project
● Ensure codes and categories support strategic and corporate information needs
● Match codes and categories to HR system codes etc.
● Match codes and categories to the organisation's management structure
● Integrate codes and categories in all aspects of the PSO infrastructure

The following is an example of such as description – it must be tailored to meet the specific requirement of your PSO implementation project.

Deliverable/Product Description

Product name

Standard Resource and Deliverable/Task Code and Categories.

Purpose

To support the efficient and effective strategic and tactical planning and management of the organisations resources

Format

A list of agreed codes and categories (with supporting descriptions) for the:

- *employees of the organisation;*
- *deliverables, products and tasks involved in executing programmes and projects;*
- *business-as-usual and non-project work;*
- *expenditure incurred when executing programmes and projects;*
- *expenditure incurred when undertaking business-as-usual and non-productive work;*
- *sickness, authorised absence and holidays.*

Content

The codes and categories will be defined in a document which describes:

- *the structure of the codes and categories;*
- *their numbering or other identifying system;*
- *a description of what is included in that code and category.*

Quality Criteria

The codes and categories must cover the complete range of skills, resources, deliverables, products, tasks and expenditure undertaken by the organisation.

The codes and categories must conform to the organisation's management and budgetary control structures.

The codes and categories must interface with all human resources, finance, accounting and purchasing etc., so that no data transformation is necessary between these departments.

The codes and categories must support and match the requirements of all other relevant parts of the PSO infrastructure.

5.2 Ensure the Codes and Categories Support Strategic and Corporate Needs

It is essential that the codes and categories address the strategic and corporate needs if the PSO infrastructure is to become an integral part of the business support functions. Therefore the research into what codes and categories are required starts with the corporate planning and budgeting functions.

The support needed for the planning and decision making process can often be the same as that provided for the planning and budgeting, however it is also usual to find that in addition to the other requirements a range of business benchmarks are required.

Identifying what information is needed to support these processes not only provides a good start point, it also identifies where the PSO infrastructure may fill any gaps in information in the current processes.

5.3 Match the Codes and Categories to the HR System

When researching the staff resource codes and categories it is vital that they either line-up with, or match, those used in the Human Resources (HR) management function and its supporting process. This is relatively easy to achieve where the HR system has no existing system of codes and categories - however with the widespread use of Enterprise Resource Planning software (ERP) packages such as *SAP* and *Peoplesoft* it is likely that some codes and categories already exist. In these cases a degree of negotiation and compromise will be required to successfully interface the two systems of codes and categories.

5.4 Match the Codes and Categories to the Organisation's Management Structure

The research and development of codes and categories must take into account the organisation's management structure. This is vital if the information is to be of use to other departments. This matching process can prove to be a major problem if a "flat" code and category structure is used as it is difficult to identify if a code and category exists that matches the requirement.

5.5 Integrate the Codes and Categories in all aspects of the PSO Infrastructure

This final point is often missed when designing the codes and categories, particularly where the codes and categories will be used in software tools. For example, planning and scheduling tools often have a limit on the formats (number of characters) of the codes that can be used. The interface and impact on the estimating guidelines, data dictionary, skills and deliverable/staff database must also be considered.

6. Keeping Them Up-to-Date

The first point to consider in designing the codes and categories is to ensure that they can be easily updated. Therefore it is vital to design the mechanism by which they will be updated.

6.1 Have an Instant Update Mechanism for New Skills or Tasks

The mechanism by which these codes and categories are updated must be quick and efficient. It is advisable to set them up as a look-up table or small database which is used (referred to at run time) by all the components in the infrastructure. This ensures that no out-of-date codes or categories are used and new ones are implemented and available to all infrastructure users.

6.2 Control Updates Centrally

However it is important that these changes are not implemented until they have been reviewed by the equivalent of the database administrator. This role ensures that the new or updated code and category is documented, to the agreed standard, and does not overlap any previous codes and categories. In addition this role must ensure that the relevant staff in the organisation are aware of the new or updated codes and categories.

6.3 Review the Codes and Categories Every 12 Months (Budgeting Cycle)

In addition to the regular updating, a major review of the codes and categories is required every year to ensure that they continue to provide the correct support.

This review must be included in the description of the code and category update process and incorporated into the design of the infrastructure. For example, this review can be included with the reviews of other components of the infrastructure.

6.4 Measure Success (and Failures) and Amount of Support Provided

To facilitate the annual review process it is advisable to incorporate into the code and category design process mechanisms to capture information on what use is being made of the codes and categories and their successes and failures. It is vital to capture this information because it proves their value and provides evidence to support any maintenance.

One of the principle measures of success is the number of parts of, or processes in, the organisation which use the codes and categories. To encourage other parts of the organisation to become users of the codes and categories invite as many of the potential users as possible to take part in the development process during the PSO implementation project. This involvement, in perhaps design or consultation workshops, will ensure they understand what the project is trying to achieve through the codes and categories; they can also identify new or additional uses for them in their departments.

7. Summary

The key to the successful development and implementation of codes and categories to support the PSO infrastructure is for them to be integrated into as many other functions of the organisation as possible. Their design and development needs to consider a number of factors. The most important of these is the ability of any software tools to work with the numbering and naming convention adopted.

It is also vital that the codes and categories are designed to be easily maintainable and that the need for a regular and an annual review process is incorporated into its design.

Chapter Five

Programme and Project Control Documents

1. Introduction

"More projects fail from lack of control than anything else": this is a common adage within programme and project management communities.

This chapter looks at the structure of documents which address control, including:

- **programme or project lifecycles;**
- **programme management methods;**
- **project management methods.**

However, the production of these documents alone does not mean that the programme or project is under control. Documents only provide the relevant members of the organisation with sufficient information to decide if control action is needed, and, once taken, to measure the effectiveness of that action. They also define the uncertainty in the programme or project at their inception. Thus by examining these documents it can be seen if the programme or project manager has succeeded in reducing the uncertainty.

2. The Reason for Programme and Project Control Documents

The most effective methods of control contain the following steps.

- **Step One:**   **Decide what is to be achieved.**
- **Step Two:**   **Prepare a plan of how to achieve it.**
- **Step Three:**   **Execute that plan.**
- **Step Four:**   **Assess what has been achieved.**
- **Step Five:**   **Compare the achievements to the plan and what was intended to be achieved.**

- Step Six: Define any action that is needed.

Then either stop or go back to Step One.

This monitor/review control cycle exists in all programme and project lifecycles and methods. It is used in the programme and project lifecycle to check that the masterplan portfolio is delivering what it promised.

It is used in programme and project management methods to ensure they are delivering what they were commissioned to provide, within the agreed time and resource profiles.

Whilst in the project or system development method, the monitor/review/control cycle is used to assess progress in the detailed execution of the development of the agreed and defined deliverables.

The programme and project control documents which are used to facilitate steps 4,5,6 are therefore a vital element in all these lifecycles and methods.

3. What are Programme or Project Lifecycle Control Documents?

There are typically six sets of documents used to control the programme or project lifecycle. In some organisations additional documents are added such as budget approval and business cases. It is important that, whatever the organisation chooses as its control documents, they are defined and agreed in format and content. Also their development should be an integral part of the programme or project management methods or the project or system development method.

The six control documents featured in this section are:

- **the programme or project idea form;**
- **the programme and/or project contribution matrix;**
- **programme or project feasibility study report;.**
- **programme definition statement (PDS) and project initiation document (PID);**
- **end of tranche and end of stage reports;**
- **programme closure report and project closure report.**

3.1 The Programme or Project Idea Form

The programme or project idea is developed by the programme or project requester and, in some organisations, by the corporate planning department. The form describes in brief terms the aims and objectives of the programme or project, and is used as part of the high level planning process for the strategic plan.

See example document **13**: *A programme or project idea form.*

The masterplan committee, which oversees the creation and management of the masterplan portfolio of programmes and projects, approves the programme or project idea forms after satisfying themselves that the programme or project supports the strategic plan. The programme or project idea form is then given to a programme or project manager to undertake a feasibility study, and associated report, and if possible prove the economic and technical viability of the programme or project.

3.2 The Programme and Project Contribution Matrices

The programme and project contribution matrix assesses the contribution that each programme or project makes to the business strategy plan or the contribution of the project to a programme.

See example documents **14**: *Business strategy / programme / project contribution matrix and* **15**: *A project/programme contribution matrix.*

The matrices are developed after the programme or project idea form is completed and is refined as other documents are developed. The format of the matrices and the method of assessment vary in each organisation but typically it contains:

- **a list of the programme or projects;**
- **a brief description of their aims and objectives;**
- **a high level estimate of their costs and timescales;**
- **details of who is the sponsor and requester;**
- **an assessment of what the programme or project will provide**
- **an assessment of the contribution it will make to strategic goals or to a specific programme.**

3.3 Programme or Project Feasibility Study

As with most of the documents in this chapter, the exact format and contents of each document varies between organisations. However to ensure that the control process operates effectively all should contain the:

- **aims and objectives of the programme/project;**
- **execution options that were examined;**
- **recommended method of approach or execution;**

- technical, programme/project and business risks;

- initial programme or project plan;

- probable costs of the programme/project and its benefits.

This document is developed by the programme or project manager, in conjunction with the programme or project requester and the sponsor, with support and information provided by the PSO.

See example document **16**: *A feasibility study report.*

If there is an embryonic programme or project board, it can approve the feasibility study report before the masterplan committee's approval. The masterplan committee must approve the feasibility study report to ensure the programme or project will provide what they require to fulfill the business strategy.

In exceptional situations (i.e. where the programme or project provides a critical part of the strategic plan, or involves a significant expenditure) the feasibility study report may need board approval. This report is also part of the programme and or project management method.

3.4 Programme Definition Statement and Project Initiation Document

These come from refining and re-defining the feasibility study to reflect the reduction in the uncertainty of the programme and project from the programme or project idea form.

The document is developed by the programme or project manager and provides the baseline for the rest of the programme or project. Having agreed the feasibility study, the next step in the programme and project lifecycle is the formal initiation of the programme or project. This is not only a significant step in the programme and project lifecycle, it is also a major point in the programme and project management methods.

These documents contain the:

- **programme or project organisation structure;**

- **the business case;**

- **programme or project plan with tranches and stages defined;**

- **programme or project risk analysis;**

- **quality and other management plans;**

- **progress reporting arrangements.**

See example documents **17**: *A programme definition statement and* **18**: *a project initiation document.*

As with the feasibility study report, the programme or project board approves these documents before they are submitted to the masterplan committee for formal approval. The programme and project contribution matrices will also be updated as necessary. In exceptional situations this document may reveal that some form of control action needs to be actioned by the masterplan committee.

3.5 End of Tranche and End of Stage Reports

The production of a report at the end of either a tranche or stage summarising progress made-to-date and a prognosis for the remainder of the programme or project is required. Once reviewed and accepted by the programme or project board these reports are then reviewed by the masterplan committee. The masterplan committee review updates, the programme and project contribution matrices and, in exceptional situations, it decides if any control action is needed.

The typical contents of these documents are:

- **planned progress – costs, resources, deliverables;**
- **actual progress – cost, resources, deliverables;**
- **an analysis of the differences and reasons for the differences;**
- **problems encountered during the tranche or stage which have not been resolved;**
- **a prognosis for the remainder of the programme or project in respect of costs, resources and timescales.**

See example document **22**: *End of tranche and* **27b**: *End of stage report.*

3.6 Programme and Project Closure Report

The programme and project closure report is generally the final control document in the programme and project lifecycle. However some organisations also have a further document – the post programme or project review report.

The programme or project closure report is produced by the programme or project manager as part of the programme or project management method. It is usually submitted to the masterplan committee after obtaining approval from the programme or project board. In some organisations the masterplan committee reviews the report first and then instructs the programme or project board to close, or otherwise, the programme or project.

These reports contain:

- **a comparison of the programme or projects objectives (as defined in the PDS or PID) to its acheivements;**
- **a list of the lessons learnt during the programme or project, subdivided into:**
  - *the management of the programme or project;*
  - *the development or execution of the programme or projects;*
  - *risk analysis and management;*
  - *quality management.*

These observations are further subdivided into those pertinent to the particular programme or project and those that are applicable to all programmes and projects undertaken by the organisation.

A programme closure report also includes a section on the benefits realisation and sustainability plan. This describes what benefits have already been obtained, the plan for the realisation of the remainder, and the arrangements to ensure that they are sustained.

See example document **21** *and* **21b**: *The programme and project closure report.*

The masterplan committee reviews this report to update the programme and project contribution matrices. It also ensures that any lessons learnt, which affect on-going or future programmes and projects, are passed on and appropriate action taken.

4. Programme Control Documents

The programme control documents are usually defined in the programme management method. As can be seen from the previous section, many of these documents are also an integral part of the programme lifecycle. They also form an integral part of the project management method.

The names given to these documents vary in the various programme management methods. However the functionality and control process they provide is reasonably consistent.

The typical programme control documents are the:

- **programme brief;**
- **programme definition statement;**
- **regular programme progress report;**

- **end of programme tranche report;**
- **exception report;**
- **programme closure report.**

4.1 Programme Brief

The programme brief is developed by the programme manager from the programme idea form and refines it into a more definitive statement of the programme's objectives etc. The programme brief reduces the uncertainty by expanding on the idea form. It provides sufficient information to guide the programme manager who will produce the programme definition statement.

The typical contents of the programme brief are:

- **programme background;**
- **benefits framework or profile;**
- **risk analysis;**
- **constraints and assumptions that apply;**
- **required implementation timescales;**
- **programme organisation structure;**
- **outline business case;**
- **funding and a plan for the programme definition phase.**

The programme manager, assisted by the programme director and the PSO, produces the document and submits it to the programme director or the embryonic programme executive/board.

Occasionally the programme brief is also submitted to the masterplan committee for information and to assure it that the programme is proceeding according to their requirements.

4.2 Programme Definition Statement

The programme definition statement (PDS) is the programme equivalent of the project initiation document in the project management method.

The programme manager, assisted by the PSO and senior and departmental managers, refines and expands the programme brief and programme idea form into the baseline plans for the whole programme through the PDS. These form the basis for the remainder of the programme monitoring and control documents.

This document further considerably reduces the uncertainty associated with the programme.

The document is submitted to the programme executive/board for approval. It gives this once it is satisfied that the PDS is within the terms of reference for the programme, the programme idea form, the programme brief, and the programme feasibility study.

Often the feasibility study report is produced as the first deliverable in the programme once it has been initiated so at this point it may not be available to the programme executive/board.

The typical contents of the programme definition statement are:

- **programme background;**
- **future business blueprint or vision statements;**
- **transition plan;**
- **risk management plan;**
- **project portfolio;**
- **design management plan;**
- **quality plan;**
- **resourcing plan;**
- **programme organisation structure;**
- **business case and funding requirements;**
- **PDS review plan.**

See example document **17**: *The programme definition statement.*

4.3 Regular Programme Progress Report

As the programme is executed the programme manager works to a pre-defined timetable to produce regular progress reports which are submitted to the programme executive/board for their review and approval.

These reports are designed to provide assurance that the programme is proceeding as defined in the PDS, to identify emerging trends and where the programme manager needs assistance from the members of the programme executive/board to deal with problems which have arisen.

The frequency, content, and format of these reports are defined in the PDS. What is vital is that the majority of the information used to develop these reports comes from the portfolio of projects that the programme is controlling. Indeed programme level reports can be fed directly from the regular progress reports produced at project level. When designing the infrastructure to support programmes and projects, the interfacing of the reports should be carefully considered. It is essential that these systems work well, given the considerable number of reports produced during a programme.

In some organisations the information collection and collation is either done electronically or by the PSO. The programme manager must always be responsible for the analysis and interpretation of this information and verify its accuracy.

Typical reports contain:

- **the achievements (milestones or other major deliverables) that were planned to be completed during the reporting period;**
- **the actual achievements;**
- **the planned consumption of resources and costs;**
- **the actual consumption of resources and costs;**
- **an analysis of the overall status of the tranche;**
- **problems encountered which need to be drawn to the programme executive/boards' attention;**
- **an outlook or prognosis for the remainder of the tranche and programme.**

These reports are not usually sent to the masterplan committee, unless there is a specific need. For example where a programme is of vital importance or is consuming a large amount of resource.

See example document **19**: *A programme progress report to the masterplan committee.*

4.4 End of Programme Tranche Report

At the end of each tranche of the programme the programme manager produces an end of tranche report. This is similar to a regular progress report, with an added re-assessment of the programme. The end of tranche typically marks one of the points in the programme, often referred to as "islands of stability".

The 'island' concept reflects the arrival of the programme at some significant achievement of part of its aims and objectives. As a consequence, it is a prudent time to review the programme's remaining aims and objectives to ensure that they are still needed, or to re-align them if appropriate.

The programme manager prepares this report in conjunction with the programme executive/board and those parts of the organisation that are responsible for the commissioning of the programme.

Once approved by the programme executive/board, the document is passed to the masterplan committee. The masterplan committee use the document not only as an indication of the progress made, but also as part of their regular re-assessment of their portfolio and the contribution each of the programmes and projects make to strategic goals and targets.

The reports typically contain:

- **the progress made, as compared to the plan, in the delivery of the programme;**
- **the benefits realised to date and the plan to achieve the remainder;**
- **a review of the programmes aims and objectives and whether these are still required by the organisation;**
- **a review of the programme plan;**
- **a review of the remainder of the arrangements described in the PDS – risks, reporting, organisation structure etc. In some instances an updated PDS may be developed.**

Because of the importance of these reviews it may also be necessary to involve the organisation's board in this review process.

*See example document **22**: End of programme tranche report.*

4.5 Exception Report

An exception report is a programme control document because it is produced as part of the programme management method in which progress is measured and control action taken as required.

Exception reports are produced by the programme manager when something occurs which will prevent delivery of the objectives, or agreed budgetary or other limits will be exceeded.

The exception report is first reviewed by the programme executive/board who decide whether the problem is serious enough to be escalated to the masterplan committee for action.

The typical contents of these reports are:

- **description of the problem;**
- **the causes;**
- **the impact on the programme;**
- **what remedial actions have been considered;**
- **the implication of the actions on the programme;**
- **the recommended course of action.**

See example document **23**: *Exception report and plan.*

4.6 Programme Closure Report

The final document in this section is the programme closure report. This document is produced by the programme manager and is used by the programme executive/board and the programme director to mark the end of the programme and possibly their responsibility for its management and operation.

This report is produced in conjunction with the project managers from each of the constituent projects and the PSO, together with the departmental managers responsible for realising and sustaining the business changes that the programme is designed to achieve.

It is important to note that in some programme management methods the programme may not cease at this point. For example, the control and monitoring of the changes that the programme was to achieve may pass on to a new organisation structure responsible for its full implementation, sustainability and continued performance monitoring. Also some programme management methods contain a post programme review once the benefits realisation has been completed.

5. Project Control Documents

The typical project management method contains a similar structure of control documents to those used in a programme management method. However, their role is two fold. Not only do they control the projects but, when the project is part of a programme, they also work with, and feed to and from, those used in the control of the programme.

This section explains their use in controlling the project and the interface with those in the programme management method.

The typical project control documents are:

- project mandate;
- project brief;
- project initiation document;
- regular progress reports;
- end of stage report;
- exception report;
- project closure report.

5.1 Project Mandate

The project mandate provides the organisation with sufficient information to develop a project brief and is usually the basis of the project idea form.

The project mandate typically contains:

- the trigger for the project;
- the authority responsible for the project;
- high level terms of reference for the project;
  - *background,*
  - *objectives,*
  - *scope,*
  - *constraints,*
  - *interfaces,*
  - *quality expectations,*
  - *outline business case,*
  - *and other associated documents or products.*
- indications of the user and customer interests;
- the project organisation structure.

If this document is not supplied in full to the project manager, it is essential that it is completed before proceeding through to the production of the project brief.

*See example document **24**: A project mandate.*

5.2 Project Brief

This document is produced from the project idea form submitted to the masterplan committee, the project mandate, or as a consequence of the programme definition phase where the portfolio of projects needed to facilitate a programme are identified or defined. The project brief can also be generated as a result of an end of tranche report which identifies that a new or re-targeted project is needed to enable the programme to complete its stated objectives.

The purpose of the project brief is to prove to the project board that the project has sufficient merit to proceed to the project initiation stage. This document removes a large degree of the initial uncertainty of the project and provides the basis for the production of a project initiation document. It is important, as it supercedes the project mandate as the terms of reference for the project and is, therefore, used at a large number of points during the project's execution to ensure it is under control.

The project brief, once approved by the project board, is submitted back to either the programme manager or the masterplan committee as the definition of the project's objectives.

The PSO, the user and customer departments, who will be using the project's deliverables, assist the project manager in the production of the document.

The project brief should contain:

- **project definition;**
  - *background,*
  - *scope,*
  - *objectives,*
  - *project deliverables or outcomes,*
  - *exclusions,*
  - *constraints,*
  - *interfaces.*
- **an outline business case;**
  - *definition of the support it provides to the business strategy,*
  - *reason for the selection of a particular solution or approach,*
- **customer expectations (quality);**
- **acceptance criteria for the whole project;**
- **risks that have been identified;**
- **an outline project plan.**

*See example document **25**: A project brief.*

5.3 Project Initiation Document

Once the project brief has been approved by the project board, the masterplan committee and the programme manager, the project manager can produce the project initiation document.

The project initiation document has two main purposes. The first is to provide the basis for the management and control of the project. It achieves this with the detailed plans which have been put into place for the project – including not only the project deliverables but also its management structures and supporting systems.

The second purpose is to define the project success criteria – those vital elements of the project that must be satisfied if the project is to be regarded as a success by the organisation.

The project initiation document is the major control document and must reduce the uncertainty associated with the project so that the organisation fully understands what the project is, what it involves, and what it is designed to achieve.

The document is developed in consultation with a large number of people and is an amalgamation of a series of separate documents. As with all documents, the exact composition of the document will vary from organisation to organisation and project to project – however it must cover the following fundamental questions:

- **what does the project aim to achieve?**
- **why is it necessary?**
- **who is involved /responsible for managing the projects and their responsibilities?**
- **how and when will the project be executed?**

Once completed by the project manager, the document has to be approved by the project board. The project initiation document is approved only if it confirms and concurs with the project brief and project mandate.

The document is then submitted to the masterplan committee, or the programme manager, to enable them to update the programme definition statement, the programme plan, and the project or programme contribution matrices.

Control action may be needed at this point by the masterplan committee or the programme manager, if they identify that the project is not on track as regards its contribution to the strategy or programme.

This action can be a modification to the aims and objectives which requires the project manager and project board to go back and redraft the document. However the vetting of the project mandate and project brief by the masterplan committee, or the programme manager, should reduce the need for this type of action.

The typical content of the project initiation document is as follows:

- **–a background to the project;**
- **–a project definition, including:**
  - *objectives,*
  - *defined execution method,*
  - *project deliverables /products or workpackages,*
  - *scope of the project,*
  - *constraints,*
  - *assumptions,*
  - *exclusions,*
  - *interfaces;*
  - **a business case;**
  - **a project organisation structure;**
  - **a project quality plan;**
  - **a project plan;**
  - **a plan for the first stage of the project;**
  - **project control structures and reports;**
  - **exception, issue, change control processes;**
  - **a risk analysis and risk management process;**
  - **a contingency plan for any major risks or false assumptions that may arise;**
  - **project filing and document management systems.**

See example document **18**: *A project initiation document.*

5.4 Regular Progress Reports

The typical project management method contains two forms of regular progress report, which support the control process. The first of these are internal to the project team, and are either deliverable completion, acceptance reports or checkpoint reports. These reports are generated by the project team and officially notify the project manager of the completion of specified deliverables or the attainment of a checkpoint (a mini milestone). The frequency and contents of these reports are defined in the project control section of the project initiation document. It is a control document because, based on the report, the project manager can instigate action to rectify any deficiencies or, if the situation is serious enough, can escalate the situation to the project board through the exception process.

The second type of regular progress report is external to the project team. Examples of this are the monthly report to the project board – often referred to as a highlight report. This report is developed by the project manager in conjunction with the project team and the PSO and reports to the project board progress made during the last reporting period, with a projection of the progress planned for the next period.

It often contains an analysis of any relevant statistics such as the average overspend in terms of time and effort on each deliverable. The project manager will also include any problems, issues or risks that need to be brought to the attention of the project board.

This document is not usually sent to the masterplan committee or the programme manager, unless they use it to report progress to another part of the organisation.

The typical contents of regular progress reports are:

- **period covered;**
- **budget status (planned and actual);**
- **schedule status (planned and actual);**
- **products, workpackages or deliverables produced;**
- **actual problems encountered and not dealt with;**
- **problems expected in the next reporting period that the project board can help with;**
- **products, workpackages or deliverables to be produced in the next reporting period;**
- **project issues and their status;**
- **forward projection on the stage and the project of any budget or schedule variances to date.**

*See example document **20**: A project progress report.*

5.5 End of Stage Report

At the end of each stage of the project, the project manager develops an end of stage report. This report collects together all the information from the regular progress reports that were circulated during the stage, and gives an overall analysis of the performance to date.

This report also previews the next stage and the remainder of the project. The project manager uses the project team and the PSO to develop the report and the supporting information and analysis. It is then reviewed by the members of the project organisation structure responsible for project assurance. Their role is to verify that the facts and figures are correct.

The report is presented first to the project board, then to the masterplan committee or the relevant programme manager. As with the regular progress report, the interface between the report and the masterplan committee and the programme managers' reporting systems must be carefully designed so that they are efficient and effective.

A vital part of most project management methods, the report is the basis on which the project board either authorises the project to proceed to the next stage or not. The project board could, as a consequence of the report, redirect the project or revise the contents of the next stage. In addition it is at this point that the board sets the tolerance, or contingency, for the next stage.

The masterplan committee or programme manager can also exercise similar control at this point by directing the project board to take specified action.

The typical contents of an end of stage report are:

- **a comparison of the stage plan and the actual position as regards deliverables, and resources consumed;**
- **an update of the project plan for the remaining stages;**
- **an updated risk assessment;**
- **an updated business case (if relevant);**
- **an analysis of the project issues, change control and quality processes;**
- **a report of any lessons learnt during the stage.**

It could also include:

- **the next stage plan;**
- **a list of deliverables and key dates and events;**
- **any changes proposed to the arrangements defined in the project initiation document (e.g. changes to the project organisation structure).**

5.6 Exception Report

As with the programme management method, there is a need for a control document which enables the project manager to identify that the project either has, or will, not keep to its agreed schedule, costs or deliverables. The exception report, developed by the project manager assisted by the project team and the PSO, is submitted to the project board. The board decides whether to deal with the situation or send it to either the masterplan committee or the programme manager. This pre-consultation process cannot be used if the problem is extremely serious.

If the exception report reveals a serious problem, the project board can call for a premature end to the stage in order for them to gain control of the situation. Similarly the programme manager may call an unplanned end of tranche review if the situation warrants it.

Thus the exception report from the project management method also interlinks with the programme management method.

The typical contents of an exception report are:

- a description of the problem (and its cause);
- the consequences and impact of the problem on the project;
- the options available to the project board to rectify the situation;
- the effect of each of the options on the problem and the costs, resources and schedule;
- risks associated with each of the options and any other effects their adoption may have on the project;
- a recommended course of action.

See example document **23**: *An exception report and plan.*

5.7 End of Project Report

The final control document examined in this section is the end of project report, produced by the project manager assisted by the project team and the PSO. This document also interlinks with the programme management method, as it provides much of the information for the report. Members of the project organisation structure responsible for project assurance also review the report. Their role is to verify that the facts and figures are correct – similar to the end of stage report.

The report is first approved by the project board and then passed to the masterplan committee or the programme manager to update their records. Of particular interest to the masterplan committee and the programme manager are any lessons learnt which are relevant to new, or current, projects in the portfolio.

The typical contents of the end of project report are:

- **a comparison of the project's planned aims and objectives and those actually achieved;**
- **an assessment of whether the project has matched or achieved its critical success factors or acceptance criteria;**
- **an analysis of how the project performed, as compared to its plan, in respect of its delivery, use of resources and costs;**
- **the final statistics on project issues, quality performance and change control activities;**
- **the date and arrangements for any post project review.**

See example document **21b***: A project closure report.*

In some project management methods a further control document is produced - that of a post project review report. This report, similar to the end of project report, reviews the overall effectiveness of the project and its management to identify if any further lessons learnt should be taken into account for future projects.

6. Summary

Project failure usually occurs because the organisation failed to operate the many control process available in programme and project lifecycles and methods.

The structure of control documents described in this chapter will ensure that programme and project managers are in control from the start, and throughout the programme's/project's execution.

As the control documents support each other, it is vital that the supporting infrastructure is effective and efficient – providing interlinks without major data transformation.

Any tailoring or tuning of the control structures should only be undertaken after careful thought, ensuring that the structural integrity of this powerful aid to the management of programmes and projects is not undermined.

Chapter Six

Progress Reporting And Timesheets

1. Introduction

One of the main reasons why an organisation establishes a PSO is to ensure that it has an efficient and effective way of monitoring the progress of programmes and projects in its masterplan portfolio.

In addition to this traditional role, many organisations have extended this monitoring and reporting role into the business-as-usual and non-project work. This is because the processes and systems used to collect information for programmes and projects can be applied to other activities. This is important because up to 70% of organisation resources can be devoted to non-programme and project activities.

This chapter examines programme and project progress reporting systems and how these can be applied to other activities – business-as-usual and non-project work.

2. Why Are They Needed

Before examining how to install and operate an efficient and effective progress reporting system, it is important to establish its purpose.

2.1 Measuring What Has Been Achieved

An organisation's first reason for installing a progress monitoring system is to measure what has been achieved. However, this apparently simple phrase is often misinterpreted as what has been done or spent – indeed in many organisations the emphasis is on activity monitoring not achievement. Resource consumption is important, but the achievements made are what matter, rather than the activities performed or the resources expended.

2.2 Assessing What Is Left

Similarly, the second reason organisations install progress monitoring is to assess what is left to do. This, again, is often misunderstood. What is needed is an assessment of what is left to be done, based on what has been learnt to date – a newer updated plan is required. An assessment of what is left to be achieved compared to the original plan can provide information – it should not be dismissed as irrelevant – but it is important that it is not the only measure used.

2.3 To Update Plans

One of the most important functions that the programme or project manager performs is the regular updating of the plans. This updating function includes three processes. The first is to include on the plan the achievements made and resources consumed to date. This enables the programme or project manager to complete the second process – to identify if the plan needs to be updated to reflect the lessons learnt to date. The third and final process is to assess if any other amendments need to be made to the plan to reflect any changes in the development approach.

2.4 Is Control Action Needed?

Having used the progress information to update the plan, the programme or project manager can then use the updated plan to assess if any control action is needed to keep the programme or project within the agreed target dates and resources. If the assessment reveals that control action is needed, the updated plan is part of the report which assists the programme or project board to decide what control action should be taken.

2.5 To Provide the Basis of Lessons Learnt

One of the major components of the end of tranche, end of stage/phase reports and the programme and project closure reports is the lessons learnt section. The information collected through the progress monitoring process supplies a large proportion of the statistics included in the report. The subsequent analysis and actions taken by the programme or project manager based on the progress monitoring also provides valuable material for this report.

3. Types of Programme and Project Progress Reports

This section examines the various types of programme and project reports and recommends what information is needed to support these reports.

3.1 Programmes

There are typically three types of progress reports in a programme which need to be supported with information:

- **regular progress reports;**
- **end of tranche reports;**
- **programme closure.**

3.1.1 Regular progress reports

The regular progress report is prepared for the programme board by the programme manager. This report is designed to provide assurance (or not) to the programme board that progress is to plan. For the period covered by the report, the information included is:

- **the planned achievements;**
- **the actual achievements;**
- **planned and actual expenditure for:**
  - *manpower resources,*
  - *expenditure,*
  - *other resources.*

The report must also contain an analysis of the progress made to date and a projection of remaining activities for the rest of the tranche.

In addition to this information the report must contain for the next period:

- **the planned achievements;**
- **planned expenditure for;**
  - *manpower resources*
  - *expenditure*
  - *other resources*

3.1.2 End of tranche reports

At the end of each tranche the programme manager prepares a report for the programme board, which enables it to both assess the progress achieved to date and to review the programme as a whole.

This report typically contains:

- **the planned achievements;**
- **the actual achievements;**

- planned and actual expenditure for:
  - *manpower resources,*
  - *expenditure,*
  - *other resources.*

The report must also provide an assessment of the successes and failures of the management of the programme and any lessons learnt. In addition it needs an up-to-date review of the changes in business benchmarks and any other performance measures that the programme is designed to achieve, particularly:

- the original benchmarks or performance measures;
- the current benchmarks or performance measures.

The report should also contain an updated plan for the remainder of the programme and, for the next tranche, the following information:

- the planned achievements;
- planned expenditure for:
  - *manpower resources,*
  - *expenditure,*
  - *other resources.*

*See example document **22**: An end of tranche report.*

3.1.3 Programme closure report

At the end of the programme, the programme manager prepares a report for the programme board which summarises the whole programme. This report contains:

- the planned achievements;
- the actual achievements;
- planned and actual expenditure for:
  - *manpower resources,*
  - *expenditure,*
  - *other resources.*

In a similar way to the end of tranche report, but for the whole programme, the report contains:

- the planned achievements;

- the actual achievements;
- planned and actual expenditure for;
  - *manpower resources*
  - *expenditure*
  - *other resources.*

The report must also provide an assessment of the successes and failures of the management of the programme and any lessons learnt. In addition it contains an up -to-date review of the changes in the business benchmarks and other performance measures that the programme was designed to achieve. In particular it must contain:

- the original benchmarks or performance measures;
- the current benchmarks or performance measures.

The report should also include any further actions to be carried out after the programme has closed.

See example document **21**: *A programme closure report.*

3.2 Projects

There are usually four types of progress reports in a project that need to be supported with information:

- weekly or checkpoint reports;
- highlight or monthly reports;
- end of stage reports;
- the project closure report.

3.2.1 Weekly or checkpoint reports

The purpose of the weekly or checkpoint report is to provide the project manager with a status report on the deliverable, products or tasks that have been allocated to the team. The reports can be either time triggered – at the end of each week, or event triggered – e.g. when the deliverable has been completed or when X resources have been consumed.

This report should contain:

- the planned achievements;
- the actual achievements;
- planned and actual expenditure for:

- *manpower resources,*

  - *expenditure,*

  - *other resources.*

*See example document **26**: A checkpoint report.*

3.2.2 Highlight or monthly reports

At the end of each month, or at a prescribed date, the project manager prepares a report for the project board. This enables them to assess the progress achieved to date and to review the rest of the stage or phase.

This report contains:

  – **the planned achievements;**

  – **the actual achievements;**

  – **planned and actual expenditure for;**

  - *manpower resources,*

  - *expenditure,*

  - *other resources.*

The report also provides an assessment of the successes and failures of the management of the project to date and any lessons learnt. In addition it must include an update of the plan for the remainder of the stage or phase and other issues of note for the project board.

*See example document **27**: A highlight report.*

3.2.3 End of stage reports

At the end of each stage or phase the project manager produces a report for the project board which summarises the work of the previous stage. The report also contains a plan for the next stage or phase and an updated project plan. It must contain the following information for the previous stage or phase:

  – **the planned achievements;**

  – **the actual achievements;**

  – **planned and actual expenditure for:**

  - *manpower resources,*

  - *expenditure,*

  - *other resources.*

The report also provides an assessment of the successes and failures of the management of the project and any lessons learnt.

In addition it contains an overview of the next stage or phase of:

- **the planned achievements;**
- **planned expenditure for:**
  - *manpower resources,*
  - *expenditure,*
  - *other resources.*

*See example document **27b**: An end of stage report.*

3.2.4 Project Closure Report

At the end of the project the project manager prepares a project closure report which is a summary of the end of stage or phase reports.

The report contains:

- **the planned achievements;**
- **the actual achievements;**
- **planned and actual expenditure for;**
  - *manpower resources,*
  - *expenditure,*
  - *other resources.*

The report also provides an assessment of the successes and failures of the management of the project and any lessons learnt.

*See example document **21b**: A project closure report.*

4. Measuring Progress

All of the reports described in the previous section require measures of the progress achieved. This section examines what measures could be used and the advantages and disadvantages of each. The measures described in this section can be applied to programmes, projects, business-as-usual and non-project work.

4.1 Milestones

One of the most commonly used measures of progress is the milestone. Milestones can either tell you how far you have come or how far it is to go. In project management terms, a definition is "a significant date or event in a project which serves as a reference point in time for measuring a projects progress"

(*ABT Corporation's PMW manual 1997*).

Examples of milestones include:

- **the points in the project or system development method at which some significant deliverable, product or task has been completed.**
  e.g. user requirements agreed;

- **the points in the project or system development method where a major logical step has been completed. e.g. design now completed;**

- **the points in the programme or project which marks significant steps in its completion. e.g. in a programme the realisation of a benefit or part of a benefit, in a project the acceptance of the business case and authorisation to proceed;**

- **the points in the programme or project at which defined expenditure on resources (all the M's) will be reached;**

- **those points in the annual operations cycle where major parts of the business as usual activity have been completed.**
  e.g. first cut budget approved, staff appraisals completed;

- **those points in the annual operations cycle where a significant part of the business as usual budget or other resources has been consumed.**

What is important when using milestones as an assessment of progress, is to decide what types of milestone are required to convey real meaning to the operational management or programme or project board. For example, what means more to senior management, a point in the project where a deliverable is produced or a significant point when benefits or changes are achieved?

Therefore, there may well be a need to use several different "types" of milestones - each aligned to specific audiences. The adoption of this flexible approach can be very effective; however it can cause problems of consistency when comparing projects in the masterplan portfolio.

4.2 Deliverables, Work packages, Products

Another measure of progress favoured by many organisations is the deliverable, product or work package. The reason for their use rather than milestones is that they represent a measure of achievement – not just activity.

The size and importance of these vary, as do the various terms for deliverables, products and workpackages.

The definitions which have a common acceptance are:

Deliverable:

An output from the business-as-usual operations, programme or project which represents a significant part of the operational plan or the programme or project's objectives.

Work package:

A collection of one or more products which together contribute to a deliverable. The decision for what products are included in a workpackage is organisation, department or project specific.

Product:

A single output from the business-as-usual operations, programme or project given to an individual or team to produce. It may require more than one task or activity to produce and, in exceptional situations, be subdivided into sub-products.

4.3 Activities Completed

In some organisations this term is used to describe the unit of work required to complete a deliverable or product and consists of many tasks. While others adopt the classical definition; the activity is the operations performed to complete a task, where a deliverable or product consists of one or more tasks.

Because of this inconsistency, it is important that the definition of the term is agreed first. It is important that this measure is predominately a measure of activity, not achievement. This is because it is very easy to find new or additional activities to complete a deliverable.

4.4 Resources Consumed

This measure can be used to assess business-as-usual and non-project work situations, as well as programmes and projects. In the business-as-usual and non-project work, the resources consumed are compared to the planned consumption of the total annual plan or forecast of the many types of resources. This form of progress reporting can be particularly useful in ensuring the business-as-usual or non-project work utilises its budget allocation, but does not exceed it.

In the case of programmes or projects, the resources consumed provide a useful indication of both the progress to date and the eventual outcome. On its own the information about resource consumed is interesting but not very informative, it requires them to be used in conjunction with other information.

A good example of this is where resources consumed are used to calculate "burn rate" indicators. This term describes the following calculations:

> **Step One:**
>
> *Calculate the ratio of the total planned manpower resources required (in man days), to the programmes or projects elapsed days or duration.*
>
> **Step Two:**
>
> *Calculate the ratio of resources actually used to date to the elapsed days or duration to date.*
>
> **Step Three:**
>
> *Calculate the ratio of the estimated resources required to complete the project to the elapsed days left.*

An examination and analysis of the three ratios can provide some interesting information – for example if the third ratio is far higher than the other two, it probably means the programme or project will be late.

The same measurement system can be used for other types of resources e.g. costs, deliverables in isolation, but a comparison and analysis of the three ratios for all these measures can give an amazing amount of information about the status of the programme or project.

4.5 Earned Value

This term is also applied to a number of different measurement systems. Most of the software tools which support programme and project planning and scheduling have this as a function. In simple terms, earned value analysis provides a mechanism to compare and assess a product's worth to the resources used to develop it. Those figures are then compared to those planned to date, or for the project as a whole.

These comparisons can be carried out in number of ways – some of the most common calculations use the following components:

ACWP (Actual Cost of Work Performed)

Resources used to date x their actual cost rate

BAC (Budget At Completion)

Total planned resources x their budgeted cost rate

BCWP (Budgeted Cost of Work Performed)
also known as the earned value

BAC x the percentage of the work completed

BCWS (Budgeted Cost of Work Scheduled)

Resources planned to be used to date x their budgeted cost rate

EAC (Estimate At Completion)

Actual resources to date plus estimated resources needed to complete the project x their actual cost rate.

x = multiplied by

These formulae are used to plot tables or graphs of the planned and actual situation.

Organisations have found other, perhaps simpler methods to calculate earned value reports including:

- **assigning each deliverable with a "worth" and then calculating the ratio of what was spent to achieve the deliverable, with the value or worth. (This is done for planned and actual to date);**
- **assigning a "worth" to each hour or other unit of work performed on the programme or project – based on the total benefit the programme or project is to achieve – then calculate how much worth has been generated by multiplying the resources consumed by the worth. (This is done for planned and actual to date).**

Earned value can also be used in assessing business-as-usual and non-project work in a similar way.

The major problem with using earned value methods to assess progress is that it can lead to false assumptions about the programme or project. However, used wisely in an organisation which understands the principles and how to use the information, it can provide real benefits.

5. Designing an Effective Reporting System

After deciding what measurement method will be used to report progress, the next, and equally important step – convey the information to its intended audience. This section examines the factors to be considered when designing an effective reporting system. These are:

- **decide and agree who wants what and when;**
- **decide and agree the format;**
- **design Progress Information Collection / Collation;**
- **allow for flexibility;**

5.1 Who Wants What and When

The first and most important point to consider and agree is: who wants what report, about what and when? This is not as easy as it sounds, it is not just a question of asking the intended audience. Normally the potential audience does not know what to ask for and the different formats available.

Therefore when planning how to achieve this definition, it is vital that an education process is included.

The definition of these requirements should be carried out as part of the design of the PSO and its supporting infrastructure, ensuring that the information can be provided efficiently and effectively. The key to obtaining a successful design for this process is to ensure that the generation of the progress reporting information is integral and integrated into the whole of the infrastructure.

5.2 Decide and Agree the Format

Deciding and agreeing the format of these reports involves a tremendous amount of work. Experience has shown that most organisations go through three major stages with the formats of these reports.

The first stage usually entails the production of a number of sets of statistics about the progress achieved. The use of milestones planned and delivered, resources and expenditure and even earned value charts are used. This is because the organisation is still on a learning curve and believes that it needs all these figures to ensure that its has control of the situation.

With this type of reporting format the organisation can become preoccupied with what has already passed and the figures themselves, rather than what the figures tell them – the 'all information but no analysis syndrome'. After using this sort of reporting format for a period of time the organisation realises that what it needs is not a mass of figures, but a simple way of identifying the areas of concern and reports providing an analysis of the situation.

CASE STUDY

A large supermarket's information systems department used its PSO to collate and publish the progress reports from its programmes and projects. This process was achieved by extracting information from the project plans and importing this data into a standalone database. This data was then supplemented with further data supplied by the project manager and the information was used to calculate a large number of statistics about each project (over 100). These statistics were sent to the project managers for verification and, once they cleared them, circulated to the department executive and senior management.

A review was carried out to establish whether this process was achieving value for money for the organisation. The review identified that most managers only used one or two of the statistics.

As a result the organisation introduced a far simpler reporting system in which the project managers completed a simple one-page report and distributed it direct to the relevant managers.

The organisation then typically moves to the second stage of reporting – the Traffic Light System. This format takes the information provided and analyses it to make a judgement whether it is on target (Green), encountering problems that the organisation should be aware of (Amber), or has substantial problems that require management to take control action (Red). Some organisations also have a "doing better than expected" category (Blue).

The difficulty with this type of reporting format is deciding the boundaries for the different areas. There is a further problem that if these traffic lights are used for different viewpoints of the same situation – say delivery, costs, quality, risks – which one of these, or combination of them, should be used to describe the overall situation?

Diagram 11 **Traffic Light Report**

Programme Performance				Overall Status		

	Costs £	Benefits £	Benefits non-financial	Progress	Risk	Status
PROGRAMME						
PROJECTS						
1						
2						
3						
etc.						

CASE STUDY

The Post Office identified that it had a wide range of progress report formats used by its programme and project managers. It decided to rationalise and simplify these and also to make them available on the organisation's intranet system.

A project was commissioned to install a central database to which project managers would input progress data at prescribed intervals. An analysis and graphical output package was applied to this database, which produced the traffic light reports. The organisation tackled the problem of deciding the boundaries between the red, amber or green, by letting the individual project boards and project managers set them for their own projects.

These boundary problems are further compounded when multi-project programmes require the combining the individual project reports into an overall one for the programme.

After using this approach for some time a further problem emerges – that of the relationship of the projects. For example, if a project or business-as-usual activity costing £50,000 has a Red traffic light, and another costing £1,000,000 is at Amber, where should the organisation devote its time and resources to rectify the situation? Also, most traffic light systems **do not** include information enabling the organisation to identify the size or relativity of the constituent items in the reports.

This is when organisations move to the third stage of progress reporting. This type of reporting combines the traffic light system with some of the earlier metrices – however now they are value added reports or indices. For example the "Burn Rate" indicators described earlier also give some measure of the importance of the activity or programme or project.

5.3 Designing Progress Information Collection/Collation

A major factor to be considered is the design and operation of the progress information collection and collation system. This process should ideally be carried out as part of the design of the PSO and its supporting infrastructure to ensure the information is collected and collated efficiently and effectively. The key to obtaining a successful design for this process is to ensure that the collection and collation is integral to, and integrated into, the whole of the infrastructure.

There are two main approaches used for this process. The first of these is best described as the stand-alone approach. Here the information is supplied through a specific process, typical examples of this are a series of standalone reports from the project manager to the project board, programme manager and the PSO so they can collate the information into a report for the masterplan committee. This approach is not particularly efficient as the project manager could be supplying the same information to all these recipients. Also, although this approach is relatively simple, it requires a high degree of discipline to put into place and considerable effort to run and support.

The second type of approach is the integrated approach. The degree of integration depends on the number of different report formats required and the number of sources of information.

CASE STUDY

A major European organisation which supplies products and services to banks used the following approach:

The programme and project manager completed a report which contained all the information required to satisfy the requirements of the progress reports and supported the information requirements of other parts of the infrastructure – e.g. the estimating system.

The information submitted through these progress reports was supplemented by information in respect of the non-productive work and business-as-usual activities, through a system of electronic timesheets.

The information was sent electronically to the PSO who, after ensuring that the information submitted was to the required standard, completed a data transformation process, which not

only reformatted the data, but also produced the required reports and updates to the relevant
parts of the infrastructure.

This form of progress reporting, although more time consuming to set up, stands a greater chance of overall success as it is central to the PSO infrastructure and therefore generates a natural pressure on the suppliers of information to follow the agreed processes.

There are currently no off-the-shelf tools available to support this – however, several of the software companies have partial coverage of this function.

5.4 Allow For Flexibility

Whatever process is adopted initially, to design and implement an efficient system of progress reporting, it is inevitable that over a period of time the organisation will want to change the formats and even the information required. Therefore, when designing these systems, it is vital to allow for the building-in processes which allow the necessary flexibility without compromising the overall design of the system.

Of particular importance is the ability to change the format of the reports easily. It is also important to recognise and build into the design, the need for the information's recipients to carry out further analysis with the information supplied. This may mean that the output from the progress reporting process should be made available in an electronic format e.g. spreadsheet or other live text.

6. Time Sheet Systems

Of all the methods available to collect the progress information, the time sheet system is the most prevalent.

This section examines the various types of timesheet systems and the options available to operate and support them.

6.1 The Three Types of Timesheet Systems

There are three main timesheet systems used to collect progress information are:

- **push then pull;**
- **pull;**
- **pull then push.**

The push type of timesheet presents the user with a list of their activities (according to some form of plan) which they either confirm, or amend to reflect what was completed. The pull type requires the user to complete a blank sheet.

The selection of which timesheet system to use depends on which software tool has been selected to support the process. However the specific advantages and disadvantages of each system should be taken into account during the selection process for the software tool.

6.1.1 Push then pull

The "push then pull" system is a type of turnaround document. Here the timesheet system pre-loads each person's timesheet with the planned activities for the forthcoming week. The document is then sent to each person who updates it to reflect the work actually carried out. The document is then sent back to the timesheet system which updates the plans and the cycle starts again.

Diagram 12 **Push then pull timesheet**

Time Sheet	For: John Kelly			Week Number 24	Week Dates	14/06/99 – 20/06/99				
Planned Project Work	**Task Number**	**Task Name**	**Monday**	**Tuesday**	**Wednesday**	**Thursday**	**Friday**	**Saturday**	**Sunday**	**Total**
Project Astra	FE100	Data design	4hrs	8hrs						
Project Whizzkids	FD250	First draft PID			4hrs					
Project Mindsoft	EG299	Project Plan				6hrs				
Planned Non Project Work										
Absence										
Holiday							4hrs			
Total			4hrs	8hrs	4hrs	6hrs	4hrs			

This type of timesheet is very effective where all the work of the organisation is on a plan of some type that can be accessed by the timesheet system. If this is not the case, or the actual work carried out varies considerably from that planned, this type of timesheet system can require considerable manual intervention to keep it operating.

6.1.2 Pull

The "pull" type of timesheet system operates with the timesheet system sending a blank timesheet to each person at the end of the reporting period. Each person completes their

Diagram 13 **Pull timesheet**

Planned Project Work	Task Number	Task Name	Monday	Tuesday	Wednesday	Thursday	Friday	Saturday	Sunday	Total
Time Sheet — For: John Kelly — Week Number 24 — Week Dates 14/06/99 – 20/06/99										
Project Astra										
Project Whizzkids										
Project Mindsoft										
Planned Non Project Work										
Absence										
Holiday										
Total										

timesheet and sends it back to the system, which checks that the work is completed as planned. If any discrepancy is found, the timesheet is returned to the person who completed it and, after any rectification or acceptance, of the unexpected entries, is returned to the system which updates the plans the cycle starts again.

Diagram 14 **Pull then push timesheet**

Time Sheet — For: John Kelly — Week Number 24 — Week Dates 14/06/99 – 20/06/99

Planned Project Work	Task Number	Task Name	Monday	Tuesday	Wednesday	Thursday	Friday	Saturday	Sunday	Total
Project Astra	FE100	Data design	4hrs	8hrs						12hrs
Project Whizzkids	FD250	First draft PID			4hrs			4hrs		8hrs
Project Mindsoft	EG299	Project Plan				6hrs				6hrs
Planned Non Project Work										
Team Meeting					4hrs					4hrs
Customer Support Desk						2hrs	4hrs			6hrs
Absence										
Holiday							4hrs			4hrs
Training Seminar			4hrs							4hrs
Total			8hrs	8hrs	8hrs	8hrs	4hrs			44hrs

This type of timesheet system is particularly useful where a large proportion of the work undertaken is not part of a plan. To support this environment, the timesheet system usually has a "drop down" code system for a number of the activity categories. The problem with this type of timesheet is that it requires a large amount of manual intervention and decision-making to convert the data received from the source into the information needed to support the infrastructure.

6.1.3 Pull then push

This type of timesheet system operates with the blank timesheet being sent to the person as before, however, the person completing it not only has access to the plans for the current period, but also for those periods immediately prior and afterwards. As before, the completed timesheet is returned to the system and checked to ensure it meets the relevant quality criteria. It is then used to update the plans and the cycle starts again.

This type of timesheet system is equally applicable to both of the previous environments (where the work undertaken is not always part of a plan and where it is). As before, this sort of timesheet system usually has a "drop down" code system for a number of the activity categories. The problem is that the system also requires a lot of manual intervention and decision making to convert the data received into the information needed to support the infrastructure.

6.2 The Technical Options

There are a number of different types of software support tools available to support timesheet and progress reporting.

6.2.1 Specialist integrated package

This technical option supports the "Pull Me Push You" approach. To be successful the software package needs to be based around a database or repository. The repository is used to store all the information from the planning processes and the timesheet package uses the information to identify what activities are to be carried out, by who, for a particular reporting period. The information is loaded onto timesheets and sent to each individual.

This type of software usually includes a sophisticated process for information validation prior to the information being used to update not only the plans, but also other parts of the infrastructure.

Because the progress information is stored in a database, the preparation of reports is much more flexible and simplified as the choice of the information used and the software to generate the report is not as restricted as the other technical options.

One of the most popular versions of this type of software is Niku's Repository, supported by other applications such as its Team Workbench.

6.2.2 Specialist package with interfaces

This type of technical option is a halfway house between the fully integrated package and the simple packages or manual systems.

A special timesheet package reads and writes to one specific type of plan – often Microsoft's Project or Niku Workbench. Some of these types of software package can operate as full "Pull Me Push You", however most of them are "Push Me Pull You" packages. The major problem with this software is how it deals with non-planned work. Most of them allow the person filling in the timesheet to select from a list, or "drop down menu", of either preset codes or set new codes to represent unplanned work they have performed. The problems arise on two counts: the first problem is that the list of codes can grow to such proportions as to be almost unusable.; the second problem is what the package does with this non-productive work information. Often the packages simply total the information and present a list which add no extra value at all.

An example of this type of package is Innate's timesheet software.

6.2.3 Simple e-mail document with interfaces – do it yourself

This technical option is relatively low-tech and is often developed in-house using simple tools such as Microsoft's Excel or Access and standard e-mail packages. Typically this option operates as follows: Each person has a "stock" of electronic timesheets and once completed they are sent via e-mail to their manager for authorisation, who then sends it to the PSO, or direct to the PSO. The PSO extracts the information from the individual sheets and consolidates it to provide the required progress reports and also information for the relevant managers to update their own plans.

CASE STUDY

A subsidiary of a large electrical supply company developed its own timesheet system based around an Oracle database. To operate the system the organisation used a series of preset codes for its projects on the timesheets. The timesheets were submitted to a central point where they were consolidated and input to the database.

The database was then used to provide information for progress reports and expenditure and to raise invoices for the work performed to the organisation's customers.

This option is often adopted because it uses in-house technology and is simple to install and maintain. The problem is that it is not particularly efficient and does not support the concept of the integrated PSO support infrastructure.

6.2.4 Manual process

The final option is manual. Timesheets are produced on paper and submitted to the line manager for authorisation and input to the plans, then manually generated progress reports are produced. However in some organisations the PSO is sent these timesheets and they perform the updating process and the generation of the progress reports. This option can be extremely effective and flexible, but is time and resource intensive.

CASE STUDY

A major police force installed a PSO to act as a clearing house for information about the projects in its masterplan portfolio. The PSO first established a database of all the projects in the portfolio, then collected progress information. The PSO discovered, as they did with the database of projects, that a wide range of timesheets and progress reports were in use. The varying formats meant that they were unable to use automatic or semi-automatic consolidation methods and therefore had to resort to manual methods.

The effort required to complete this manual consolidation was considerable – initially they finished one consolidation cycle only a few hours before the next set of information arrived. To rectify this, they standardised the reporting mechanisms and got the project managers to send "consolidated" reports on behalf of their projects. The new reports fully met the organisations requirements.

Often this option is not considered and organisations go straight to one of the other options. Experience has shown that to dismiss this option without careful thought is ill-advised, as the full cost to the organisation of the purchase, implementation and operation of the more "efficient" systems can be extremely high.

7. Applying These Systems to Business-as-Usual and Non-Productive Work

In most organisations the time and resources devoted to programmes and projects only account for 20-30% of the organisation's activities. Many organisations now realise that it is equally important to have plans and to monitor and report progress on these other activities as it the programmes and projects.

7.1 Why These Areas Need to be Planned and Monitored

The organisation's strategic plan is realised through both programmes and projects and also business-as-usual activities and non-project work. The need for a planning, monitoring and control process for programmes and projects is understood by most organisations, however the need to have similar functions and processes for business -as-usual activities and non-project work is not.

In many organisations the only monitoring performed on these activities is unstructured and usually centered around only finance and budgetary issues. The reasons for the lack of a management function is because many organisations do not understand how it would be achieved and they do not believe that it is the "done thing" to demand such control for what they believe are management activities.

However, these types of activities can consume far more resources than programmes and projects and also, unless the demands of these activities are taken into account, the programme and project plans can become unrealistic.

This is because it is not uncommon for the project or programme plan to be developed ignoring the support activities which members of the development team have to undertake. Some programme and project managers attempt to take account of this other work by reducing the hours available for someone, or apply a factor of less than one to their efficiency. However, these are compromises. What is actually needed is a plan that really does take account of these other activities.

7.2 The Planning and Monitoring Methods

To effectively manage and control these activities using the same methods as those used for programme and project management, it is first necessary to realign a few basic concepts and principles.

Most managers will tell you that it is impossible to plan these activities because they are random etc. This is true, so new principles are applied to the planning methods.

The first of these new principles is to recognise that detailed plans, like those used by programme or project managers, are not applicable. The basic concepts are followed including progress reporting – the use of milestones, resources and outputs – but they are less prescribed and precise than those used in programme and project management.

The second principle is that this form of planning and monitoring provides some defined and agreed level of control over the activities – not total control as in programmes and projects. One organisation uses the term "results management" to describe this process. The remainder of this section describes the approaches used for business-as-usual and non-project work under such a regime.

7.2.1 Pseudo project plans

One of the most popular approaches is to establish "pseudo project plans" for all these activities. These plans are designed to cover all the various types of activities that are generally regarded as business-as-usual and non-project work such as:

- **business process operation;**
- **business process support;**
- **business process and operational management;**
- **problem and fault fixing;**
- **investigation and pre-programme or project analysis;**
- **sickness;**
- **holidays;**
- **authorised absence;**
- **training;**
- **special leave;**
- **attending seminars.**

The plans are constructed as organisation-wide, or based on individual departments. The selection of which of these two routes to follow depends on a number of factors – the most important of these is the structure of progress reporting supplied by this function.

For example, if the organisation only wants departmental-based progress reports for these activities then it is sensible to have departmental-based plans. However if the organisation believes that organisation-wide reporting is more beneficial, then this plan structure should be selected. Which ever option is followed, it is important to design the contents of the plans in a similar way to that of the project and system development methods. In particular, it is vital to use a structure for these plans which incorporates a standard resource and task coding system and a data dictionary to ensure that they are under control and the use of the codes are consistent.

The main problem with designing and installing these plans is to ensure that managers who are involved in the design and implementation, fully understand the purpose of the new function and, importantly, how to use the information. This ensures that the structure of the codes is designed to provide maximum benefits to the whole organisation.

CASE STUDY

While assisting an organisation in Belgium to adopt this approach, the manager responsible would not listen to the advice offered and demanded that the design contained just six codes for all the activities of the whole organisation. The PSO dutifully co-operated with the edict – while realising that approximately 200 codes in a five level hierarchical structure were needed for real control of the process. However, once the senior manager responsible for the six-code edict understood that the PSO was right, he then swung the other way and insisted that over 500 unstructured codes were installed. The staff became confused as to which code to use and as a result the information was inaccurate and inconsistent. The end result – the organisation lost confidence in the information and control of situations and as a result had to start the process all over again.

Diagram 15 **Business as usual coding system**

Code	Top Level	Code	Second Level	Code	Bottom Level
M	Management Activities	B	Business Planning	W	ISD Workplace Meeting
				M	Management Meetings
				L	LMA/STATS
		P	Performance reviews	R	6 monthly review
				F	Group Finance Lunch
O	Operational Support Activities	S	Systems Advisor Function	X	System X
		A	Application Support	S	SPJAM team mtg.
				J	JAM/CGS meeting
				R	Release Control Group
		H	Help Desk	X	System X
				Y	System Y
N	New Business Support	F	Forward Planning	I	IBM quarterly mtg.
				C	Compaq quarterly mtg.
				X	System X mtg.
				O	RCG/other mtgs.
				N	Review network issues
				F	Customer Services Open Forum
				M	Cross Function Meetings

The approach for building these pseudo plans is:

First Step: Design the task and resource code structure

This task code structure should be designed to meet the progress reporting and monitoring requirements. As with codes used for programmes and projects these should be aligned to budget and other organisational processes if possible.

This code structure should be supported by a data dictionary entry for all the tasks and their application. This ensures that duplication and overlap does not occur. When designing this structure it is strongly advised that you follow the advice set out in chapter 3. If possible, the task codes should also be aligned to those used in the programmes and projects.

Diagram 16 **Task and resource coding system**

Activity Code	Activity	Required Resource Code	Annual Total Effort in Man Days
MB	**Management Activities – Business Planning**		
MBW	ISD Workplace Meetings	SAG	40
MBM	Management Meetings	SAG	25
MBL	LMA/STATS	SAG	30
MP	**Management Activities – Performance Reviews**		
MPR	6 monthly review	MLT	10
MPF	Group Finance Lunch	MLI	20
OS	**Operational Support – Activities – Systems Advisor Function**		
OSX	System Y	SAX	50
OSY	System X	SAY	35
OA	**Operational Support – Activities Application Support**		
OAS	SPJAM team mtg.	OSS	25
OAJ	JAM/CGS meeting	OSP	50
OAR	Release Control Group	OSS	75
OH	**Operational Support – Activities – Help Desk**		
OHX	System Y	OSP	15
OHY	System X	OSP	20
NF	**New Business Support – Forward Planning**		
NFI	IBM quarterly mtg.	MLT	37
NFC	Compaq quarterly mtg.	MLT	44
NFX	System X mtg.	MLI	33
NFO	RCG/other mtgs.	MLI	31
NFN	Review network issues	MLT	22
NFF	Customer Services Open Forum	MLT	33
NFM	Cross Function Meetings	MLT	15

The resource codes should be treated similarly; however, it is vital that the same person has the same resource code in both programme and project management and business-as-usual and non-productive work systems.

Second Step: Build the skeleton project plans

In this step, the codes are transferred to a project plan using the organisation's planning software package. The resource pool allocated to the plans must include all the employees allocated to those particular tasks. It is important to ensure that this plan is given the same global calendar settings as the programme and projects. Failure to keep calendars in synchronisation can cause major problems when collating the information from the programmes and projects with these other plans.

Third Step: Allocate resources

This step requires a lot of tact and understanding. Each of the line, resource or department managers is visited and asked to estimate the amount of effort they want spent on each of the tasks/code, and who will be involved in, or perform the task.

A reasonable level of accuracy is required – not precision. For example, if the manager says the amount of time required on a task for the whole year is 20 days, and one person will do that part time over the year, then spread the effort over the whole year. This will ensure that the code will appear on the person's timesheet every reporting period.

Apply the same principle and process to non-project work such as sickness, holidays and authorised absence.

7.2.2 Resource management systems

This approach to planning, monitoring and progress reporting is similar to the "pseudo plan" approach, except there are no plans. The same steps are carried out, except in this case the information is stored not in a plan, but in a calendar spreadsheet or diary system.

The approach operates as follows. The line or resource manager has a resource management system which is used to record details of all the work which their staff undertake on programme, projects and business-as-usual and non-productive work.

The programme or project manager, after developing the first version of their plan, meets the manager and agrees when the required resource will be made available. The resource or line manager then includes this "booking" in the resource management system. The timesheets are generated from the resource management plan, which is also the driver for the progress reports. The programme and project plans are simply working documents for the programme and project managers.

Diagram 17 **Resource Managers Plan**

Description	Res Cat	Res Name	Effort/Period	M	T	W	T	F	T	M	T	W	T	F	T	M	T	W	T	F
				W/C 25/11						W/C 2/12						W/C 9/12				
PROJECTS																				
New O/S	SX	JAM																		
Win 98	SX	NFP																		
Lan Etn	SX	RUW																		
SST	SN	SGS																		
TASKS																				
Support (HD/Mitre/Pall)	SX	JAM	3.5 days week		8	8	8			8	8	8	8	8		8	8	8		
Support (HD/Mitre/Pall)	SX	NFP	3.5 days week	8	8	8	4				4	8	8			8	8		8	4
Support (HD/Mitre/Pall)	SX	RUW	3.5 days week		8	8	8			8	8	8		8		8		8	8	8
Support (Network/HD)	SN	SGS	2 days week	8			8				8			8			8		8	
Month end/Gti	SX	??	1.5 days month					1.5												
Runsheets	SX	??	1.5 days month									4								
Task Total				##	##	##	##	##	##	##	##	##	##	##	##	##	##	##	##	##
Business As Usual																				
LMA/STATS	SX	??	.5 day week					0.5						0.5						0.5
SPJAM team mtg	SX	JAM	2hrs per Mnth															0.5		
SPJAM team mtg	SX	NFP	2hrs per Mnth															0.5		
SPJAM team mtg	SX	RUW	2hrs per Mnth															0.5		
Systems Advisor Function	SH	TMN																		
Systems Advisor Function	ST	LAB																		
Systems Advisor Function	SP	DAR																		
Systems Advisor Function	SX	JAM	.5 day per qtr															0.5		
Systems Advisor Function	SN	SGS	.5 day per Mnth															0.5		
Systems Advisor Function	SR	CGS																		
JAM/CGS meeting	SR	CGS	2hrs per fontnight																	0.5
JAM/CGS meeting	SX	JAM	2hrs per fontnight																	0.5
Release Control Group	SP	AH																		
Release Control Group	SX	JAM	.5 day week					0.5						0.5						0.5
Release Control Group	SR	CGS																		
Release Control	ST	LAB																		
Group Finance Lunch	SR	CGS	0.5 per Qtr															0.5		
ISD Workplan Meeting	SR	CGS																		
Management Meetings	SR	CGS	0.5 per Mnth															0.5		
6 monthly review	SR	CGS																		
6 monthly review	SH	TMN																		
6 monthly review	ST	LAB																		
6 monthly review	SP	CPJ																		
6 monthly review	SP	DAR																		
6 monthly review	SX	JAM																		
6 monthly review	SX	NFP																		
6 monthly review	SX	RUW																		
6 monthly review	SN	SGS																		
IBM quarterly mtg	SR	CGS	2hrs qtrly															0.1		
IBM quarterly mtg	SX	JAM	2hrs qtrly															0.1		
Help desk																				
Customer Services Open Forum	SX	??	1 hr fortnightly															0.1		
System X mtg	SX	JAM	1hr fortnight															0.1		
System X mtg	SN	SGS	1hr fortnight															0.1		
RCG/other mtgs	SN	SGS	.5 day week															0.5		
Review network issues	SN	SGS	.5 day week															0.5		
Review network issues	SN	RUW	.5 day week															0.5		
Office move (pre/post work)	SN	SGS	2 days Mnth															0.5		
Weekend working	SN	SGS	3 days Mnth									0.5								
Cross Function Meetings																				
Business as usual				##	##	##	##	##	##	##	##	##	##	##	##	##	##	##	##	##
Grand Total				##	##	##	##	##	##	##	##	##	##	##	##	##	##	##	##	##

A venture capital company wanted to provide its line managers with a simple system to ensure that it did not over commit its staff who worked on a mixture of programmes, projects, business-as-usual and non-project work.

This was achieved by giving each resource manager a spreadsheet on which they "booked out" their staff to the various work. A system of standard names for all these tasks was used so that, if required, a report could be produced which consolidated information about all the activities on a specific task across the whole organisation.

When this consolidation was performed the organisation was amazed – they had no idea how much time was being spent on these activities!

This type of system is used where the source of power resides in the line or resource function and where resource utilisation and management is a major issue. The software used to support this process is usually built in house – although some of the commercial off-the-shelf software systems now provide support to this approach.

Diagram 18 **Integrated personal plan**

Integrated Personal Plan			W/C 25/11					W/C 2/12					W/C 9/12				
Projects			M	T	W	T	F	M	T	W	T	F	M	T	W	T	F
New O/S	SX JAM		8.0	8.0				8.0		8.0			4.0				
Business As Usual																	
Support (HD/Mitre/Pall)	SX JAM	3.5 days week			8.0	8.0	8.0	8.0		8.0			8.0		8.0	8.0	8.0
SPJAM team mtg	SX JAM	2hrs each 3 weeks													2.0		
Systems Advisor Function	SX JAM	.5 day per qtr													2.0		
JAM/CGS Meeting	SX JAM	2hrs per fortnight															2.0
Release Control Group	SX JAM	.5 day week				4.0					4.0						0.5
6 monthly review	SX JAM																
IBM quarterly mtg	SX JAM	2hrs qtrly													1.0		
System X mtg	SX JAM	1hr fortnight													1.0		

7.2.3 Ignore the boundary systems

The final technical option that can be adopted for this process is to ignore the boundaries between the programme, projects and business-as-usual and non-productive work – and use personal plans for all the resources. This is a specialist version of the previous option, but this time use a plan for each person.

The plan includes all the work undertaken by the individual and the system has pseudo project plans, which again are mainly working documents. To make this system work all the codes used in the plans must be carefully controlled and centrally administered. Indeed, the plans can also be centrally administered.

This method can be particularly effective where the organisation wishes to keep control of what work is scheduled to each employee. It demands a high level of co-ordination and may be regarded as inefficient because it has a high proportion of duplicated information, but this type of system can be very useful.

8. Summary

The progress reporting and timesheet system adopted by an organisation is at the heart of how it monitors and controls activities and is used so much that it **must** be right.

The key to getting it right is to include it in the design of the PSO infrastructure. There are many options open to the organisation and it is vital that the selection process takes account of all the options before a final decision is made.

All of the decisions and processes must endeavour to provide value added information and concentrate on the analysis, not just provide raw information.

Chapter Seven

Issue, Change and Configuration Management

1. Introduction

Programmes and projects are like a voyage of discovery. The purpose of the voyage is agreed, a plan is developed, the resources allocated or obtained, and the journey begins. From then on the captain, or the manager of the programme or project, has to deal with issues and changes to the plan. This chapter examines what these issues are and why changes occur. It then describes the supporting infrastructure and sub-processes that can be installed and used by the PSO to support the programme and project manager in managing issues. It also looks at the purpose and function of the configuration management system employed to help the voyage succeed.

2. What Are Issues?

"Issues" has a number of possible meanings. The PRINCE project management method defines it as "anything which could have an affect on the project (either detrimental or beneficial)".

This definition covers anything that can affect either a programme or project, so the sources of such issues derive from anywhere, or anyone, affected. With these extremely wide parameters it is conceivable that the programme or project manager could be swamped with thousands of issues – some critical to the success of the programme or project and the others trivial. To control this situation most programme and project management methods demand that while an issue must be formally acknowledged and recognised, only those that are documented will become part of the issue management process.

This restriction is not designed to make submitting an issue for consideration a major hurdle, but to put a "checkpoint" in the process. This "checkpoint" asks the person who wishes the issue to be considered, to reflect whether it is important enough to spend five minutes expressing the concerns on paper or e-mail. It also provides the programme or project manager with a mechanism of recording what has been raised, and by whom, so that they can acknowledge that the issue has been received and given due consideration.

The content of these issues can be specific, such as suggesting that something in the programme or project needs to change; or generic, perhaps reporting that one of the programme or project's objectives will not meet the agreed requirements. The remaining issues are generally just information or potential risks which need to be managed or closely monitored. Finally, an issue may be so complex that it cannot be neatly placed in one of these "slots". It may consist of several separate smaller issues. Therefore, issues can lead to requests for change, exception situation reports and even new entries in the risk register.

3. What Are Changes?

Nearly every programme or project strives to reduce the number of changes by ensuring that the requirements, which the programme or project is to satisfy, have been discussed, and agreed by all the relevant stakeholders .

Also the programme or project plan must be based on the best information available, carefully assembled, and agreements made with the suppliers of resources. However, even with all these safeguards, the need for change to the arrangements will always occur.

The most common change requests are those affecting the:

- **deliverables or workpackages;**
- **timing of the deliverables;**
- **scope of the programme or project;**
- **method of approach used to execute the programme or project;**
- **resources to be used.**

4. Managing Change

There are number of reasons why issues and changes need to be managed. This section examines the following perspectives:

- **the potential direct impact on the programme or project;**
- **the indirect repercussions which can arise;**
- **how the changes can assess the "health" of the programme or project.**

4.1 Direct Impact

Obviously issues and changes need to be examined because they can severely affect the programme or project. There may be a direct impact from possible delays and additional costs when redeveloping completed or partially completed deliverables to meet the revised requirements. Or, an issue, or change, may substantially change the whole basis of the programme or project in its aims, objectives, risks, business case, or its impact on the user or other communities.

The most important of these is the overall impact that issues or changes can have on the programme or project – failure to manage these can cause failure.

CASE STUDY

The failure of the London Ambulance Service Computer-Aided Dispatch System was so serious that a formal inquiry was held to determine the causes.

The inquiry revealed;

"in their eagerness to please users, [they] often put through software changes "on the fly" thus circumventing the official project issue report procedures whereby all such changes should be controlled. These "on the fly" changes also reduced the effectiveness of the testing procedures, as previously tested software would be amended without the knowledge of the project group. Such changes could, and did, introduce further bugs."

The case for effectively controlling and managing issues and changes is obviously overwhelming.

4.2 Indirect Impacts

The most crucial indirect impact may come from a demoralised development team and the problems of increased expectations of management. If the issues or changes mean redeveloping previously agreed components, the development team will very quickly start to adopt the attitude: "it does not really matter about getting it right as it will change anyway". A symptom of this is that the "quality" of the deliverables starts to slide rapidly and more errors arise, which in turn leads to more issues and changes.

The attitude of the organisation's management can also change considerably and may include the belief that they do not need to think out their requirements - that a commitment given is only a temporary thing. Finally, their expectations for the programme or project may become out of control as they lose "the vision" of what the programme or project is designed to deliver.

4.3 Using Issues and Changes to Assess the Health of the Programme or Project

Issues and changes provide a useful guide to the overall health of the programme or project. For example, if a programme or project has received no issues, or made no changes, it can mean that it is being superbly managed; or else the organisation is not interested or aware of its existence; or even, it does not know that it can raise issues and request for changes.

Similarly, a high level of issues or changes can indicate that the users are not sufficiently involved in the acceptance processes of the programme or project; or that the communication strategy or plan is not operating effectively – it can, of course, also mean the complete opposite!

The most important indication of the programme or project's health is the number of issues and changes that are raised and how quickly the programme or project management process deals with them.

Sudden changes in the numbers of issues and changes received by the programme or project management team indicate that something has changed. The programme or project manager should investigate and identify the causes of these variations and report the findings to the programme or project board at the first available opportunity. The "clear up" rate indicates the internal efficiency of the programme or project management process and, also, the level of access that the programme or project has to high level management when major decisions are required.

5. How do Issues and Changes Need to be Managed

An efficient and effective method of managing the evaluation and implementation of issues and changes is vital.

This section describes the typical process adopted by a programme or project. The process is applied to both issues and changes. Indeed most changes come from issues and in some project management methods all changes must be first registered as an issue. This insistence of dealing with everything initially through the issue route is to ensure that there is a consistent interface with the "outside world". Also, with just one procedure the process is simplified and ensures that nothing is overlooked.

The remainder of this chapter explains the processes and steps on the basis that all changes start life as an issue. If your organisation does not do this and maintains a separate system for changes, the same steps and output apply.

5.1 The Issue and Change Management Process

As with all processes, the issue and change management process can be sub-divided into a number of steps and is supported by a series of outputs. The typical steps are:

- **acknowledge and register;**
- **first level evaluation;**
- **first level decision, or;**
- **second level evaluation;**
- **passed to relevant decision authority;**
- **decision;**
- **inform author;**
- **action and update records.**

5.1.1 Acknowledge and register

The first step consists of recording the receipt of the issue in the issue log and acknowledging the receipt of the issue to its author.

At its simplest the issue log is either a sheet of paper or computer document on which are recorded the:

- **reference number allocated to the issue;**
- **type of issue (issue, change request, exception situation);**
- **authors name and contact details;**
- **date the issue was received;**
- **date the issue was acknowledged;**
- **the current stage of the issue's evaluation;**
- **the history of the evaluation process and the location of supporting documentation;**
- **date the issue was closed.**

See example document **28**: *The project issue log.*

5.1.2 First level evaluation

The first level evaluation of the issue is the next step. The purpose of this first level evaluation is to ensure that any programme or project threatening issues are quickly highlighted and appropriate action started immediately. This evaluation involves assigning a priority for the issue. The categories used vary, but typically are: must; important; nice to have; cosmetic; and no change.

In addition this evaluation establishes whether it is a change request, exception situation report, new or changed risk, or an issue and the impact it may have on the programme or project. This assessment uses the information from the programme definition statement and, or, project initiation document, which identifies who in the organisation is empowered to make a decision about changing the plans and other agreed arrangements to deal with the issue raised.

Where the issue can be resolved without the programme or project being delayed, outside of its agreed plan and accompanying tolerance, the programme or project manager can be empowered to make the decision. If the issue is more serious, it can be assessed by the programme or project board, or the main board. At this point the issue log is updated to reflect the evaluation.

5.1.3 First level decision or second level evaluation

This is used when the first level evaluation reveals that the issue lies within the programme or project manager level of authority. They then commission whatever actions are required to implement their decision and inform the author of their decision and the action being taken. The issue log is then updated.

If, however, the first level evaluation has revealed that the issue cannot be decided by the programme or project manager, the issue proceeds to the next step.

5.1.4 Second level evaluation

The second level evaluation ensures that important issues are thoroughly researched, and the impact fully evaluated, before they are presented to higher management for a decision. This second level evaluation is led by the programme and project manager who identifies what the evaluation process should be and who should be involved in it.

This second level evaluation may lead to the issue being converted to an exception situation report or formal change request.

5.1.5 Passed to relevant decision authority

When the second level evaluation has been completed, the programme or project manager passes it to the relevant level of management for a final decision. The issue log is again updated and the author notified of the progress made-to-date in the evaluation of the issue.

5.1.6 Level two decision

The programme or project manager attends the meeting at which the decision about the issue is made – in some organisations the person who raised the issue is also invited. At the meeting, the relevant managers receive the details of the evaluation made by the programme or project manager and any recommendations made. They decide on the required course of action and the programme or project manager is authorised to make any amendments, or changes required, to action their decision. The decision is again noted on the issue log and a copy of the minutes of the meeting either attached or cross-referenced.

5.1.7 Inform author

Having received the decision the programme or project manager then informs the author of the decision and action to be taken. Where possible this should be carried out face-to-face so that the programme or project manager has the chance not only to thank the author, but also to explain what has happened.

5.1.8 Action and update records

The issue is then formally closed and the actions carried out. It is at this point that the responsibility for managing the resultant changes passes to the configuration management system.

6. What Infrastructure and Sub-Processes are Needed to Support the Management of Issues

To support the management of these issues a supporting infrastructure and sub-processes are required. A number of the components of this infrastructure and sub-processes are also part of the configuration management system described later in this chapter.

6.1 The Infrastructure Required

One of the fundamental elements of the infrastructure required to support issue and change management is the issue log. In a programme or project that is relatively small this can be a simple paper-based or electronic-paper system. However in more complex situations a computerised database application should be considered. It is important to remember that even such a small system as a database to support issue management needs to be treated as a mini-project and not built "on the fly".

Whatever infrastructure is installed to support the issue management system, it must interface efficiently and effectively with those used for the change and configuration management system. Indeed, the documents used in the issue management system should be incorporated into the configuration management system.

At its simplest the configuration management system can also be a paper-based system. The key elements of the configuration management system used to support the issue management process are:

- **the register of all documents;**
- **the filing system supporting the storage and retrieval of master copies of documents;**
- **the history file of all the documents.**

See example document **29***: The configuration management record.*

6.2 Evaluation Processes

The issue management process involves two sub-processes in whichever type of evaluation is carried out – first or second level evaluation. The support needed for both these evaluations are:

- **a defined process for the evaluation;**
- **a defined team of staff who carry out the evaluation;**
- **rules or agreements to cover who makes what decision;**
- **standard or template documents.**

This process is usually standard in all programmes and projects and documented in the programme definition statement and, or, project initiation document.

6.3 Decision Processes

In a similar way to the evaluation process, this process involves two sub-processes – first and second level decision. Both of these sub-processes need to be supported by:

- **a defined process for the decision making;**
- **rules or agreements to cover who makes what decision;**
- **standard or template documents.**

The definition of these processes, and how they are operated, can be standard to all the organisation's programmes or projects – or special arrangements are agreed. These arrangements, both the standard and any special arrangements, are specified in the programme definition statement (PDS) and or the project initiation document (PID).

7. Configuration Management

Configuration management is essential. A real life example illustrates why:

CASE STUDY

A passenger jet had a cracked windscreen. The fitter assigned to replace the windscreen looked up in the parts manual the equipment needed – a new screen, seals and bolts to hold it place. He obtained the spares and fitted the windscreen. Later that day, as the plane took off, the new windscreen became detached from the plane and the pilot was sucked part way out of the cockpit – he was saved by a stewardess who grasped hold of him.

After landing safely, the resulting enquiry found that the manual that the fitter had consulted was out of date. New components had been introduced making the windscreen "thicker". As a result the bolts specified to hold the windscreen were now too short to allow for the new "thicker" windscreen and the windscreen blew out.

Configuration management ensures that all the deliverables and products are built to fit together and remain so when changes occur.

7.1 The Processes of Configuration Management

Once the programme or project has been completed, the deliverables or products will be absorbed into the organisation. It is therefore vital that the following processes are operated on an organisation-wide basis, as well as in the individual programme or project.

Configuration management consists of four processes:

- identification;
- control;
- status accounting;
- audits or verification.

7.1.1 Identification

The identification process is used to ensure that all the deliverables and products are uniquely identified and that any revised or updated versions produced or made, are numbered and identified as such, so that they are not confused with the original version. It also ensures that any other products that interface with the deliverable or product are defined and their relationship is both agreed and documented.

This numbering system helps ensure that if any deliverables or products change, interfacing

Diagram 19 **Configuration Identification Numbering**

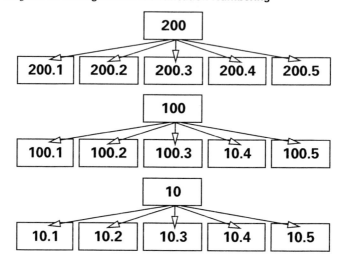

can be checked to ensure that they still "work together" as expected, or are modified as required.

7.1.2 Control

The control process ensures that once a deliverable or product has been completed and passed as fit for purpose, this version is stored and any changes made are carried out only when appropriate approval is obtained from the relevant level of management.

It also ensures that the reason for those changes are documented and that changes required to other deliverables or products that interface with it, are also updated. The level of control to be exercised is summed up in this quote from the PRINCE Manual, "Once a product has been approved – nothing moves, nothing changes without authorisation".

7.1.3 Status accounting

Sufficient documentation should exist in the configuration management system and infrastructure so that a complete history of each deliverable or product is available. This information should be to such a standard so that an audit can be carried out to ensure that the contents of the programme or project configuration matches the documentation.

*See example document **30***: *A configuration status account.*

7.1.4 Auditing or verification

This process is carried out at regular intervals throughout the programme or project. It provides assurance to the programme and project management team, and the organisation, that there is conformity between the deliverables and products and their authorised state as described in the configuration management system.

See example document **31**: *Configuration audit report.*

7.2 Infrastructure Required to Support Configuration Management

As with the issue and change processes described earlier in this chapter, the configuration management process needs to be supported by an infrastructure. One of the key elements of this infrastructure is the storage of records. It is possible to handle quite complex configurations with a simple card index system. However, increasingly organisations are resorting to in-house built database applications and packages supplied by commercial software houses.

The other major infrastructure component is that of the physical storage of the deliverables or products (usually referred to as configuration items). In the past this posed a major problem – but is now rarely a problem with low cost electronic storage media.

7.3 Interfacing Configuration Management with Issue and Change Processes

It must be obvious that the three processes described in this chapter – issue, change and configuration management – must be designed and installed so that they interface with each other efficiently and effectively.

It is also essential that these systems interface with other components of the PSO infrastructure, for example the deliverable library, the deliverable/staff database and the estimating guidelines.

Therefore, the design must be careful to ensure that, in supporting these three processes, the infrastructure does not duplicate data held elsewhere and that it ensures your programme or project does not have the wrong bolts fitted to your windscreen.

8. Summary

The effective management and operation of the issue, change and configuration management processes is of vital concern to the programme or project manager. Ideally the design of these processes and the supporting infrastructure and system should be included in the overall design of the PSO and its infrastructure. What is essential however is that these elements of programme or project management must be formal, efficient, and effective.

Chapter Eight

Risk Management

1. Introduction

All human activities are subject to a degree of risk. When assessing the level of this risk, a general rule can be applied:

The greater the size, novelty or complexity of the task – the greater the risk.

There are two further landmark rules that must be observed:

Murphy's Law – Things will always go wrong when you least expect, or want, them to.

No two activities are ever the same therefore experience only guides us.

This chapter first examines risks – why they need to be managed; how they should be managed; and the types of risk management methods commonly used. It also explains the supporting infrastructure and processes needed to support the programme and project manager in managing risk.

2. What Are Risks?

Although often seen as negative, programme and project managers have come to recognise that not all risks are bad – indeed they can have a positive effect on the programme or project. As a point of reference the EC commissioned a project under its EUREKA initiative to develop a risk management methodology called RISKMAN. This set out to design a standard risk management methodology which could be used in all EC countries. What is interesting about this methodology is that it deals with both positive and negative risks and defines risk as follows: "a risk involves uncertainty and has an impact".

Following this definition to absurd proportions could mean that every programme or project is affected by everything that happens everywhere. However, in this chapter the areas of potential risks dealt with are those which directly affect the programme or project. Areas of risks included are those from the:

- **business environment;**
- **market place;**

- **method of approach used for execution;**
- **availability or quality of resources;**
- **development of the deliverables.**

Nearly all programme and project management methods include a formal risk management process. However, as with issue management, risks can be identified by anyone directly associated with the programme or project. Therefore management processes must also be included in the programme and project management method to handle risks identified outside of the formal risk process. The issue management process provides this channel as any issues that are in essence "new risks" are classified as such. They are then passed to the programme or project manager for consideration and inclusion in the method's formal risk management process.

3. Why Do Risks Need to Be Managed?

There are many obvious reasons why risks need to be managed, this section examines the most common of these:

- **reduces the programme and project uncertainty;**
- **increases the chance of success;**
- **reduces the chance of increased cost and delay (10 to 1 rule);**
- **reduces the impact (stitch in time);**
- **increases the visibility of the risk to management.**

3.1 Reducing the Programme and Project Uncertainty

Because a programme or project undertakes new ventures, they have more risks to their success than activities which repeat something already achieved. There is a lack of knowledge (hindsight is wonderful) of what really needs to be done and the team has not experienced the specific programme or project before.

To reduce the level of risk, the team uses its experience and knowledge from previous programmes and projects to identify as many of the uncertainties as possible. The risk management process then enables them to propose actions to remove, reduce or limit the effects of these risks. They try to build into the new programme or project previous knowledge and experience, thus reducing some of the uncertainty associated with its management and control.

3.2 Increasing the Chance of Success

The process of risk management also increases the chances of the programme or project being viewed as a success. This is partly due to the removal of some uncertainty, but perhaps even more importantly it exposes the concerns of the programme or project managers to the organisation's management. Deciding whether or not a programme or project is a success is not a science – perception, belief and values are the deciding factors.

One of the skills that truly great programme and project managers practice is that of "expectations management". Experience has shown that failing to manage expectations will guarantee that the programme or project will be viewed as a failure by at least part of the organisation. Risk management is one the important tools used to ensure that the organisation's management has a realistic expectation of the programme or project.

3.3 Reducing the Chance of Increased Cost and Delay (10:1 Rule)

In addition to assisting the programme and project manager in their management function, risk management also helps reduce the chance of increased cost and delay to the project. As with reducing the uncertainties, the risk management process helps, using previous knowledge and experience, to identify where delays and increased costs may occur. The same knowledge and experience will help the programme and project team prepare contingency and alternative plans and strategies to deal with the risk.

The 10:1 rule refers to the level of cost reduction and time over-run typically achieved by such planning. Risks identified and dealt with early on increase the cost or timescales – but they generally reduce the effects of the risk if it had materialised by a tenth .

3.4 Reducing the Impact (Stitch-in-Time)

As well as cost and delay, risk management reduces the impact of risks in other ways. The identification of a risk to the user community, for example, that it cannot deal with the changes the programme or project will provide, can be reduced by ensuring the affected department has additional staff over the change period.

This stitch-in-time approach often has the same rule of 10:1 as described in the previous section. Another point is, should such risk avoidance actions be costed and included in the business case for the programme or project?

3.5 Increasing the Visibility of the Risk to Organisation's Management

Programme and project managers recognise that all programmes and projects have an element of risk. If they are to succeed they will need to devote considerable effort to managing them.

Many other senior managers who have risen up in the organisation through the normal management route, may not understand why risk management is required. By involving them in the risk management process, the programme or project manager ensures that the risks are visible to the decision makers and increases the importance and role of risk management.

4. What Is The Risk Management Process?

Whichever risk management method is used in a specific programme or project, they all follow the same basic process. What varies is the way that the process is carried out.

Diagram 20 **Checklist of Steps in Risk Management Process**

Areas of Activity Covered by Risk Management

● Identify and formally record Risk
● Assess Impact
● Decide on Risk Management Strategy
● Allocate relevant actions
● Monitor success of actions and re-assess the Risk

4.1 Identify And Formally Record Risk

The first step is to identify and formally record the risk. This process can be carried out in many ways – the most common of these are:

- **risk identification workshop (unstructured);**
- **risk identification workshop (structured);**
- **risk identification "Delphi technique".**

The majority of these approaches use some form of knowledge base to support the identification process. These knowledge bases come from a variety of sources, including specialist suppliers.

This chapter includes a generic knowledge base, which could be used during a risk identification workshop. The risks identified in the processes are usually classified into four main types:

Business risks *– those risks to the business that the programme or project will cause if it fails to deliver what is required with the agreed resources.*

Programme or project risks – *those risks which can cause the programme or project to fail to meets its agreed objectives with the agreed resources.*

Security risks – *those risks to the security of the organisation, and other processes used by the organisations, caused by the new programme or project.*

Maintainability risks – *those risks which affect the ability of the organisation to maintain and support what the programme or project delivers.*

These classifications are used to help identify which area of management should be involved in their assessment and the strategy and tactics used to control them.

4.1.1 Risk identification workshop (unstructured)

This method of risk identification is usually a brainstorming meeting where interested parties identify potential risks.

These are then documented and the workshop continues with the assessment of their impact, or the programme or project manager and their team are tasked with preparing that information for a separate assessment workshop.

4.1.2 Risk identification workshop (structured)

The organisation can use a formal structure to the workshop. This structured workshop uses a checklist generated from the organisations' records of previous risks (the risk register), or a software tool which can provide a similar structure to identify the possible risks.

*See example document **32**: The risk register.*

4.1.3 Risk identification – Delphi technique

In this approach the risk identification is performed by the same group of people (authors) individually, or in small groups, using the structured or unstructured approach. The results are then collated together and any major discrepancies identified. The authors of the "exceptional results" are then asked to explain their reasons for the differences and the other authors asked if they wish to modify their assessment. If needed, the results are recalculated.

4.1.4 Generic knowledge base (checklist)

The identification of the areas of risk to be managed are usually addressed through the use of a predefined risk register or checklist. These ensure that each potential area of risk is examined and thought about.

Failure to use such a checklist can result in important areas of risk not being examined or inadequately analysed.

These checklists can be provided through some form of automated software tool, which can integrate this assessment stage with the latter probability and impact assessment stage.

What is vital, when using such checklists, is that the user is allowed to update and, or, personalise them, to reflect any risks of special interest to the particular organisation. In addition the checklist must be updated to include any new risks gained by the organisation from contemporary and previous programmes and projects.

These checklists group risk into five sections:

- **business environment – external;**
- **business environment – internal;**
- **programme and project organisation and management;**
- **programme and project delivery mechanism;**
- **programme and project content.**

Business Environment – External

There are a number of issues in the external business environment that need to be considered when assessing the risks to the project .

1. Is there likely to be any major governmental or political changes during the development of the project that may effect:

    - **the stability of the market place?**
    - **the reason for the project?**
    - **the scope or content of the programme or project?**

2. Is there likely to be any major change in the economic environment during the development of the programme or project that may effect:

    - **the financial aspects?**
    - **the current market place for the programme or projects?**
    - **the future market place for the programme or project's products?**

3. Is there likely to be any major change abroad during the programme or project's development that may effect:

    - **the reason for the programme or project?**

- **the financial aspects of the programme or project?**
- **the scope or content of the programme or project?**
- **the stability of the market place?**
- **the current market place for the programme or project 's products?**
- **the future market place for the programmes or project 's products?**

4. Are there likely to be to any significant new developments in technology or other process improvements during the programme or project that may effect:

- **the reason for the programme or project?**
- **the financial aspects of the programme or project?**
- **the scope or content of the programme or project?**
- **the stability of the market place?**
- **the current market place for the programme or project 's products?**
- **the future market place for the programme or project's products?**

5. Are your competitors:

- **undertaking any major new investments?**
- **re-organising themselves?**
- **undertaking similar programmes or projects?**
- **carrying out any other form of competitive edge improvement activities?**

Business Environment – Internal

There are a number of issues to be examined in the organisation's internal business environment when assessing the risks to the project.

1. Are there likely to be any major internal changes e.g. re-organisation during the programme or project's development that may effect:

- **the parts of the organisation the programme or project is provided for;**
- **the reason for the programme or project;**
- **the scope or content of the programme or project.**

2. Is there likely to be any major change in the internal economic environment

during the development of the programme or project that may effect:

- **the financial aspects of the programme or project?**
- **the cost benefit analysis of the programme or project?**
- **the rate of return required for the investment to be considered viable?**

3.   Is there likely to be any major change in personnel, departmental structure, or internal procedures in the organisation during the development of the programme or project that may effect:

- **the reason for the programme or project?**
- **the financial aspects of the programme or project?**
- **the scope or content of the programme or project;?**
- **the stability of the market place?**
- **the current market place for the programme or project 's products?**
- **the future market place for the programme or project's products?**

4.   Are there likely to be to any significant new developments in technology, or other process improvements in other parts of the organisation during the programme or project that may effect:

- **the reason for the programme or project?**
- **the financial aspects of the programme or project?**
- **the scope or content of the programme or project?**
- **the stability of the market place?**
- **the current market place for the programme or project 's products?**
- **the future market place for the programme or project's products?**

5.   Are the technical and business aims of the programme or project:

- **compatible with existing business strategies?**
- **compatible with existing IT/IS strategies?**
- **compatible with other relevant strategies?**

6.   Is the data which has been used in the estimation of the resources required by

the programme or project:

- **from a known, tried and trusted source?**
- **encompassing all associated quality and management control activities?**
- **relevant to the programme and or projects?**
- **allowing for a calculated amount of tolerance?**

7. Have senior level management taken ownership of the programme or project and ensured that this is communicated to all members of the organisation?

Programme or Project Organisation and Management

There are a number of issues that should be examined in the programme or project organisation structure when assessing the risks to the programme or project.

1. Has the organisation put in place the necessary organisation and other infrastructure components to:

- **produce an agreed brief or terms of reference for the programme or project?**
- **develop and agree a blueprint for the changes the programme or project is to achieve within the organisation?**
- **ensure the programme or project has the necessary finance and skilled resources?**
- **ensure the reasons for the programme or project are still valid and the progress made is regularly reviewed?**
- **resolve any priority clashes?**
- **monitor progress of the programme or project and the constituent projects?**

2. Are there likely to be any changes to the management environment that are responsible for the programme or project during the development of the programme or project that may effect:

- **the senior managers who are sponsoring the programme or project?**
- **the amount of time these senior managers can devote to the programme or project?**

- the launching of other projects that interface or interfere with the programme or project?

- changes in the priority given to the programme or project?

3. Is there likely to be any major change in the organisation during the development of the programme or project that may effect:

- the sponsors of the programme or project;

- the position of the recipient parts of the organisation;

- changes to the investment profile/decisions of the organisation.

Programme or Project Delivery Mechanism

There are a number of issues that should be examined in respect of the programme or project delivery when assessing the risks to the programme or project.

1. Has the programme or project delivery been defined in terms of:

- an agreed statement of the aims/objectives and costs/benefits of the project – a programme or project brief, terms of reference or blueprint?

- support from an agreed and documented programme or project management method?

- a series of tranches, stages, milestones or phases?

- the business products to be produced?

- the other components of the programme or project, such as management of change?

- linkages with other related programmes or projects or change initiatives?

2. Will the programme or project be:

- controlled by a group of senior managers who are responsible for its delivery?

- managed to a defined programme or project management method?

- developed to a defined programme, project brief or terms of reference?

- monitored by senior management?

- employing tried and trusted planning and control systems?

3.	Are the technical development strategies to be used in the programme or project:

	–	**established?**

	–	**well known to the organisation?**

	–	**well known generally?**

4.	Are the members of staff with responsibility for delivering the programme or project :

	–	**experienced in such activities?**

	–	**empowered with the necessary span of control and authority?**

	–	**allocated the necessary resources?**

	–	**aided by a PSO?**

5.	Have soft, human or change management elements been included in:

	–	**the responsibility matrix for the programme or project?**

	–	**the definition of the programme or project?**

	–	**the list of products or deliverables to be developed?**

6.	Has the organisation ensured that there are:

	–	**effective communications between the programme or project manager and managers of related programmes or projects?**

	–	**estimating systems used in the programme or project which are accurate and up-to-date?**

Programme or Project Content

A number of issues should be examined in the programme or project's content when assessing the risks to the programme or project.

1.	Has change management been included in the programme or project in:

	–	**the programme or project brief, blueprint or terms of reference?**

	–	**any human resource issues?**

	–	**ensuring that staff experienced in this discipline are involved in the programme or project?**

- ensuring that the organisation is equiped to deal with the situation.

2. Are the technical development strategies in the programme or project:

- established?
- well known to the organisation?
- well known generally?

3. Are the members of staff responsible for delivering the programme or project deliverables or products:

- experienced in such activities?
- empowered with the necessary span of control and authority?
- allocated the necessary resources?
- supported by a programme or project support office?
- able to deliver "soft" programmes or projects, e.g. personnel or attitude change?

4. Are the programmes or projects interdependent with others to such an extent that:

- failure or delay of another programme or project places this programme or project at risk?
- a total or partial failure of one component of another programme or project means this programme or project is at risk?

4.2 Assess Impact

The assessment of the impact is also called the "evaluation of the risk". This can be combined with the identification process, but most organisations prefer to keep the processes separate. This is due to the amount of research necessary to evaluate the possible impact of the risk and the need to model the knock on or collective effects.

This impact or evaluation stage consists of assessing the probability of the risk occurring and its impact on the programme or project.

The assessment of the probability of the risk occurring is usually made with predefined guidance, based on previous experiences. This is one area of the assessment and management process where the use of software, or other tools can be very useful. These tools provide the programme or project manager with an assessment based on a larger information source than their own.

The probability of an identified risk turning into an event can be expressed as either a qualitative or quantitative value.

In the case of a qualitative assessment, the risk is usually expressed as a judgement – e.g. it is certain to happen, unlikely etc.

The quantitative assessment assigns a probability in either a percentage, or a value of points out of 10, for example. In addition, a number of methods use a weighting factor to convert the assessment to an expression of its overall importance to the programme or project.

A further form of quantitative assessment is the effect of the risk materialising expressed as a variation to the expected duration or resources needed. This then enables the project manager to recalculate the expected costs and duration of the projects using a PERT (Project Evaluation and Review Technique) approach.

Diagram 21 **Risk Pert Evaluation**

		Duration	**Cost**
Project Plan	Base Case	18 months	1.5 million
Project Plan	Worst case	36 months	4.0 million
Project Plan	Best case	15 months	1.3 million
Project Plan	Worst 2 standard deviations	30 months	3.5 million
Project Plan	Best 2 standard deviations	16 months	1.4 million

These statistical based probability and impact quantification measures can be used manually, but normally the amount of calculation and information necessitates a specialist computer-based tool.

4.3 Decide on Risk Management Strategy

Having identified and assessed the impact of the risk, the risk management process needs to decide how the risks will be contained, eliminated or managed. Again it is common for checklists to be used as the basis of the decision. It is also vital that the user is allowed to tailor these lists to reflect the particular organisation's experiences from previous projects.

These measures usually seek to either:

- **contain the risk by insulating the project from its effects;**
- **eliminate the chance of the risk occurring by implementing remedial action;**

or

- impose procedures and assign the monitoring and management of such a situation to a specific person or group.

The following factors determine which of these routes is adopted:

- the value of the programme or project to the organisation;

- the value of the programme or project's deliverable to the organisation;

- the costs of correcting the risk's impact if it occurs;

- the costs of the strategy in relation to the value of the risks;

- the availability of resources to eliminate, contain or manage the situation.

The use of decision tables, cost benefits analysis and impact assessment techniques are common in this part of the risk management process.

One of the critical success factors for using risk assessment and management successfully, is that the findings are the responsibility of both the programme or project manager and the senior managers who are responsible for the programme or project. Therefore it is vital that

Diagram 22 **Risk Conditions Summary**

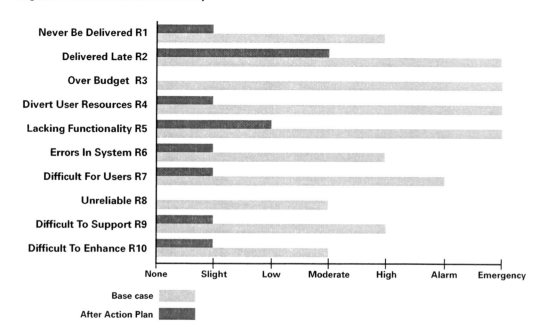

these senior managers are involved in the approval of the risk management plans and take an active role in the risk identification and assessment process. Indeed, in some organisations it is the senior manager's responsibility to perform all three sub-processes described in this chapter.

4.4 Allocate Relevant Actions

This next sub-process is where many organisations fail – ie, they do not put in place relevant risk actions. Having agreed what actions are needed to address a potential situation, and by whom, the programme or project manager must ensure that the actions are included in the plan, and are monitored and controlled. The most successful programme and project managers either:

- **include the actions as tasks in the relevant projects;**
- **create a new project, which contains all these risk management activities,**
  or
- **treat the risk actions as standalone work packages in the programme plan**
  or portfolio.

The risk activities can then be managed, monitored, reported on and controlled in the same way as other activities in the programme or project.

*See example document **33**: A risk action plan.*

4.5 Monitor Success or Actions and Re-Assess the Risk

The assessment of the risks and its management will need to be updated as the programme or project progresses. This reappraisal is needed for four reasons:

- **the completion of parts of the programme or project may increase or decrease the probability of the identified risks happening;**
- **the environments surrounding the programme or project may change, presenting new risks or changes to existing ones;**
- **the team can consult the appraisal to ensure it reflects knowledge gained during the initial parts of the programme or project;**
- **to identify the successes and failures of the risk management actions.**

The key decision is the frequency of such reappraisals – some of the programme or project management methodologies prescribe this for the end of each tranche, phase or stage, or when a significant event has occurred, either internally or externally to the project. The general recommendation is a six-weekly review.

All reviews must, as with the initial review, be discussed and agreed with the senior managers responsible for the programme. Most of the software tools available allow for the comparison of this reappraisal with that carried out in stage two. A comparison helps communicate to senior managers the changes in the risk management strategies.

5.   The Main Types of Risk Assessment

The main methods used to assess the impact of the identified risks are qualitative and quantitative.

5.1 Qualitative

Qualitative methods assess the risk's potential impact on the programme or project in terms of quality. The term quality here is used to its maximum meaning - fitness for purpose.

The assessment covers the usual factors – being late or over budget etc., but also examines other measures such as the reliability of the deliverables, the level of difficulty in maintaining or supporting them and their usability.

The method works by asking the evaluation or assessment team to answer some questions, each of them with a multiple choice answer.

The answers are measured against a database of values. At the end of the evaluation process the scores or values are calculated and compared to a further table.

*See example document **34**: A scored risk assessment.*

The key to these methods is the research and database that underpins them. For example one company researched over 400 projects and conducted multiple regression and factor analysis techniques to identify both the questions and scoring that should be adopted for their method.

The fact that these methods are based on known situations and real programmes and projects is a major strength. Such methods knowledge bases are bigger than most individual programme or project managers possess and therefore the results have a high validity.

However, be aware of possible inherent weaknesses in the database. Unless it was constructed in house, you will not know what kinds of projects it was based on, the age of the data – and therefore whether it is applicable to your programme or project?

5.2 Quantitative

The quantitative approach to risk management assesses the risks to the programme or project in terms of delays, costs, problems with functionality and maintainability, or the possible time and financial consequences of the risk actually occurring.

A risk panel is used to perform the first of these types of quantitative assessment. This group, a mixture of senior management, programme or project team members and other managers with an interest in the programme or project, assesses and allocates a level of probability of each of the risks occurring. Information from previous programmes and projects is used to support this process. The information from the assessment is then used to prepare charts or tables which summarise the results.

These charts are used by the organisation to identify which risks should be managed. The risk assessment process should then be repeated to measure the reduction or elimination of risk and to assure the organisation that the risk management plan has not caused any new risks.

*See example document **35**: A quantitative risk assessment.*

The second quantitative approach uses a statistical method to predict the range of potential outcomes of the programme or project if risks occur. This approach first identifies which of the programme or project deliverables, products or activities are likely to be affected by which risk. To each of these a probability curve is applied which, based on previous programmes or projects, provides a range of possible estimates for their time and cost.

This information is then used, in conjunction with an assessment of how likely it is that this risk will materialise, to prepare a series of revised estimates for the overall time and cost of the programme or project.

This analysis is similar to the Project Evaluation and Review Technique (PERT) in the planning process.

As with the other quantitative approach, the results are used to identify the required risk management activities and evaluate the effects of these activities by repeating the assessment.

The complexity of the mathematics and statistics used in these approaches mean that the use of a software tool is essential. There are a number of commercial software tools available – notably @Risk and Predict.

This approach is extremely useful in drawing management's attention to the risks and their possible consequences. It is also useful in evaluating which are the most important risks and the effects that the deployment of specific risk management activities would have on the programme or project.

The only concern here is an over reliance on the figures generated by this process. The use of complex statistical approaches can mean that the assessments assume a pseudo-scientific validity. This is a false premise as they only provide an indication, based on estimates and probabilities. Nevertheless, if used with care and understanding they are extremely useful.

6. Infrastructure and Processes Required

6.1 The Basis of the Infrastructure – Manual or Computer Systems

The risk management process can be supported by manual systems, computer software tools or a mix of the two. The following factors help decide which to adopt:

- **the numbers of programmes and projects that need supporting;**
- **the potential impact on the organisation if the risks materialise;**
- **the level of sophistication of the risk management process that the organisation can deal with.**

The general rule is that the more factors present, the more the organisation is likely to implement software tools to support their process.

There are many types of tools that can be deployed ranging from those based on, and using, complex statistical models, to simple automated questionnaires. The choice of which tools to employ is again dependent on the three factors described previously – the more sophisticated the requirements, the greater the need for complex tools.

6.2 Integration With Other PSO Infrastructure Systems

It is vital that whatever infrastructure is installed to support the risk management process, it must be integrated with the other components of the PSO infrastructure.

The obvious links are with the issue and change control, and configuration management systems. The change control process must ensure that actions needed are included in the various deliverables, products and activities in the programme and project plans and an issue can obviously be part of the risk process.

The other components requiring links are the estimating matrices, deliverables/staff database and the processes and standards used in developing the business case.

6.3 Supporting Infrastructure for Risk Assessment and Management

The risk assessment and management process itself needs a supporting infrastructure. The major components of this are:

- the risk register or library;
- the risk log;
- the risk management history file.

6.3.1 The Risk Register or Library

The risk register can be used in two ways. The first is to store all the risks identified in previous programmes and projects so that they can be considered during the risk assessment. This form of risk register needs to be designed to ensure that the risk is stored in an easily identifiable way for the programme and project manager. They must also hold as much supporting information as possible, including which programme or project the risk originated from, why the risk was selected for special consideration, the risk management actions used and the success or failure of those actions. The supporting information could also include the number of times that the risk has been included, or a ratio or percentage indicating if the risk should be considered for an average project.

The second use of the risk register is to collate and provide a consolidated list of risks on all the programmes and projects in the organisations portfolio that have been identified and are being managed.

This consolidated list enables the organisation to rationalise its management actions. For example, one action could support one or more projects or similar actions can be allocated to one person.

6.3.2 Risk log

Each programme or project should have its own risk log. This log contains:
- the reference number allocated to the risk;
- the type of risk (business, project, security, etc);
- date and method of how the risk was identified;
- date of the last update;
- description of the risk;
- an assessment of how likely it is the risk will materialise;
- an assessment of the impact or severity of the risk;
- the management actions being used;
- the current status of the risk.

See example document **36***: A risk log.*

6.3.3 History file of the risk management process

The history file can be a separate support system, or it can be combined with the risk register.

History files contain the detailed records of the history of each risk with cross-references to relevant documents. This file is particularly important to the programme or project manager when they are preparing the end of programme or project report.

*See example document **37**: A risk history file.*

6.4 Evaluation Processes

The risk evaluation process requires support to enable the programme or project manager to perform a "what if" analysis, identifying the potential impact on the project if the risk materialises, on the programme or project plans, the business case and the requirement specifications.

This supporting infrastructure includes providing information from a wide range of sources and the tools to enable the alternative scenario evaluations to be carried out efficiently and effectively.

6.5 Management Strategy Decision Processes

Once the impact of the risks have been assessed, the organisation will need to define a strategy for the management of the risks.

To support this process, the person responsible for deciding the strategy must have access to the risk register, risk history files, and risk logs. This enables them to assess what actions should be included in the strategy and how they should be implemented.

6.6 Action Decision and Monitoring Process

Having decided the risk strategy, the required actions, and the processes used to monitor them, must be chosen.

There are a number of strategies that can be deployed to manage risk and each of these requires support.

6.6.1 Containment

A wide range of actions can be used to contain a risk. These actions include containing the impact of the risk by preparing alternative action plans – redesigning the programme or project plan to ensure the component facing potential risk is not on the critical path. Actions can also be directed at containing the chance of the risk occurring. Some of the actions used to address this problem include pre-booking or pre-allocation of resources and monitoring the issues that the risk identified.

Diagram 23 **Risk Management Monitoring Sheet**

Risk No.	Risk	Action	Responsible	Start	Complete	Report Method
1	Delay due to inexperienced staff	Additional staff to be allocated to the nominated key products	Mr. D Purves (Project Manager)	09/08/99	16/11/99	Report when cleared to P Board
2	Failure in quality review of key products	Use of external advisors during the development of these key products	Mr. D Purves (Project Manager) and also Mr. D Smith Manager Department X	09/08/99	16/11/99	Include QR stats in weekly Report to P Board
3	Lack of funds to carry out risk avoidance	Obtain additional tolerance for the project from the programme	Mr. D Marsh Executive member of the project board	15/08/99	15/08/99	Report when cleared to P Board
4	Failure of prefabrication company to deliver on time	Weekly visits to the supplier by the procurement department to assess progress	Mr. G Strange Head of procurement	09/08/99	Delivery Date 20/11/99	Include status in weekly Report to P Board
5	Delays due to protesters on site	Construct 3 metre fence and employ security staff	Project manager and head of procurement	09/08/99	12/09/00	Report when cleared to P Board
6	Possible problems with capacity of concrete plant	Set up standby arrangements with local suppliers	Head of procurement	09/08/99	31/08/99	Include production report weekly Report to P Board

The selection process for which containment actions should be used need to be supported with information from a number of sources including the risk register, the programme and project plans and the business case.

6.6.2 Eliminate

When deciding what actions are needed to eliminate a risk, the risk register provides considerable help. It may be necessary to re-plan a part, or the whole, of the programme or project; use a different development method or approach; or to change the scope of the programme or project.

Whichever of these approaches is selected, the programme or project manager needs access to the PSO infrastructure to decide on the necessary actions.

6.6.3 Reduce

If the reduction route is adopted, the programme or project will need to be re-planned or redirected in some way, or contingency funds or arrangements employed to minimise the effects of the risk. This contingency can be used to obtain different or more manpower resources or to use alternative materials or equipment etc.

To support the implementation of this strategy it is essential to have access to all parts of the infrastructure which support the planning processes, the acquisition and deployment of resources and alternative sources of materials and equipment.

6.6.4 Insure

The use of an "insurance" strategy can be literal, or can describe other activities which provide compensation if the risk materialises.

In respect of insurance, it may be possible to obtain insurance from either a specialist organisation or from the suppliers involved in the programme or project, if the project is late or fails to meet expectations. Specialist help is required, not just to find such organisations, but also to ensure that the insurance will pay if the worst happens.

The same critical approach must be taken to any such insurance or penalty clauses entered into with suppliers. Experience has shown that it is difficult to enforce such clauses and, even if enforced, they do not often solve either partys' problems. As before, specialist help is needed to ensure that such contracts are enforceable and adequately compensate if the risk occurs.

6.6.5 Live with it

The final strategy is to accept that the risk is too small to warrant any form of control action or that is impossible to deal with satisfactorily.

The support needed for this strategy is increased monitoring of the situations that lead to risk occuring. Also an amendment of the control processes can allow action can be taken quickly if the risk materialises.

6.7 Action Monitoring

Experience has shown that most organisations involved with the risk management process identification, usually perform the activities with efficiency and effectiveness. However, one area which they nearly always neglect is the monitoring and controlling of the chosen actions. This is where the PSO infrastructure can provide real assistance.

One of the most successful ways the PSO provides support is to create a special project in a programme where all the risk actions are included. The risk actions are then planned, monitored and reported as in any project.

The risk actions can also be built into the relevant projects and, as in the special project above, they are planned, monitored and reported. Whichever method is used, monitoring the risk management actions is essential.

6.8 Include in the Programme Definition Statement or Project Initiation Document

All arrangements to deal with the risks identified in a programme or project must be documented and submitted to the programme or project board for their approval. Initially this is done in the programme definition statement (PDS) or the project initiation document (PID). Any changes made to the risk management strategy and tactical plans must be incorporated into updates of the PDS and PID. In addition, the results of these strategies and tactics must be evaluated and documented in the risk registrar so that the experiences gained can be recycled for future programmes and projects.

7. Summary

Risk management is a vital component of a programme or project. Indeed some maintain that programme and project management is risk management in disguise.

Risk management needs to be carefully considered and treated with a level of formality which ensures that it is taken seriously and managed effectively and efficiently. The risk management process will require considerable support from the PSO infrastructure and its information needs must be incorporated in the design of that infrastructure, as well as its interfaces with other components.

Although it can be supported and carried out using manual processes or computer software, it is important that these do not eliminate the need to think.

One of the key support components is the configuration management process and systems. The deployment of a risk management process and the control action means a large number of items in the configuration library will need to be amended. Major problems can ensue unless the systems can cope with these changes.

Finally, it is better to ensure that the actions are controlled, rather than spending effort on evaluating every possible scenario. It is impossible to identify all the risks – concentrate on making sure that the ones identified are actioned and the action is monitored, controlled and recorded in the risk register, ready for the programmes and projects of tomorrow.

Chapter Nine

Business Cases

1. Introduction

Every organisation requires a business case for any significant investment.

This document is necessary for two reasons: firstly to ensure that there is sufficient justification for the investment and, secondly, to ensure that the various options for delivering the product or service have been examined and the most cost effective option selected.

2. What is a Business Case?

A business case is a document which provides all the relevant information about a programme or project. This information is translated as far as possible into financial terms so that a decision can be made whether to comission the work, and, if so, which is the best proposed option.

It provides all the information relevant to the decision, such as the reasons for, and objectives of, the programme or project. It must also explain what will happen if the investment is not made. The most important component of the business case is the description of the benefits the organisation will realise from its investment and the critical success factors which will judge the result of the investment.

The business case must also define the resources to be consumed by the investment. In some organisations the term "investment appraisal" is used rather than business case . Indeed, the term can be applied to all investment opportunities, to identify where the available funds are best applied, rather than appraising the options within a single programme or project. The same approach and technique is used in both the investment appraisal and business case.

3. Why Do We Need A Business Case?

The business case provides the organisation with the information needed to decide whether the benefits of the proposed programme or project merit the investment, and which options should be adopted.

In addition, the business case also provides the organisation and the programme or project manager with an initial estimate of the required resources. These estimates, together with the timescales, provide the programme or project manager with the basis of the programme or project plan.

The estimates also provide the organisation with the basis of the monitoring and control processes – i.e. the agreed targets for expenditure and delivery.

Moreover, the business case provides a level of assurance that the investment is sound and the programme or project will deliver the requirements.

4. Developing The Business Case

4.1 The Background And Objectives Of The Programme Or Project

The first step in developing the business case is to define the background to the programme or project. This may be a simple statement that is part of the organisation's strategic plan, or a lengthy explanation of the ideas behind the programme or project. This definition must contain sufficient information to illustrate to the organisation's senior managment the reasons for the programme or project, and show the programme or project manager why it is needed and what it must provide.

The business case also includes the aims and objectives of the programme or project. This must be a description of the functionality required and not a description of the solution. For example, it may state "The aim of the programme is to implement new business processes and supporting systems for the invoicing with the objectives of reducing errors to .001% and ensuring no invoices are unpaid after 25 days, etc." Whereas presented as a solution it would state "to implement X invoicing software systems and associated new processes".

By describing its functionality it encourages the document's author to identify real alternative ways of providing the functionality in the options section .

4.2 Identifying the Options

Having agreed the background and objectives of the programme or project the business case's author must identify and define the options that are available to the organisation to deliver the required benefits.

These options must represent the classic options of:

- **Do very little or almost nothing radical to achieve the objectives:**
  - *For example implement new manual processes or carry out minor business process re-engineering rather than develop a computer system, or purchase a complete solution from an external source to meet the objectives.*
- **Do something a little more radical to achieve the objectives.**
  - *For example develop and implement not just new manual processes, but also some increased automation of a process or a major business process re-engineering assignment. Even implement a tailored software package to meet the requirements.*
- **The third option is do everything.**
  - *This refers to options that implement radical changes – perhaps automating a complete process or implementing a bespoke application.*

Each of these options must provide the required functionality and benefits and each will have a different costs and benefits profile, level of risk, and acceptability to the organisation. What is vital is that these are true options, not just sub-options.

As an example of true options, imagine the programme or project is to provide a new method of transporting you to work.

Option one could be to use public transport, option two, personal transport, and three, a chauffeur-driven limousine. These are true options because they represent radically different ways of achieving the end result. If sub-options had been identified they might have been a small, medium or large car. To ensure that you have identified real options, a useful guide is that true options can be sub-divided into sub-options.

But here is a problem: just how many options should be identified and examined? In an ideal world the answer would be as many as possible, but in reality the the business case is best restricted to three real options.

For each option, the cost and benefits are identified and compared to the current situation using a completely consistent set of processes to evaluate them.

5.   Costs

5.1 Introduction

This should be the easiest part of the analysis, but take care to ensure that each element of cost is consistently evaluated for each option examined. To ensure that this is achieved most organisations use a proforma, or standard spreadsheet, to prepare a statement of the costs. The proforma subdivides the costs into a number of standard categories and ensures that a common approach is used on all the options, acting as a checklist to ensure that no costs are omitted. The following section describes some of the general rules and conventions which ensure consistency in the business case.

5.2 The Rules

Rules are needed to deal with:

- **timing;**
- **inflation;**
- **taxation;**
- **costs already incurred and benefits already obtained;**
- **future costs and benefits.**

The following section looks at the typical rules that are applied to the identification and definition of both the costs and benefits of the above elements.

5.2.1 Timing

What is an appropriate duration for the programme or project? It should be defined and agreed by senior management and take into account a number of factors including any specific rules that the organisation has for business cases – for example, all IT projects 3 years, for capital equipment 10 years, etc.

The issue of timing is of crucial importance for two reasons:

- **money is worth more today than tomorrow – even with zero inflation – because of that, money can be invested elsewhere to gain benefit;**
- **there is a cone of increasing uncertainty in the future. A potential benefit is much more likely to be realised now than the same benefit in five years' time.**

The effect on the business case of these two factors is dealt with in the financial analysis, and risk and sensitivity sections discussed later.

5.2.2 Inflation

In considering the impact of inflation, the recommended approach is to perform the assessment at constant (present-day) prices. This ensures that a wholly consistent set of assumptions is used across all costs and benefits. The only exception to this universal approach, is where it is expected that some costs or benefits may increase at a different rate to other parts of the business case. For example the organisation may expect that computer equipment costs will not inflate as much as salaries. In such circumstances an allowance is made in the business case to cover what is known as "differential inflation" by increasing or reducing the expenditure accordingly.

5.2.3 Taxation

Taxation will occasionally have an impact on the choice between options in the business case, especially when capital expenditure is high. However, such analysis should never be attempted, except by a taxation specialist who also has knowledge of the organisation's specific circumstances. Hence, the business case generally leaves out tax considerations.

5.2.4 Costs already incurred and benefits already achieved

It is vital that costs already incurred or committed, and all benefits already obtained, must be excluded from the analysis. It is only future costs and benefits, beyond the decision point, that should be considered.

5.2.5 Future costs and benefits

In all the assessments of costs and benefits discussed below, three important principles must be applied:

- **each line item of cost or benefit should be separately identified and recorded (preferably in a spreadsheet);**
- **the analysis should show the cost or benefit in each year or half-year;**
- **great care must be exercised to consider the likely causes of changes in both costs and benefits over time. For example, a benefit may be to increase sales volume over time and this itself increases costs over time.**

5.3 One-off Costs

The majority of costs will be incurred through the performance of the tasks identified in the programme or project plan and schedule. It is a common mistake to estimate such one-off costs only up to the day when the system goes live. However, when the system is "bedding in", there may be some additional costs such as temporary staff. These, and like costs, should be anticipated.

Typically, standards are set by the organisation's finance department for calculating costs.

The following section describes the one-off costs included in the business case.

5.3.1 Programme or project team costs

In order that these costs are assessed realistically, it is important to decide how to deal with the following:

- **what cost rates are to be used, the specific cost of individuals, i.e. salary & National Insurance (NI), or the generic cost of the class or category of the resources;**

- **what man-days will be included, actual workdays planned or the weeks that each resource is made available to the project;**

- **how will the costs for non-project time, e.g. holidays, be included;**

- **how will the costs of overheads, e.g. space and management, be included?**

5.3.2 User costs

As with the programme or project team costs, it is important that user effort is fully reflected in the programme or project costs. e.g. in assisting with the development of user requirements, specifications, acceptance testing, user training, etc.

5.3.3 Incidental costs and expenses

Again, a standard approach needs to be used to ensure that these are dealt with consistently across all the options.

5.3.4 Capital expenditure

Many programmes or projects require the purchase of hardware and software. These should be shown at their full capital cost at the time of purchase. Some key points to consider here are:

- **any grants against capital cost should be shown explicitly as a negative cost and timed at the date the cash should be received;**

- **see also residual values below.**

5.4 Recurring Costs

These are the additional items of cost resulting from the new system. The following cost categories are recommended to be used:

- **staff costs (use the same subdivisions as in one-off costs);**

- **consumables;**

- **maintenance of equipment;**

- **system enhancement and maintenance.**

Remember that all the above costs are to be calculated as those costs over and above the current situation.

5.5 Residual Value

Assets purchased under capital expenditure decline in value over time. Residual value is the price at which such assets could be sold at the end of the analysis period. So it is a negative cost, but it falls logically on the cost (not the benefits) side of the analysis.

The residual value of each asset purchased should be calculated using the organisation's formal standards for depreciation. For example, if the standard for hardware depreciation is a straight line to zero after 5 years, then the residual value 3 years after acquisition is 40%.

*See example document **38**: A cost analysis.*

6. Financial Benefits

In exceptional situations there may be nothing under this heading. For example, if the programme or project is solely to comply with new regulations and has no other benefit, then it is a waste of time trying to quantify the benefits. However, many benefits can be quantified financially.

The single most important point about all such benefits is that the most senior users must be involved in their evaluation and committed to their achievement.

As with the costs section of the business case most organisations use a proforma or standard spreadsheet on which to enter the benefits. Some organisations use a proforma which includes the calculation of the benefit by comparing pre and post programme or project costs, others only use the net figures (the difference).

6.1 Displaced Cost

This is the most straightforward benefit to identify (e.g. personnel, equipment or materials). Some of the savings will arise naturally, e.g. costs paid externally to run and support the system that the programme or project is to remove or replace. However other displaced costs are only potential benefits – they need a plan to realise them. This is true of any personnel costs, where it is important to establish and verify that the potential savings can actually be achieved. Where the notional saving is only part of a person's time, or perhaps release of capacity on a mainframe computer, it is not always obvious that the savings can be realised. The released capacity might have zero value. Guidelines for valuing such savings must be set by the organisation.

6.2 Increased Revenue

The programme or project may be an enabler or pre-requisite for increasing revenue; rarely will it directly increase revenue. So, as above, plans must be in place to realise the increase in revenue that the new service, product or business system enables.

6.3 Other Financial Benefits

The direct benefit of a new service, product or business system will often lead to other indirect benefits that can themselves be quantified. For example:

- better debtor records enabling debtor days to be reduced;
- improved supplier communications, hence reduction in supply lead times and therefore stock reduction.

In each case the user should estimate the immediate measure of benefit e.g. debtor days reduced from 50 to 40, supplier lead times reduced by 50%; these then form the basis of the calculation of financial benefit.

For example, if current debtors are £1m, then reducing debtor days by 20%, as above, will produce a cash benefit of £200,000.

6.4 Other Intangible Benefits

There will be benefits to which it is impossible, or unwise, to assign financial value. You must recognise that fact, but still list and explain them.

For example:

- government regulations demand it;
- without a system like this we will go out of business;
- better, faster management information will allow better strategic decisions to be made;
- customer service will be demonstrably improved, hence our competitive reputation.

Some of these "intangible benefits" can be partially converted to some form of financial value by applying the "So What" test. This test works as follows:

Customer service will be improved.

So What?!

We will keep our existing customers.

So What?!

We can reduce our advertising costs, as we will not require so many new customers to replace those we lost.

So What?!

It will save us £x per year. That's what!!

These partial measures are useful, however there will always be some benefits, or parts of benefits, that cannot be assigned a quantitative value of any sort.

*See example document **39**: A benefits analysis.*

7. Financial Analysis (Discounted Cash Flow)

The purpose of the financial analysis is to create a meaningful summary of the financial measures of the programme or project.

Usually the organisation's finance director will specify which set of financial measures should be used. A set of measures is required, because no single measure provides all the information needed.

The shape of the cash flow for most programmes and projects is that the costs come at the start and the cumulative costs rise to a peak, until the benefits arrive. These benefits continue to accrue over the life of the system and the cumulative benefits begin to exceed the cumulative costs. Thereafter the benefits continue to grow and provide the positive balance of benefits over cost that is the justification for the programme or project. However, benefits are worth less in later years than in early years, and this must be incorporated in the analysis.

The major measures used are:

7.1 Maximum Cumulative Cost

This is the cumulative cost at the end of the project implementation, before the benefits start. If the whole project fails to deliver any benefit, it is the maximum sum that will be lost. This is very simply calculated.

7.2 Break even Period

This is the period from the present until the cumulative benefits exceed the cumulative costs (i.e. the time it will take for net benefits to reach zero). Again the calculation of this point is straightforward.

7.3 Net Present Value (NPV)

Both NPV and the Internal Rate of Return (IRR) take account of the time-value of money using the same principle of discounted cash flow (DCF). Typically the finance director will set a rate of return (r%), against which each project should be measured. This value (r%) represents the value the organisation places on having money now rather than in a year's time. So if r is set at 10%, the calculations are as follows:

£100 in year 1 is worth 1/(1) = £100

£100 in year 2 is worth 1/(1.1) = £90.91

£100 in year 3 is worth $1/(1.1^2)$ = £82.64

NPV is calculated using this principle, and is illustrated in the following example:

Year	1	2	3	4	5
Cash Flow in Year (£K)	-500	200	300	400	500
Discount Factor	1	.909	.826	.751	683
(r=10%)	(1/1)	1/(1.1)	$1/(1.1^2)$	$1/(1.1^3)$	$1/(1.1^4)$
Net Present Value	-500	182	248	300	273
Cumulative NPV	-500	-318	-70	230	503

So the NPV of this 5-year cash flow is £503k, and the breakeven point is in year four.

7.4 Internal Rate of Return (IRR)

This measure uses exactly the same concept of discounted cash flow as NPV. In NPV, the rate of return r% is set and the calculation of NPV is based upon that rate. The calculation of IRR reverses the process – it is the value of r where, at the end of the project or programme, the cumulative NPV is £0. The higher the IRR, the better. There is no formula for calculating IRR, but there are iterative procedures available on spreadsheets to help identify it.

7.5 The Effect of Inflation

As previously stated, inflation should be excluded from all the initial assessments of costs and benefits. Often, it is valid to exclude it altogether. It is worthwhile to include it if there are good grounds for believing that certain types of cost and benefit will incur different rates of inflation from others. If included, it should be applied to each separate line item of the cash flow analysis. However, the original (constant price) analysis should always be kept as a reference.

7.6 How Should the Rate of Return (R) be Set?

There is a plethora of guidelines on this matter. Some finance directors set r higher in order to take account of the high uncertainty in later years – the widening of uncertainty. In this way cash flows in later years have a small effect.

8. Risk and Uncertainty

All the preceding sections identify the line items of costs and benefits and give them a single financial value, where appropriate in each period of the analysis. This is the base case. However, there are many reasons why this base case can be subject to variation or uncertainty.

For example, the programme or project may:

- **cost more to deliver than currently planned;**
- **be late, so the benefits will be late;**
- **not deliver the benefits as well as planned, so the benefits will be less.**

Even if the programme or project delivers exactly as planned, the benefits are only estimates and are subject to a great deal of uncertainty, especially in the later years.

There is always a danger of "paralysis by analysis". While calculating endless sets of figures relating to different combinations of possible events, it is important to remember the ultimate objective: to present information on cost and benefits in order that a decision can be made. Keep it as simple and as clear as possible.

Looking first at the programme or project, the risk assessment performed in a consistent manner across the options and across programmes or projects, identifies the risks that the project would be late, over budget or deliver inferior benefits. In conjunction with users and the programme or project team, this risk analysis should be quantified into best, likely and worst cases.

For example:

- **at best, *it will be on plan in all respects;***
- **the most likely case, *is for a 2-month delay, £50,000 extra cost, and delivering 90% of the planned benefits;***
- **at worst, *it will be 6 months late; £200,000 extra cost and deliver 70% of the planned benefit.***

The risk assessment of a different development option, may indicate that for a slightly increased schedule and cost, the risks can be reduced and benefits increased. The two options may look like this:

	Option 1	Option 2
Best Delivery	**June Year 2**	**Aug Year 2**
Cost	£500k	£550k
Benefits	100%	110%
Likely Delivery	**Aug Year 2**	**2 Sept Year 2**
Cost	£550k	£580k
Benefits	80%	95%
Worst Delivery	**Dec Year 2**	**Dec Year 2**
Cost	£700k	£650k
Benefits	70%	80%

To decide between the options, or indeed whether either is worth pursuing, the size and the timing of benefits needs to be considered.

These vary, not only because of the inherent uncertainty of assessing benefits, but also because certain benefits are dependent on specific events. For example, if the system is not implemented by a certain date, the sales people will be unable to capitalise on the peak buying season in the market place.

Benefits vary between cases, not only because of the inherent difficulty of predicting benefits, but because of differences between what each programme or project option delivers – both in the schedule and in the quality of the delivered benefit. It is recommended that these different effects are separated.

A spreadsheet/graphics package can now be used to show graphically these net cash flows for each case.

9. Summary

The business case is not just a financial hurdle required by the organisation's bureaucrats before it can give the programme or project approval to begin. It provides the opportunity for the organisation to consider if its investment is justified after all the options have been considered. Because it is carried out on a consistent basis, it enables potential investments to be compared, obtaining the best use of scarce resources.

The document itself provides the basis of the programme or project plans and the monitoring and control process. It also defines the critical success factors - both financial and non-financial – used to judge whether the programme or project is a success or not. A well researched and considered business case provides an excellent and confident start to a programme or project.

Chapter Ten

Quality Reviews

1. Introduction

This chapter examines the two types of quality reviews the PSO could be involved with and describes the supporting processes, roles, responsibilities and infrastructure.

2. What is a Quality Review?

This term covers two completely different processes. The first is a review of the arrangements which ensure that a programme or project is managed according to accepted standards to acheive the required outputs, deliverables or products, within the agreed time and costs. This type of review is carried out at a prescribed point in a programme or project, or as the result of an apparent, or real, problem occuring. A person who is independent of the programme or project should conduct this review.

The second type of quality review scrutinises the outputs, deliverables or products of the programme or project. This review can be either a formal or informal review. The formal review documents progress at every stage and a physical meeting (with an independent chairman) is held where the producer of the output, deliverable or product, discusses any concerns that the reviewers may have.

The informal review has no formal meeting, just discussions; however there is still documentary evidence of the review process.

The formal review process is usually reserved for very important deliverables, outputs or products, as they can involve considerable expenditure. The importance of a deliverable is usually judged on the following criteria:

- is it a major deliverable identified in the programme or project plan;
- is it a major deliverable in the project or system development method;
- is it a deliverable which will be used to build other major deliverables;
- is it a deliverable that is of contractual or legal significance?

The above items are a general guide, most organisations develop their own checklists for deciding which review to use.

3. What Does a Quality Review Achieve

Both types of quality reviews are carried out for four main reasons:

3.1 Assurance

The reviews provide the organisation with assurance that the programmes and projects are proceeding according to agreed plans and processes. They both provide this assurance, but in different ways. The first type of quality review directly assures the organisation that the correct processes are being deployed to ensure that the programme or project meets it objectives. The second review, although directed at specific products, indirectly proves the validity of the plans and processes as any problems during the output, deliverable or product reviews, can be traced back to a failure in the programme or project management processes.

3.2 Measuring the Effectiveness of Programme and Project Management Processes

The first type of quality review directly assesses the effectiveness of the programme or project processes. The second type of quality review provides this indirectly – if the same problem emerges a number of times then there is obviously something wrong with either the process, or how it is being operated.

3.3 Lessons Learnt

Both quality reviews provide the organisation with the opportunity to appraise what has happened and the lessons learnt. As before, the first type of review assesses this directly, whereas in the second type of review this information is gained through both direct and indirect routes as reviewers make an observation or comment about the processes directly or indirectly. The programme or project manager analyses the statistics from these quality reviews as part of their regular progress reports to the programme or project board.

3.4 Identification of Areas of Non-Compliance and Improvement

Both quality reviews identify lack of compliance or improvements to existing process. The first review is directly aimed at this goal, although the second type can also be used.

4. Programme or Project Quality Reviews

The programme or project quality review is similar to the process used by auditing agencies that check an organisation's compliance with ISO or British Standards. In these checks the auditors are not just checking conformance to the agreed processes and standards, they are also looking for evidence that these are being maintained and updated, as required, to reflect changes in the business.

The review process normally follows a methodical examination of the documents, processes and standards used to ensure that the programme or project is being operated under a quality regime. Each organisation has its own particular examination method – this section uses a generic approach to describe the principle components of such an examination.

4.1 The Quality Plan

The programme or project quality plan or any standard quality management system (QMS) is first assessed by a review or audit.

The audit establishes that there are such documents and that they are recognised as the definitive statements on the company processes. The assessment also looks at whether the organisation has designed the quality plan, or QMS, to cover all the work normally undertaken – or are there areas of activities performed by the programme or project management staff that are outside of the documented processes and standards. Also, the review will asses the compliance of the programme or project quality plan or QMS to the relevant standards – using specific methodology or internationally-recognised guidelines and standards. Any shortfalls, or potential areas of improvement, are noted and researched later in the review process.

4.2 The Processes Used to Deliver The Plan

Having assessed the applicability and coverage of the quality plan, the quality review then ensures that the documented processes are being operated as defined and the relevant supporting standards applied. This is usually performed through discussions and observation of actual procedures as compared to the prescribed processes and standards.

While performing this assessment the auditor looks for evidence that the processes have been, or are, amended to reflect any changes in requirements. Attempting to constrain or fit new requirements into inappropriate processes causes additional work and means the reason for employing a quality plan or quality management system is ineffective.

During this part of the assessment the auditor also evaluates any areas of concern that emerged during the desk research from the first part of the review, to see if they are still relevant. Any non-compliance with the documented processes and standards, or lack of coverage of the processes, is noted.

4.3 Lessons Learnt

The review process must pay special attention to the way that the organisation's built-in mechanisms to incorporate lessons learnt are included in the processes and standards. This is where organisations that have adopted national or international standards programme and, or, project management methods can have problems. This is because standards need to be tailored to meet the specific requirements of each organisation. Indeed they can often actively discourage this tailoring and rigidly enforce compliance to the defined method, even when the method does not support specific organisation requirements.

4.4 Areas of Non-Compliance

It is at this point that areas of non-compliance are defined. However, before any formal decision is made, the auditor verifies the findings with discussions or observations and informal meetings with the relevant members. The auditor then has to identity the reasons for the non-compliance – is the process or standard no longer needed, carried out in a different way, or is there a lack of training or knowledge about it?

Often a small change will put the situation right. However, the auditor must appreciate that the knock-on effects of a small change can be substantial – and it is the organisation that owns the processes and standards, not the auditor.

4.5 Areas of Improvement

Also at this point, and sometimes simultaneously with the previous step, the auditor identifies where areas of improvements are required. Again the auditor has to take the difficult path between identifying areas of improvement and stating what must be done. It is vital that the auditor leaves the management of the organisation to identify how it will deal with the areas identified for improving.

The auditor is the key to a successful quality review or audit of the programme and project management process. The auditor selected must have sufficient in-depth knowledge and experience of programme and project management to identify any defects in the processes. They must also have considerable experience of carrying out such audits, the political repercussions of these reports can be wide-reaching.

5. Deliverable or Product Quality Review

The deliverable, output or product quality review process has two main functions. The first of these is to ensure that the outputs, deliverables or products are as specified. The second function, as discussed previously, is to check indirectly the validity of the supporting processes.

5.1 Direct Reviews

The direct review process compares the output, deliverable or product to its original specification. The process is conducted by reviewers who were not part of the team that either developed or purchased it, but are knowledgeable about the particular output, deliverable or product. The reason for using reviewers with experience and knowledge is that, even with the most exhaustive specification, there will still be gaps which may need to be dealt with by the reviewers. It is important that reviewers are trained in the quality review process and direct their attention to those parts of the quality review process that provide added value.

5.2 Indirect Review

In addition to the review of the item, this appraises the process used to plan the quality review process, select and train reviewers, prepare specifications, ensure the developers have the specification and ensure the build or procurement process is operating correctly. It also checks that the reporting process is operating as well as the planning processes. Any deficiency in these supporting processes become apparent as the review process will experience problems or fail.

For example, if the reviewers are not available then it shows that the planning and reporting processes are not operating correctly. If the reviewers find a large number of faults with an item, the specification or development process is not operating sufficiently. Any problems with the quality review process therefore indicates that one or more of these supporting processes are not operating satisfactorily.

6. Output or Product Quality Review Process

The process for this type of quality review has four major steps. The same steps and outputs are used in both the formal and informal quality review, however they are performed in a slightly different way.

Diagram 24 **Checklist of steps in a Quality Review**

	●	Preparation – Phase one
	●	Preparation – Phase two
	●	Review meeting
	●	Follow up

The support provided by the PSO to this process varies from organising the whole process to providing administration support. Once the level of support has been agreed, the steps can be modified accordingly. This section has been written with the PSO not providing support, which allows for a less complicated description of the steps.

6.1 Preparation – Phase One

This step occurs as part of the planning process for the programme or project. The programme or project manager, together with the relevant members of the programme or project team, decide:

- **Which products will be subjected to what type of quality review (formal or informal)?**
- **At what point in the programme or project will the review be scheduled?**
- **Who the reviewers should be.**

This information is then used when completing the programme or project plan in the planning process and also added to the relevant deliverable, output or product description.

The same process is used for both formal and informal reviews.

6.2 Preparation – Phase Two

This step is performed during the programme or project about 10 days before the agreed review date, although this timescale is flexible as it needs to provide sufficient time for its preparation activities to be completed. As a consequence the timescales can be shorter for small or uncomplicated reviews or extended where the deliverable, output or product is large or complex.

The programme or project manager confirms with the developer of the deliverable, output or product that it will be ready for review. The programme or project manager then checks with the chairman of the review and the reviewers that they will be available. Any amendment to the plans, or arrangements, are performed.

Once the deliverable, output or product has been completed and passed its internal review by the development team, it is made available for the reviewers. The deliverable, output or product is accompanied by its specification and, or, any standard quality checklists. This processes is usually documented with an invitation to the reviewer to inspect the deliverable, output or product and send written comments to the developer, at least two days before the formal review meeting takes place.

A room or venue has to be arranged by the programme or project manager for the review.

In an informal review the above activities are still performed, but the room is not required as the review usually takes place face-to-face with the item's developer at their workplace.

Having delivered the item to the reviewers, the developer prepares the material that will be needed for the review meeting. At the same time the reviewers appraise the deliverable, output or product and document their comments or questions in the form of an error list or annotating the item itself.

These comments should not be "fixes", but questions or queries. The review error lists are sent to the developer of the output, deliverable or product at least two days before the meeting so that the errors can be examined and any research completed before the review.

Once the review error list has been completed, the programme or project manager finalises the agenda for the meeting with the review chairman and communicates it to all the review participants. This list can include additional observers such as internal auditors or members of the programme or project assurance team or quality department.

In an informal review the product is still examined and the errors noted on the error list. However the arrangements for the discussion and the preparation for the meeting by the developer are usually not needed.

6.3 Review Meeting

The review follows a prescribed order – normally an organisation standard. However the following section describes the typical way these meetings are conducted.

See example document **40** *The agenda for a quality review.*

6.3.1 Chairman's introduction

This explains the purpose of the meeting and thanks everyone for their efforts. The chairman should also remind everyone that the purpose of the meeting is aimed at fault detection – not necessarily correction.

6.3.2 Developer's presentation

The developer of the deliverable, output or product gives a short presentation on the item's background and any relevant information about the development process.

6.3.3 Reviewer's comments

The chairman then asks the reviewers if they consider that it is worthwhile holding the review – i.e. do they consider the deliverable, output or product sufficiently acceptable so that they will formally accept it provided their comments are addressed.

This is needed to ensure that the meeting is not a waste of everyone's time. If the deliverable, output or product is so bad that no amount of error correction will put it right the review can be abandoned.

6.3.4 Walkthrough and comments

The developer of the item under review then explains the deliverable, output or product dealing with the errors on the error list, either by way of explanation and discussion with the reviewers, or by accepting their comments. The decisions made about each of the errors are recorded by the administration support, particular attention is given to what actions are needed and which of the reviewers will check that the changes have been made satisfactorily.

The chairman asks the administrator to read back the agreed actions either at the end of the meeting, or at a series of convenient points if the list is long.

6.3.5 Review decision

The chairman then asks the reviewers for their overall decision on the deliverable, output or product. Is it:

- **fit for purpose as is;**
- **fit for purpose once the errors have been corrected;**
- **needs significant work and a new review.**

The reviewer's decision is discussed and documented on the quality review result form. The chairman also asks the reviewers if they have any comments on the quality review process itself – in particular the quality of the deliverable specification. These points are also included on the quality review result form and, if necessary, the chairman ensures that the information is conveyed to the programme or project manager. The chairman again thanks all the participants for their efforts and formally closes the meeting.

In an informal review the paperwork described above is completed, but the review is conducted without a chairman, usually at the workplace of the item's developer. The same decisions are made and documented.

All the paperwork from these reviews, both formal and informal, is sent to the programme or project support assistant who includes them in the relevant files. As required, they use information from these documents for the programme or project manager's progress reports.

6.4 Follow-Up

The follow-up step consists of the reviewers and developer completing their allocated actions and obtaining the necessary sign-offs. Once this work has been completed, the item's developer notifies the chairman, who communicates to the programme or project manager that the review is completed and the item is fit for purpose.

Again all relevant documents are sent to the programme or project support assistant who files the information and extracts information for the programme or project manager.

*See example document **41**: The documents/forms used to support the quality review process.*

In informal reviews this step is completed but, once again, without the involvement of the chairman.

7. The Roles and Responsibilities in the Quality Review

There are four specific roles needed to fulfil the quality review process:

- **the chairman of the review;**
- **the developer of the deliverable, output or product;**
- **the reviewers;**
- **the programme or project support assistant.**

As with other aspects of the review process described previously, the roles and responsibilities are usually standard in each organisation. The following section describes the typical roles and responsibilities.

7.1 Chairman of the Review

The Chairman runs (on behalf of the organisation, not the programme or project) the quality review process for the specific deliverable, output or product. This is a senior management role, designed to provide assurance to the organisation that the item is fit for purpose.

The specific responsibilities of the role are:

- **to ensure the review is carried out in accordance with the organisation's standard process;**
- **to set the agenda for the review meeting;**
- **to chair, manage and control the review meeting;**
- **to ensure that the review keeps its focus and results and actions are documented and agreed;**
- **to ensure the programme or project manager is aware of the outcome of the review process;**

- to ensure that any comments about the review process are acted upon.

The importance of this role must not be underestimated. A good chairman makes the review process operate well and provides motivation to the programme or project team. The involvement of such a person illustrates the value the organisation places on the programme or project.

This role is not normally required for an informal review.

7.2 The Developer of the Output, Deliverable or Product

The role of developer or procurer of the output, deliverable or product under review, is usually filled by the leader of the team that produced it.

This role, as before, has standard responsibilities. The following list is a typical example:

- **to supply the reviewers with the relevant deliverable, output or product that conforms to the agreed specification;**
- **to prepare materials for the review that will explain the background of the development of the deliverable, output or product;**
- **to review the list of errors identified by the reviewers and to research these for the review meeting;**
- **to answer questions on the deliverable, output or product at the review meeting and explain the implications of the errors and any other comments raised;**
- **to discuss and agree follow-up actions with the review team;**
- **to carry out the review action and obtain sign-off for the errors as they are resolved;**
- **to obtain the overall sign-off for the deliverable, output or product from the chairman of the review once all errors have been rectified.**

This role is almost identical in an informal review, except there is no review meeting.

7.3 The Reviewers

The reviewers are selected on the basis of their knowledge and experience of similar deliverables, outputs or product. They have the most important role in the quality review process. As well as the technical knowledge, the reviewers must also understand the politics and sensitivities at work during this process. The politics include the pressures that can emerge from the programme or project team, and the organisation, not to delay the development process unnecessarily. The sensitivities revolve around the undeniable fact that they are there to find fault with someone else's work. The reviewers must be sensitive about the work, effort and dedication that has been used to develop the deliverable, output or product. Also taking criticism at any time is not easy, particularly when your mistakes are exposed to the whole organisation. However, they must not let these considerations detract them from their responsibilities which include:

- **when preparing for the review, they must understand the specification for the item under review and also conduct any required research to perform the review;**

- **to assess if the item conforms to the agreed specification and will be fit for purpose;**

- **to identify and judge the importance of any non-conformance to the specification or its fitness for purpose;**

- **to discuss non-conformances and any other relevant topics at the quality review meeting to their satisfaction;**

- **to monitor any allocated follow-up action to their satisfaction;**

- **to formally sign-off the whole corrected deliverable, output or product once the item is fit for purpose.**

7.4 The Programme or Project Support Assistant

This role is also sometimes called "the scribe". This person takes notes of the decisions and agreed actions at the review and confirms these with the attendees at the end of the meeting.

However, this role can be widened. Often "the scribe" assists the chairman in the administration of the review by arranging the venue, dealing with the agenda and papers and also acting as a progress chaser for the chairman to ensure all the follow- up actions are completed. The programme or project support assistant could be a member of the PSO or the programme or project team.

In addition to these formal roles the programme, project or team manager responsible for developing the item under review, must ensure that the review activities and resource requirements have been included in the plan. They must also ensure that the plan includes resources and activities to deal with any possible follow-up actions, including a complete rework of the item. They must also make sure that before the deliverable, output or product is submitted for review the development team has reviewed it and judged it fit for review.

In some circumstances the programme, project or team manager can also perform one of the roles in the review process. However this should be only in exceptional situations, as the review process must not be open to subjective pressure.

The members of the programme or project assurance team also have a part to play, performing some of the review roles. However the assurance team's main function is to ensure, on behalf of the organisation, that:

- the review was carried out according to the agreed standards and processes;

- the reviewers were themselves "fit for purpose". They can even recommend who the reviewers should be or act as reviewers themselves;

- the review team is adequately trained in the review process;

- the whole process and, in particular, any follow on actions are completed satisfactorily;

- any areas of improvement in the quality review process, or the supporting programme or project management processes and standards, are identified and acted upon.

In an informal review the same roles and responsibilities exist, but they are adjusted to take account of the lack of a formal meeting. Note, however, that a lack of formality must not mean lack of rigor. This is a real danger and the programme and project assurance role must ensure that standards do not slip.

8.0 The Supporting Infrastructure

For the quality review process to be effective and efficient it needs to be supported by an infrastructure provided as part of the PSO's services, or from the relevant programme or project.

8.1 Training in the Process

One of the most important factors in conducting a successful quality review is for the participants to have had training in the review process and their role and responsibilities. This training can be provided by the PSO, or organised by it.

8.2 List of Skills Available

One of the major problems facing the programme or project manager is identifying who in the organisation has the necessary skills to be a reviewer. The PSO infrastructure can assist the identification process greatly by providing a database that shows which members of the organisation have what specific skills, and what deliverables, outputs or products they worked on previously.

8.3 Product Descriptions

The specification of the output, deliverable or product should also be supplied or supported from the PSO's infrastructure. The provision and maintenance of a set of standard output, deliverable or product descriptions, which are used by the individual programmes and projects, is extremely useful.

In addition, such a central record means that any recommended improvements to the description, made as part of a review, can be built back into the subsequent review processes. This central system also provides the mechanism for storing information about the numbers and types of faults found. This assists both the programme or project manager in preparing reports to the programme and project boards. It also enables the PSO to identify which deliverables, outputs or products should be subject to a method improvement project to reduce the level of faults.

8.4 Reviews Included in the Plan

The infrastructure can also be used to include automatically the review process in programme and project plans. This is achieved by inserting in the project or system development methods the review process and outputs as a standard with relevant deliverables.

For example, if using a product-based lifecycle the sequence might be:

product 1.1 – draft (team reviewed) user requirements

product 1.2 – quality review report user requirements

product 1.3 – signed-off user requirements

8.5 Meeting Administration

Both the formal and informal methods of quality review will need to be supported with standard forms and documents. The PSO infrastructure should provide, maintain and update them.

8.5 Technical Support and Advice

Another useful function provided by the infrastructure is technical support and advice to the process. This may, at its simplest, be the production, collection and collation of information about the standards to be applied to the items under review, or a list of internal and external experts who can advise. This support and advice can also apply to the quality review process itself – perhaps providing support in the training of staff in their roles and responsibilities.

8.5 Follow-up

At the end of each review a number of actions may have been agreed. Although it is the chairman of the review's responsibility to make sure that these are completed, the infrastructure can assist by ensuring that these actions are included in the relevant programme or project plans and their associated progress reporting system. In some programmes or projects the PSO infrastructure could be allocated the role of this progress chaser.

8.7 Configuration Management Systems

An essential part of the supporting infrastructure is the configuration management system. This is because the system ensures that the pre- and post-review versions of the deliverable, output or product are kept and differentiated. The details of the follow-up performed, and also the documents produced during the review process, must also be included in the configuration management system. This enables an audit of the item illustrating the history of the changes made throughout the review process.

9. Summary

There are two types of quality review process performed in programmes and projects. It is vital that the PSO and others involved realise which of these processes are being employed.

In the second type of review – that of a deliverable, output or product – it is important to ensure that the correct level of review is applied, formal or informal. The formal review process is expensive and time-consuming, it should be reserved for those items that **need** such a review.

All quality reviews must be supported by an appropriate infrastructure of information systems and standards. Without such an infrastructure the full benefits of the review process will not be realised. The most important of these is the ability to build into the specifications for subsequent programmes or projects lessons learnt from the review process.

Example
Documents

EXAMPLE 1 BUSINESS STRATEGY PLAN

Paper to the Board of United of United Diggers

From the Business Strategy Business Planning Team

The Business Strategy 1999/2003

Introduction

The business strategy of United Diggers Plc. has now been updated to reflect the results of the business planning process and to incorporate the results of the business review report produced by McMarsh and company (document ref. ztz 2219).

Strategy Review Process

This strategy will remain in force until December 1999 when a full review will be performed. It will be reviewed in June 1999 to effect the projected changes in benchmarks included in the strategy and also in response of the updated business review report from McMarsh and company.

The major elements of the strategy

Large Diggers
United Diggers currently hold 15% of the UK market for large diggers. The strategy for the period up to 2003 is to expand this to 17.5% in the UK and to develop a European presence, which is equal in size to the current UK sales.

Intermediate targets are as follows

June	1999	First European sales
Feb	2000	European sales equal to 2%
June	2000	European sales equal to 5 %, UK sales up to 15.5%
Feb	2001	European sales equal to 7.5t%
June	2001	European sales equal to 10% UK sales 16%

Targets for years 2002 and 2003 will be set in June 2001

Small Diggers
United Diggers currently holds 65% of the UK small digger market. The strategy for this area is subdivided into existing models and new models (the EH101)

Existing Models
Existing models are to expand their market share in UK to 70 % over the period of this plan and increase the profit contribution they make from 5% of sales process to 12%.

New Models

The new EH101 is due to be launched in 2000 and is aimed at the garden centre and market gardener market.

Targets sales to garden centres 50 units year one, 200 units year two and 400 units thereafter.

Target sales to market gardeners 25 units year one, 100 units year two and 150 units thereafter.

Efficiency Savings

The current cost of developing each digger will be reviewed and methods identified to reduce these costs to ensure that United Diggers remains the digger company with the lowest percentage cost of production to sales price in the market place.

It is estimated that this will require a year on year reduction of 1.5%. This figure will be reviewed at each review point.

EXAMPLE 2 PROGRAMME PLAN

Activity ID	Activity Description
PROJ01	Transfer of Budget
PROJ02	Business Processes
PROJ05	Training
PROJ06	Transfer of job clubs
PROJ04	PC's
PROJ03	Change Process
PROJ07	Development of WAN
PROJ09	Administrative Processes
PROJ08	Equipment upgrade
PROJ10	Re-engineering library function:
PROJ11	Implement revised locations
PROJ12	Implement business processes

Planned end of tranche one

Planned end of tranche two

Planned end of tranche three

Planned end of tranche four

1999 2000 2001 2002 2001

Baseline Programme Plan

Project Start	01JAN99
Project Finish	24FEB03
Data Date	01JAN99
Run Date	24FEB99

Early Bar
Progress Bar
Critical Activity

Sheet 1 of 1

© Primavera Systems, Inc.

LIST OF INTERDEPENDENCIES

Project	Product or Workpackage	Interdependency With
1	Agreement must be reached with government and local authorities about transfer of budget/funds	Spending commitments in projects 4, 5, 7, 8 and implementation of new processes in projects 2 and 9
2	Installation of new processes	The operation of the new process must be included in the retraining in project 5, and the transfer of the job clubs in project 6.
3	The management of change report must in place and operating to support.	Wave one of the changes project 4,5,6 and a second wave projects 7,8 and the third wave projects 10,11,12.
4	The selection of the model and software. The installation of the equipment	Included in project 5 - the training course design and contents. In place to support project 5 - training and project 6.
5	Roll out of training	Equipment from project 5 must in place and any management of change activities related to this completed.
6	Transfer of job club to local library cannot be completed	Until project 3 5 and 4 are completed and also the relevant management of change activities.
7	Specification of requirements	The specification/selection of the PC's and software and Internet provider (project 4) must be complete.
8	Design/specification of upgrade to equipment	The specification/selection of the ISP provider project 4
9	Design for operation of cross charging	The completion of the upgrade (project 7 and 8) and any relevant management of change activities.
10	The agreements of the final designs	Completion of project 9.s
11	The implementation of the new processes	Agreements of the new processes project 11)
12	Purchase of new or upgrading of existing	Agreement of the new process project 10 and at least partial completion of major changes to business processes in project 11

Programme Plan

Phase One

Year One
Project 1	Completed
Project 2	Completed
Project 3	Commenced (on going until end of programme)
Project 4	Completed
Project 5	Completed

Year Two
Project 6	Completed

End of Phase One
Implementation of cross charging administrative processes for job club service.
Benefits realised £249,080K

Phase Two

Project 6	Completed
Project 7	Commenced
Project 10	Commenced

Year Three
Project 7	Completed
Project 9	Completed
Project 10	Completed
Project 8	Completed
Project 12	Commenced

End of Phase Two
Implementation of cross charging administrative processes for government information systems service.
Benefits realised £ 261,000K

Phase Three

Year Four
Project 11	Commenced
Project 12	Completed

End of Phase Three
Operation of administrative processes to support cross charging for government information systems (reduction in staff in government departments) implementation of business process re-engineering - part one - purchasing of books and new operational processes.
Benefits realised £11,025K (part)

Phase Four

Year Five
Project 11	Completed
Project 3	Completed

End of Phase Four
Implementation of business process re-engineering - part two - relocation aspects.
Benefits realised £11,025K (part)

EXAMPLE 3 PROGRAMME TRANCHE PLAN

Activity ID	Activity Description	Orig Dur	Early Start	Early Finish
Project One (Transfer of Budget)				
0001	Project One (Transfer of Budget)		22JAN99*	14JUL99
0002	Initial Meetings (Local Authority Association)		08MAR99	
0003	Initial Meetings (Ministry)		05MAR99*	
0004	Approval of draft by United Libraries Board		07APR99	
0005	Scoping Document (Local Authority Association)		23APR99*	
0006	Scoping Document (Ministry)		11MAY99*	
0007	Approval by UL board L.A. Final Negotiations		09JUL99*	
0008	Approval by UL board Ministry Final Negotiations		13JUL99*	
Project Two (Business Processes)				
0010	Project Two (Business Processes)		22JAN99*	02DEC99
0011	Required changes/additions report		28APR99*	
0012	Implement new processes		01DEC99*	
Project Three (Change Process)				
0014	Project Three (Change Process)		22JAN99	11FEB00
0015	Managements of change approach paper		17JUN99	
0016	Management of change approach report		31AUG99	
0017	Job Club Start up support		21DEC99	
Project Four (PC's)				
0019	Project Four (PC's)		22JAN99	11FEB00
0020	Survey of Existing Premises		25MAR99	
0021	Identify requirement for hardware and software		13APR99	
0022	Equipment requirement		12APR99*	
0023	Receive invitation of interest		28JUN99	
0024	Issue OJEC notice		21JUN99	
0025	Send out ITT		05AUG99	
0026	Decision by Board		09SEP99	
0027	Roll-out		21DEC99	
0028	Sign off contract		11FEB00	
Project Five (training)				
0030	Project Five (training)		22JAN99	17DEC99
0031	Survey of Existing Processes		19MAR99*	
0032	Prepare training strategy paper		22MAR99	
0033	Training Requirement Study		29MAR99*	
0034	Send out ITT		11JUN99	
0035	Award contract		11AUG99	
0036	Post Course Evaluation follow up		17DEC99*	
Project Six (Transfer of Staff)				
0038	Project Six (Transfer of Staff)		22JAN99	12JAN00
0039	Approval of United Libraries draft by United Lib		13JUL99*	
0040	First meeting with (Local Authority Association)		17JUN99*	
0041	Agreement of scoping document		02JUN99	
0042	Introductory seminars		17DEC99	
0043	END OF PHASE - Sign off of transfer		12JAN00	

Tranche 1 Plan

Project Start   22JAN99
Project Finish   11FEB00
Data Date   22JAN99
Run Date   24FEB99

Early Bar
Progress Bar
Critical Activity

© Primavera Systems, Inc.

EXAMPLE 4 PROJECT PLAN

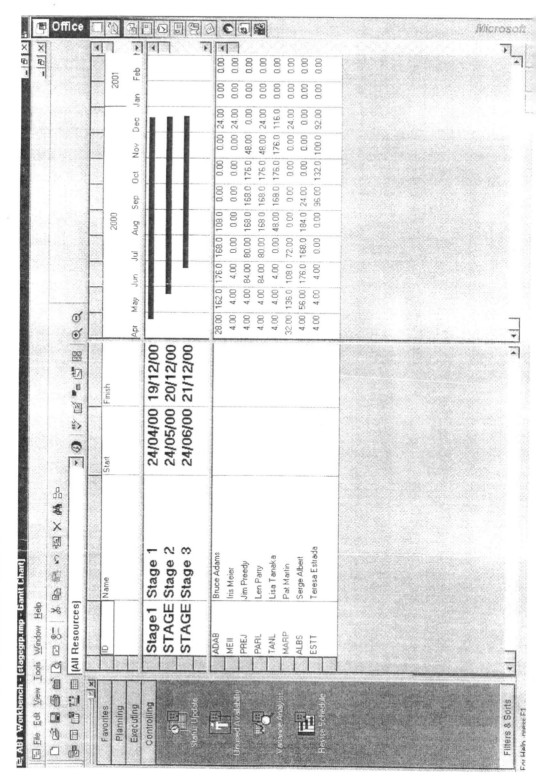

EXAMPLE 5 STAGE PLAN

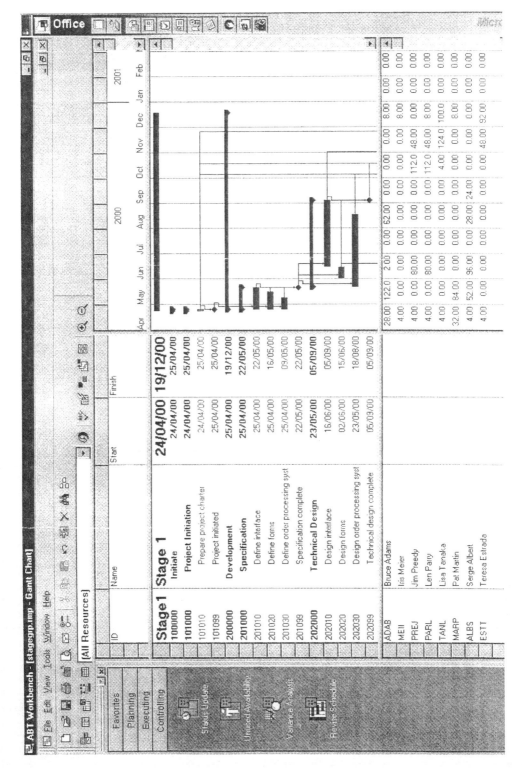

EXAMPLE 6 TEAM PLAN

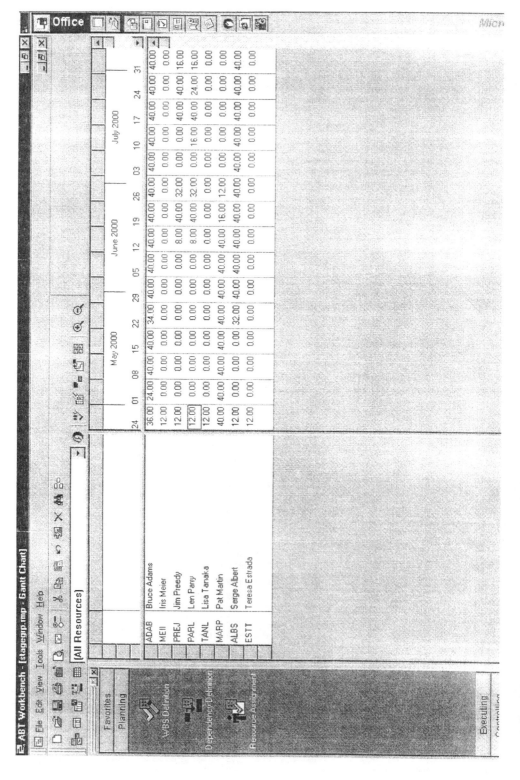

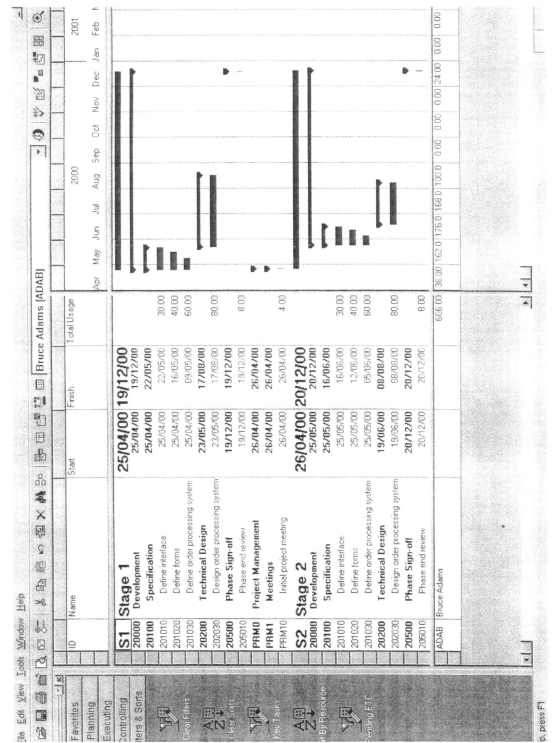

EXAMPLE 8 PRODUCT DESCRIPTION

DETAILED REQUIREMENTS REPORT   PB 01.1.04

PURPOSE
To consolidate the requirements into a single report to be used as a basis for the
Invitation to Tender.

PREPARED BY
System analyst, user.

CONTENT
Requirements overview.
Project objectives for which the package is being sought
Prioritised problems/requirements list.
Overall constraints.
Geographical locations in which the system is to be implemented.
Brief description of the existing system.
Likely hardware and software requirements.
Outline of existing hardware and telecommunications networks with
which the system must interface.
Solution model.
Performance and recovery requirements.
Acceptance criteria and targets.

DERIVATION
IT strategy, requirements catalogue, solution model, updated with
detailed inputs, outputs and processing, feasibility study report.

CROSS REFERENCES
SSADM Steps   220, 380, 420: PRISM   BBM 3.2

QUALITY CRITERIA
Functional requirements:
- Does the report fully reflect the contents defined in the output,
  input, processing and controls specification?
- Have the users agreed the contents and signed-off the document?

Technical build:
- Does the report conform to local standards?
Method:
- Formal review.

EXTERNAL DEPENDENCIES
Technical and management personnel required for review.

EXAMPLE 9 NETWORK DIAGRAM

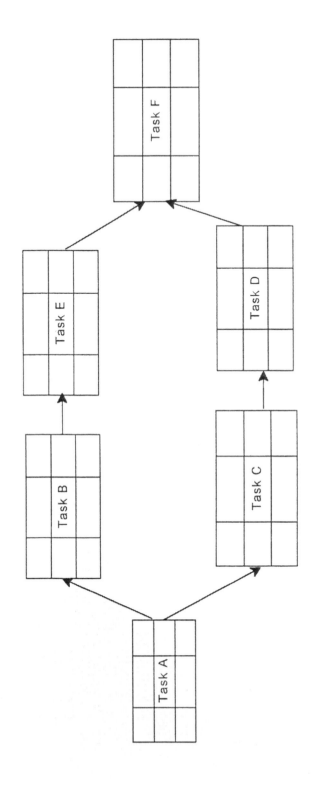

EXAMPLE 10 FORWARD PASS DIAGRAM

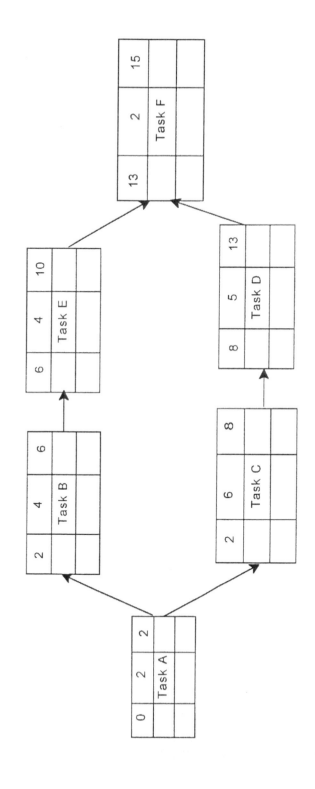

EXAMPLE 11 SECOND PASS NETWORK DIAGRAM

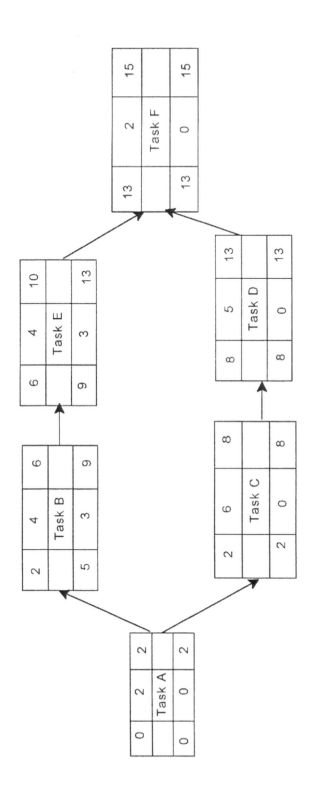

EXAMPLE 12 RESOURCE SMOOTHING

Original Network

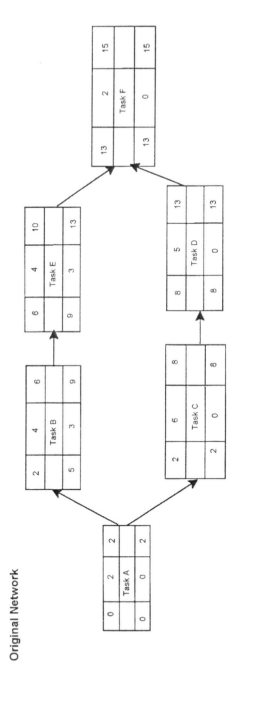

Resources Required

New Network

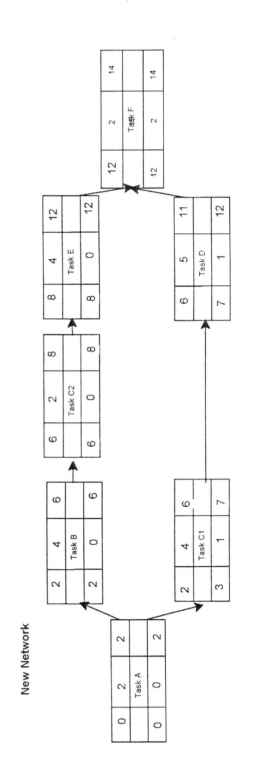

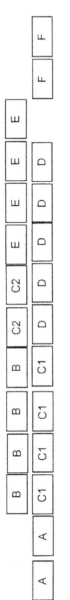

Resources Required Now

EXAMPLE 13 PROGRAMME OR PROJECT IDEA FORM

PROGRAMME OR PROJECT SUBMISSION FORM	
Submission No:	User Department/s:
Programme or Project Initiator:	Date Submitted:
Reason for/Description of Submission	

PROGRAMME OR PROJECT DETAILS	
Programme or Project ID:	
Programme or Project Title:	
Programme or Project Manager:	Programme or Project Sponsor:
Scope	
Objectives	
Benefits	
Dependencies/Constraints	
Estimated Start Date:	Estimated Completion Date:

COMMISSIONING RECORD

Masterplan Committee Meeting	Decision Taken Hold/Commission Process/Reject Priority	Reason (where appropriate)

COST ESTIMATE

	Consultancy	Internal	Bought In	Equipment	Total
Capital					
Revenue					
Budget Codes			Total Cost	£	

APPROVALS

	Masterplan Committee	Sponsor
Name		
Signature		
Date		

EXAMPLE 14 BUSINESS STRATEGY, PROGRAMME/PROJECT CONTRIBUTION MATRIX

Business Strategy To obtain 30% of the companies sales via E Commerce within 3 years.		
Programme/Project	*Contribution- Benefits*	*% Contribution to Strategy*
1. Project 1 Research report on options to introduce E Commerce. (To identify if the company should have its own Webb site , use an ISP or other companies sites (shopping mall)	Infrastructure To all the projects and programmes. Assessed as 10% contribution.	10%
2. Programme 1 To design and install new computer systems for the warehouse to operate internet as well as conventional orders.	Delivery of main functionality. Assessed as 25%	25%
3. Programme 2 Management of attitude changes needed. (To cover both internal and external changes including customer attitudes).	Infrastructure To all the projects and programmes. Assessed as 20% contribution	15%
4. Programme 3 Design of Internet Site and conversion of stock control systems to work with Internet orders. (The development of the site and also the interface between the site software and the warehouse stock control (see programme 1)	Delivery of main functionality. Assessed as 25%	25%
5. Programme 4 Development and launch of new marketing policy. (New point of sale materials, advertising)	Infrastructure To all the projects and programmes. Assessed as 10% contribution	10%
6. Project 2 New Sales Information program. (To enable sales trend data to be extracted automatically.)	Marginal benefit. Assessed at 5%	5%
7. Programme 5 Sales by credit card. (To provide the ability to handle credit card sales electronically.	Infrastructure To all the projects and programmes. Assessed as 10% contribution	10%

EXAMPLE 15   PROJECT TO PROGRAMME CONTRIBUTION MATRIX

	Project	Benefits (All figures in £K)	% Contribution to Programme
1.	Agreed arrangements for transferring budget allocation from local government authorities and government department (employment) to United Libraries.	Infrastructure basis of all three streams of benefits. Worth 20 % of Grand total of all benefits (£521,105 K x 20%) per full year plus Infrastructure basis of government information systems stream. 20 % of that benefit (£261,000 K x 20%) per full year	(156,421 K) 30.1%
2.	Development and implementation of administrative processes to support cross charging for job club service.	Infrastructure basis of job club stream. 20 % of benefits (£249,080 Kx 20%) per full year	(49,816K) 9.56%
3.	Management of change.	Infrastructure basis of all three streams of benefits. . Worth 10 % of Grand total of all benefits (£521,105 K x 10%) per full year.	(52,110) 10%
4.	Installation of standalone PC's and Internet connections in each library.	Infrastructure basis of all three streams of benefits Worth 5 % of Grand total of all benefits (£521,105 K x 5%) per full year	(26,055) 5%
5.	Retraining of existing staff to support Job clubs and other users of the technology.	Infrastructure basis of job club stream. 20 % of benefits (£249,080 Kx 20%) per full year	(49,816K) 9.56%
6.	Transfer of Job clubs from local government authorities/department of employment responsibility to United Libraries.	Realisation of job club benefits 25 % of benefits (£249,080 Kx 25%) per full year	(62,270K) 11.95%
7.	Development of wan (intranet) connections to government data network, department of Employment and employment agencies.	Infrastructure basis of government information systems stream 20 % of benefits (£261,000 K x 20%) per full year	(52,200K) 10.01%
8.	Upgrading of equipment to utilise wan.	Infrastructure basis of government information systems stream. 20 % of benefits (£261,000 K x 20%) per full year	(52,200K) 10.01%
9.	Development and implementation of administrative processes to support cross charging for government information systems.	Benefits realisation of government information systems stream. 5 % of benefits (£261,000 K x 5%) per full year	(13,050K) 2.5%
10.	Business process reengineering of library functions and locations.	Infrastructure basis of library restructuring stream 20 % of benefits (£11025 K x 20%) per full year	(2,205K) 0.42%
11.	Implementation of revised locations.	Benefits realisation of part of library restructuring stream. 20% of benefits (£11025 K x 20%) per full year	(2,205K) 0.42%
12.	Implementation of revised Library business processes. (Book procurement, installation and other operational costs.)	Benefits realisation of part of library restructuring stream. 25% of benefits (£11025 K x 25%) per full year	(2,756) 0.53%

EXAMPLE 16 FEASIBILITY STUDY REPORT

Proposed Project XXXXXXXX

Feasibility Study

Internal

1.   Document Control

1.1. Sign-off Details

Document Name	Owner	Version Date
Feasibility Study	Master-Plan Committee	

Original Author	Department	Date Written

Sign-off Authorities	Role	Date	Signature

1.2.   Distribution List

Name	Role	Reason
	Business Owner	Content Owner
	Input & Review	Key Reviewer
	Input & Review	Key Reviewer

1.3.   Contributors

Name	Role	Contribution
	Business Owner	Contents
	Input & Review	Contents
	Input & Review	Contents

1.4.   Reviewers

Name	Role	Sections Reviewed
	Business Owner	All
	Review	All
	Review	All

1.5.   Version History

Version No	Version Date	Requester of Change	Ref. Document
0.0 Draft			

1.6.   Document Change Mechanism

- Any requirement for change must be addressed to the author.

- For documents with draft status, the author may make changes at will.

- For documents with controlled status, the Sign-off authorities must approve changes.

Table of Contents

2. PROPOSAL SUMMARY SHEET

2.1. Project Identification

Project Idea Ref:
Project Code:
Corporate objective:

2.2. Project Responsibilities

Project Sponsor:
Business Owner:
Project Manager:

2.3. Deliverables Summary

3. MANAGEMENT SUMMARY

3.1. Project Purpose

3.2. Major Deliverables

3.3. Financial Case

3.3.1. *Revenue*

3.3.2. *Return on Investment*

4. ALTERNATIVE APPROACHES / BUSINESS CASES

Complete alternative analysis for each project alternative.

4.1. Alternatives Summary

Alternative	Description	Benefits	Cost
Alternative 1			
Alternative 2			
Alternative 3			

4.2.   Alternative 1 - .

       4.2.1.   *Costs vs. Realisable Benefits*
       4.2.2.   *Impacts*
       4.2.3.   *Risks*

4.3.   Alternative 2 -

       4.3.1.   *Costs vs. Realisable Benefits*
       4.3.2.   *Impacts*
       4.3.3.   *Risks*

4.4.   Alternative 3 -

       4.4.1.   *Costs vs. Realisable Benefits*
       4.4.2.   *Impacts*
       4.4.3.   *Risks*

5.   Impact Analysis of Recommended Option
The recommended option is Alternative XX

5.1.   Customers/Users

5.2.   IT & Support Staff

5.3.   Operations/Support Staff

5.4.   Third Party Suppliers/Software Houses

5.5.   Legal

5.6.   Sponsoring Department

6.   Organisation

6.1   Decision-making Bodies

6.1.1. Masterplan Committee

The masterPlan committee includes managers coming from the various divisions and departments of XXXXX. The masterplan committee's purpose is to make the interface between executive management and the project committee.

Main tasks are:

- approval to go ahead after each phase of the project based on the various deliverables ('project idea', 'feasibility report', ...) and based on budget considerations.
- put priorities on the various projects.
- solve issues escalated by the project committee.
- review closure of the projects.

6.1.2. *Project Committee*

The Project Committee include managers of the several IT departments. Main tasks are:

- review project definition before passing on to masterplan committee.
- track progress of all projects.
- solve resources conflicts and other issues reported by project managers.
- review project closure.
- escalate issues to IT management committee and to masterplan committee.

6.1.3. *Sponsoring Department*

6.2. Team Organisation

6.2.1. *Project Team*

The following is the team organisation:

6.2.2. *Project Sponsor*

The project sponsor is responsible for helping ensure the final success of the project. He/she participates in the definition of the requirements.

For this project, XXXXXX is the sponsor. The project requester is XXXXXX.

6.2.3. *Project Manager*

For this project, the project manager is XXXXXX from XXXXXXX.

The project manager has overall responsibility for the complete project, across all departments involved, for resource commitment, project schedule, control and budget follow-up.

He/she tracks the progress of the tasks performed by each department and reports progress and issues to the project committee.

He/she participates in the approval process of all main deliverables.

For this project, a monthly meeting will be held to review progress.

6.2.4. *Specialist Skills Required for the Project*

6.3. Management Control

6.3.1. *Project Reports*

The project manager will prepare a weekly project status report for the project sponsor copied to the project support office.

6.3.2. *Statement of Change Control*
No changes to the project will be considered by the project manager without written request. All change requests must be:

- submitted to the project committee for tracking.

- approved by the project sponsor.

- approved by the project business owner and/or customers.

- approved by the project committee.

The project manager has full management authority to action such requests providing they do not:

- extend the project scope.

- extend agreed time-scales.

- exceed the budget by more than agreed contingency.

7. PROJECT PLAN OF RECOMMENDED OPTION

7.1. Milestones

Extract from Microsoft Project by selecting milestones in the Gantt Chart view

7.2. Gantt Chart

Extract from Microsoft Project

7.3. Resource Requirements

8. APPENDIX A - PROPOSED CONTENTS/FUNCTIONS/SERVICES TO BE PROVIDED BY THE PROJECT

EXAMPLE 17 PROGRAMME DEFINITION STATEMENT

INTRODUCTION
The purpose of this programme definition statement is to summarise the background to the programme, its scope, its aims and objectives, and the benefits the company will derive from its implementation and the achievement of its business goals.

Following the recent report to the Amalgamated Utilities Board a programme executive board has been appointed to oversee the implementation of the programme. This programme definition statement has been prepared to enable the Board to define the portfolio of projects that will be required to achieve the business goals. It also suggests an appropriate organisation structure to facilitate management and control of the programme.

PROGRAMME BRIEF
Background
The Board of Amalgamated Utilities have agreed that their business goal is to position the Company to be among the foremost of its kind over the next five years by increasing its efficiency, improving its effectiveness, and achieving greater economy. To help meet this goal it has decided that the newly amalgamated organisation should be re-structured into one corporate body.

Programme Aims and Objectives
The aim of the programme is to unify the HR procedures, processes, and IS/IT systems to become multifunctional, covering all levels of personnel and operational activities.

The specific objectives are:

1) To reduce the management costs to the average level of the benchmarked organisations or less.
2) To reduce the cost of product and service marketing to the average level of the benchmarked organisations or less.
3) To reduce the costs of customer billing and payment processes to average level of the benchmarked organisations or less.

Scope
The programme will address the management, marketing, and accountancy functions. Any links with other functions such as the capital expenditure programme must be documented and defined.

Assumptions That Have Been Identified and Agreed
The programme assumes no increased business expansion through further takeovers or amalgamations.

The programme is to be executed and managed using internal resources.
Any changes to existing systems of work will be capable of easy implementation and operation by relatively untrained staff.

The business systems must be able to cope with the expected growth of 5% this year and each successive year for the next 5 years. Any new business system installed must incur less running costs than the existing system(s) it replaces. The first tranche of the programme will be completed within 15 months from commencement.

Responsibilities and Reporting Arrangements

Amalgamated Utilities has given overall responsibility for this programme to the Chief Executive M. Eaux who will fulfil the role of programme director. Reporting to him will be a programme executive board comprising Ms Worry, HR Director (who will undertake the role of business change manager), Mr. B Counter, Finance Director and Mr. C. Askey, IT Director (who will form the design authority) and Mr. E. Sparks, Sales and Marketing Director (who will be the programme manager).

The programme executive board has delegated authority to proceed with this programme on behalf of the full Board of Amalgamated Utilities and the programme director.

BUSINESS CASE

Programme Scope and Duration

The scope of the programme covers the management, marketing, and accountancy functions. The programme represents a major investment to achieve a long term goal and as such the programme duration has been agreed as four years.

Options Examined

1) **Improvements to the existing systems**
   This option will involve reviewing all existing manual business processes/systems and organisational structures, investigating possible improvements to unify the currently different water and electricity systems, to remove 'bottlenecks' and reduce overmanning.
2) **Installation of an upgraded computer system and any additional computer systems**
   In addition to Option 1, this option will involve examining existing IT systems and replacement possibilities, and investigating possible computerisation of existing manual systems.
3) **Full Business Process Re-engineering of all three function areas**
   This option will involve reviewing all processes throughout both constituent companies of the amalgamation, radically transforming and improving their effectiveness through fundamentally rethinking their design, their supporting IT systems, and their resourcing.

Risk and Sensitivity Analysis

Option 1

The major risks of option 1 are the potential disruption that could be caused both by the investigative processes themselves, whatever changes may be introduced and the possibility that little significant improvement may be achieved especially when compared with the cost of the effort involved.

Option 2

The major risks of this option are the possibility that the appropriate resources may not be available and the potential disruption of key systems such as the billing and revenue collection systems, any major disruption to which would seriously affect the company's cash flow and financial stability.

Option 3

The major risks of this option are the management challenges in controlling a number of simultaneous projects and in maintaining all the core business functions throughout a period of potential large-scale change. It will have a significant impact on management and staff at all levels and unless the transition is managed competently it will endanger morale.

Recommendation

The majority of the benefits to the company from the programme will come from the reorganisation of management. Such a reorganisation will require a total appraisal of all functions, processes, and their resourcing. Although this carries high risk it is recommended because of the extent of its potential contribution to the overall business goals. The recommendation therefore is to proceed with Option 3.

COSTS AND BENEFITS SUMMARY

OPTION 3	Year 0	Year 1	Year 2	Year 3
COSTS				
Mgt. Objectives				
Project 1	2,700k	300k		
Project 2	3,000k	500k		
Project 3	500k	750k	250k	
Project 4	300k	250k	200k	
Project 6		750k	250k	
Mgt. of Change				
Project 5	175k	200k	200k	225k
Billing & Payment BPR				
Project 7			1,500k	1,500K
Marketing Project				
Project 8			500k	
BENEFITS				
Reduced Mgt. Costs			50.75m	50.75m
Reduced Mktng. Costs				4.5m
Reduced Billing Costs				16.725m

PROGRAMME PLAN
This section contains an outline of the contents of each tranche of the programme.

Tranche 1

Project 1	Reorganisation of 'white-collar' staff	Budget £3m
Project 2	Reorganisation of 'blue-collar' staff	Budget £3.5m
Project 3	Management Information System (Phase 1)	Budget £0.75m
Project 4	Executive Information System (Phase 1)	Budget £0.4m
Project 5	Management of Change	Budget £0.2m

To be completed in 15 months.

Tranche 2

Project 3	Management Information System (Phase 2)	Budget £0.75m
Project 4	Executive Information System (Phase 2)	Budget £0.35m
Project 6	Manual Processes BPR	Budget £1m
Project 5	Management of Change	Budget £0.2m

To be completed in 1 year.

Tranche 3

Project 7	Billing and Payment BPR (Phase 1)	Budget £2m
Project 8	Marketing Reorganisation	Budget £0.5m
Project 5	Management of Change	Budget £0.2m

To be completed in 1 year.

Tranche 4

Project 7	Billing and Payment BPR (Phase 2)	Budget £1m
Project 5	Management of Change	Budget £0.2m

To be completed in 9 months.

QUALITY PLAN FOR THE PROGRAMME
Programme Tranche Terms of Reference
These will be prepared for each tranche of the programme and once agreed will be used to define the specific projects to be undertaken and the programme tranche technical and resource plans.

Project Briefs
These will be created for all projects at the beginning of each tranche.

Project Management and Planning
All projects will be managed using structured methods. Project plans will be prepared on a product-based approach and product descriptions will be prepared for all the products to be developed. These will be agreed with the project board when plans are being prepared and approved.

Project Controls and Reporting Arrangements

Checkpoint reports will be produced every two weeks. Highlight reports will be produced every four weeks and circulated to the project board. Mid-stage assessments will be held if a stage exceeds three months in duration. All other arrangements will be determined during plan preparation.

Project Quality Management

Quality reviews will be undertaken either formally or informally, the level of review and the review teams to be determined by the project management team when creating the plan for the particular stage in which the products are to be produced. All reviews will be fully documented.

Programme Controls and Reporting Arrangements

Monthly programme progress reports will be prepared by the programme manager, agreed with the programme executive board and submitted on their behalf to the programme director. These reports will be compiled from information derived from project board reports. A resource usage and requirements report will also be submitted along with a business benchmarks update report

At the end of each tranche the programme executive board will provide a progress review and action memo for the board of Amalgamated Utilities.

PROGRAMME PREREQUISITES

All members of Amalgamated Utilities who will have a programme or project management role must receive appropriate training.

EXTERNAL DEPENDENCIES

The implementation of the proposed programme will be affected by any change in relevant legislation or any change in government or government policy.

RISK MANAGEMENT PLAN

The risk management process operated in this programme will use a qualitative risk assessment method using the checklist/risk register provided by the programme and project office and supplemented through an unstructured workshop held at the start of each tranche.

The programme and project office together with the programme manger will produce a report for the programme executive board which describes:

The risk identified.
The probability of their occurrence.
An assessment of their impact on the programme.
The agreed action plan to manage, contain, eliminate or insure against that risk.
The arrangements agreed to monitor the effectiveness of the risk actions.

Risk No	The Risk Identified	Probability	Impact	Action Plan	Monitoring Actions
1	Change in government policy	Low	Severe	MD is to hold regular meeting with Ministers	
2	Industrial unrest	High	Severe	Inclusion of management of change project	Attitude surveys
3	Failure to achieve targets	Medium	Medium	Regular review of benefits plan by programme executive board.	Update Benchmarks every 3 months
4	Competition	Medium	High	Monitor competitors, PR campaign.	Competitor review every 3 months distributed to programme executive board.

EXAMPLE 18 PROJECT INITIATION DOCUMENT

INTRODUCTION

The purpose of this project initiation document is to provide a statement of the environment and products required from the project to support the business goals of the organisation.

The project initiation document has been prepared to ensure that the project board and the project management team have an agreed understanding of the system to be developed. It will be used by the project board to define the initial objectives of the project to develop the stock and sales administration system. It contains the baseline plan which will be used to monitor and control the development of the new system.

CONFIRMED PROJECT BRIEF

Project Background

The Board of Ace Plumbing Supplies Ltd. have agreed that their business goal for this year will be:

> *To ensure continued customer loyalty by providing a service level better than its competitors.*

To help meet this goal three major projects have been identified:

1　To install a new switchboard.
2　To upgrade the decoration of the customer area and the trade counter.
3　To develop a new sales and stock system.

This project brief is concerned with project number three.

The existing sales and stock system is now overstretched to the extent that it is inhibiting the growth of sales to both the trade and the public sectors.

The current system does not identify excess or out of date stocks and also has caused a number of errors when goods were sold when they were not in stock.

The sales manager has identified several new sales campaigns, which require a list of current customers - the present system cannot easily supply this.

Project Aims and Objectives

The aim of the project is:

To provide a new sales and stock system which will support the company's business goals.

The specific objectives are:

1   To ensure the sales section has easy access to details of the existing customers to support new sales initiatives.
2   Ensure out of date or excess stock is easily identified.
3   To reduce existing stock levels by 5%.
4   To eliminate selling of stock that does not exist.

Scope and Constraints

Scope

The project is to concentrate its efforts on the sales and stock sections and its systems. Any links with other sections must be documented and defined.

The new system is to support the sales and stock sections, any other assistance it provides to other sections is not to be regarded as having any priority.

Assumptions that have been identified and agreed

The project is to be developed by an external development team.

The system must be easy to use.

The system must be able to cope with the expected growth of 30% this year and 15% for each successive year for the next five years.

The system must be able to supply word processing facilities for the management team.

The new system must not cost any more than £10,000 to install and have a running cost less than the existing manual systems.

The project is to be completed during this financial year.

Reporting

Ace Plumbing Supplies has given full responsibility for this project to a Project Board consisting of Mr. I Balance, Finance Manager (Executive), Mr. J Yorkshire, Sales Manager (Senior User/*Customer*) and Mr. J Kelly (Senior Specialist Supplier) an external consultant engaged to advise Ace Plumbing Supplies.

The project board has full authority to proceed with this project within the limits of this document. If the project board expects to exceed this Brief then it must report to the full board of Ace Plumbing Supplies within five days of this becoming apparent.

BUSINESS CASE

Project Scope

The scope of the project is the sales and stock section of Ace Plumbing Supplies.

Project Life

The project is a long term investment and as such the project life has been agreed as four years.

Options Examined

1   Improvements to the existing system

    This option will involve improving the existing manual system by updating the records currently held by the sales section and by carrying out a full stock check every week to ensure the stock records are accurate.

2   Installation of a partial computer system

    This option will involve installing a computer system to hold details of the stocks held by Ace Plumbing or details of the sales made to its customers.

3   Installation of an integrated sales and stocks computer system

    This option is to provide an integrated computer system that will hold details of all stocks and sales made by Ace Plumbing with an on-line interrogation facility.

Risk and Sensitivity Analysis

The majority of the benefits from the project come from the computerisation of the stock control system. This area must be closely controlled. The sales information does not provide substantial benefits and if any problems occur with the project development then this aspect could be removed from the project.

The project is not critical for money. However it is important that the benefits are realised. To this end we will extend the development life cycle into benefits realisation and keep the project in place until this Product has been completed.

Recommendations

Proceed with Option 3.

COSTS AND BENEFITS SUMMARY

Option 3	Year 0	Year 1	Year 2	Year 3	Year 4
Costs					
Provision of computer System	5000			5000	
Conversion of records	5000				
	10000			5000	
Benefits					
Reduction in sales errors	8000	8000	8000	8000	8000
Reduction in stocks	2500	250	250	250	250
Additional sales	2000	2000	2000	2000	2000
	12500	10250	10250	10250	10250
Option 3					
Costs	10000			5000	
Benefits	12500	10250	10250	10250	10250
	2500	10250	10250	5250	10250
Discount Factor	1.0	.934	.877	.826	.781
Net Present Value	2500	9573	8989	4336	8005
Cum NPV	2500	12073	21062	25398	33403

DEFINITION OF ORGANISATION AND RESPONSIBILITIES

Project Board

• Mr. I Balance,	Finance Manager	Executive
• Mr. J Yorkshire,	Sales Manager	Senior User/*Customer*
• Mr. J Kelly,	External consultant	Senior Specialist Supplier

Project Manager

Jan McClelland

Project Assurance Function

- Ivor Solder   Business Aspects
- Louise Dargavel   User/*Customer* Aspects
- Trevor Whitlock   Specialist Supplier Aspects

Copies of roles and job descriptions are attached as Annex x.

PROJECT PLAN

This section contains a summary of the information contained in the project plan and the accompanying product breakdown structures, product flow diagrams and product descriptions. These are contained in Annex x.

Stage 1

Work package one: products 1 and 2.

To be completed by 16th March

Budget £1,000

Stage 2

Work package two: products 3, 4, 5, 7 and 8.

To be completed by 24th May

Budget £1,500

Stage 3

Work package three and four: products 6 and 9 to 16.

To be completed by 30th July

Budget £6,000

Stage 4

Work package five and six: products 17,18, 19 and 20.

To be completed by 16th October

Budget £1,500

Total Cost £10,000

Project Tolerance +10 days, +£1,000

QUALITY PLAN

Product descriptions: will be prepared for all the products to be developed. these will be agreed with the members of the project assurance function at the creation of the plan in which the products appear.

Quality reviews: each product will be subjected to either a formal or an informal quality review. The level of review and the review teams will be agreed by the project management team when creating the plan in which the products are created.

Documentation: all reviews will be fully documented. Examples of the documents to be used are attached as Annex x.

Controls and reporting arrangements: checkpoint reports will be produced at the completion of every product. Highlight reports every four weeks and circulated to the project board. Mid-stage assessments will be held if (in the opinion of the project manager) an exception report is raised that requires a meeting of the project board. All other arrangements will be as defined in the PRINCE reporting standards. Example proformas of all the reports are attached as Annex x.

PROJECT PREREQUISITES

All members of Ace Plumbing Supplies who will have a project management team role must receive appropriate PRINCE training.

EXTERNAL DEPENDENCIES

The development is dependent on the issue of a new version of the operating system by Mickey Mousesoft.

PLAN ASSUMPTIONS

Suitable space will be found at Ace Plumbing Supplies to locate the computer.

The current records can be converted to the new system.

Ace Plumbing Staff will be made available in accordance with the agreed stage Plans.

PROJECT RISK ASSESSMENT

A full Risk Assessment has been carried out. The results are held in Annex x. The result of the assessment is that the project risk is low.

CONFIGURATION MANAGEMENT PLAN

Note - in this project the role of configuration librarian will be shared by the project support assistant and specialist supplier team members.

Each product will be uniquely identified by a reference number allocated by the project support assistant. It will contain the Product number, version number and type.

Project support assistant, who will store and issue product copies as required, will exercise configuration control.

All project issue will be logged and controlled by the project manager. The procedures for evaluation and processing of the project issue reports will be in accordance with the PRINCE manual.

ANNEXES

Job Descriptions
  Project Board
  Project Manager
  Team Manager
  Project Assurance Function

Project Plans
  Product Flow Diagram
  Work Package and Product Breakdown Structure

Project Plan
Supporting Narrative

Quality Review Proformas
QR Invitation
QR Error List
QR Result Notification
QR Action List

Reporting Proformas
Checkpoint Report
Highlight Report
ESM Agenda
Risk Assessment Checklist

EXAMPLE 19   PROGRESS REPORT TO MASTERPLAN COMMITTEE

Summary of Programme and Project Progress Report

Ref. Number	Current Phase	Unresolved Programme or Project Threatening Issues	Plan/Actual Resources %	Plan/Actual Spend %	Plan/Actual Milestones %	Plan/Actual Delivery %	Overall Assessment of Project Status	Red Amber Green

TO DATE column spans: Plan/Actual Resources %, Plan/Actual Spend %, Plan/Actual Milestones %, Plan/Actual Delivery %

EXAMPLE 20 PROJECT PROGRESS REPORT

Project Name

Progress Report Number	Current Phase Of Project
Project Ref. Number	For Dates
	Prepared By

Overall Assessment Of The Project Status

Summary Of The Progress Made In This Period

Project Milestones/Deliverables Planned And Delivered In This Period
Milestones
Deliverables

Summary Of Planned And Used Resources Expenditure	
Resources Planned	Resources Used
Expenditure Planned	Expenditure Made

Issues Raised	Actions

Project Milestones/Deliverables Planned For The Next Period	
Milestones	
Deliverables	

EXAMPLE 21 PROGRAMME CLOSURE REPORT

To: The Programme Board
From: The Programme Manager

Programme Closure Report – United Libraries Service

INTRODUCTION

The purpose of this report is to describe the reasons why the programme has been closed and the arrangements that have been put into place to realise and sustain the benefits.

The report also describes the lessons learnt during the programme.

This report is divided into five sections:

Section One is a review of this programme against its objectives, its plan and the effectiveness of the programme management processes and standards. In addition it contains statistics for the following functions:

> Planning and control.
> Exception reports

Section Two contains the Lessons Learnt that are pertinent to this programme only and should not be taken as a global change to the programme management method on future programmes.

Section Three contains the Lessons Learnt that are pertinent to all future programmes and should be applied as a global change to the programme management method.

Section Four describes the arrangements that have been put into place to realise and sustain the benefits from the programme.

Section Five describes the arrangements and actions taken in regard of the projects that have not yet been finalised.

SECTION ONE

1.1   Programme Aim and Objectives

The original aim of the new United Libraries Service programme was to put into place business systems which would enable it to become the source of information for 75% of the UK population. The information provided by the United Library Service was to consist of all published fiction and non fiction books, other publications, government publications, and any available job vacancies publicly known. In order that this aim was met in an economic and efficient manner the following targets were set for the new service:

1. The services must be situated so that they are available within 1 mile of at least 75% of the population.
2. The number of members of each library is to be increased from 1.2K to 4K by extending the services provided to include:
   - Provision of direct access via the Internet and Intranet to UK government departments information and inquiry system's.
   - Relocating local job clubs to the library (they will use the technology provided for the Internet and Intranet service).
   - Increasing the number of publications available for members at each library from 333K to 600K.
3. Reducing the costs of the operation and provision of:
   - The library service. (Planned £11,025K)
   - Government information and inquiries. (Planned £261,000K)
   - The job club service. (Planned £249,080K)
4. Improving the quality of life of the members/general population by:
   - Increasing their average reading age and the number of books read per year. (Planned 30).
   - Reducing the time a job seeker spends looking for employment. (Planned 4 months)
   - Expanding the amount of and access to, government information. (Planned 6,000K)

1.2. PROGRAMME REVIEW

This section is subdivided into an analysis of the benefits achieved by the programme and the effectiveness of the programme management method.

1.2.1 Analysis of the Benefits Achieved

Quantitative Benefits (all figures in £ ,000)

Libraries	
Operational cost	$(0.25-0.17) \times (17-15) \times 2,000 \times 1,650 = £XXXK$
Cost of procurement of new books	$(7.5-5) \times 450 \times 1,650 = £1278K$
Repairs and replacements to books	NIL
Total	£ XXXK *Planned £xxxx*
Government Departments	
Inquiries	$(50-20) \times 5,500,000 = £ XXXXK$
Minus additional staff	$(300-150) \times 45,000$ Minus £K
Total	£ XXXXX K *Planned £XXXXX*

Job Club	
Reduction in Job Seeker allowance	(1800-1200) x 385,000=£XXXX K
Savings in cost of equipment provided	(300-100) x 385,000=£ XXXX K
Saving in revenue costs	(18.7-10.5) x 385,000=£ XXX K
Total	£ XXXK Planned £XXXX
Grand Total	**£XXXX K *Planned XXXX***

Qualitative Benefits

Libraries	
Reading age	+ 0.1 yrs
Availability of service	Nil
Number of books read per year	+ 4
Book loan period	Nil
Government Departments	
Value of Information provided	+ £400
Number of Government Departments on line	+ 45
Job Club	
Time awaiting a job	- 2.5 months
Number of information/job sources	+ 10
Availability of Job Club places	+75 x1,650

1.2.2 Summary of the Achievement of the Programme Blueprint

Aims and Objectives

The programme did not completely achieve its aims and objectives because of the following reasons.

1. The Ministry of Information removed the requirement relating to ensuring that libraries were located with 1 mile. This removed the need for tranche four of the programme and triggered its premature closure.
2. The moving of the responsibility for job clubs did achieve nearly all its objectives (X%). The variation between the planned and actual was due largely to the reduction in level of unemployment that occurred during the programme.
3. The provision of the government information service achieved X% of its targets – the failure to achieve 100% was largely due to the reorganisation in government departments that took place following the XXXX election. The new government's policy remains the same however therefore it is very likely that the full anticipated benefits will be realised during the next four years.
4. The programme was also designed to achieve substantial improvement in the operation of ULS's main business processes. These have largely been achieved.

The variation between the planned and actual benefits was due to the relocation not being carried out and therefore it was not possible to complete the proposed redesign of buildings and shelving and storage systems.

(This resulted in £xxxxx of investment having to be written of in respect of the contracts for the research into the possible sites and design contracts that had been let before the decision was made to abandon tranche 4)

1.2.3 The effectiveness of the Programme Management Method

Overall now major problems were experienced with the programme management method. The particular successes were the communication Strategy and the risk assessment method.

The standard risk checklist has been updated to reflect new risks that were identified during the programme.

1.2.4 Analysis of the Statistics

Planning

(As compared with the versions of the plan included in the final PDS Version 9)

Technical Development: Estimating variance

Resources required	Max +25%	Min 0%	Av +3.2%
Cost incurred	Max +40%	Min - 5%	Av +1.6%
Delays	Max +35%	Min -20%	Av +1.8%

Programme Management:

Resources required	Max +35%	Min -20%	Av +4.2%
Cost incurred	Max +40%	Min - 9%	Av +3.3%
Delays	Max +35%	Min - 0%	Av +3.1%

Quality Management:

Resources required	Max+135%	Min -20%	Av+45.5%
Cost incurred	Max +95%	Min - 9%	Av+36.8%
Delays	Max +97%	Min - 0%	Av+42.1%

Summary data

The planned expenditure was	£XXXX
The actual expenditure was	£XXXX
The planned delivery date was	XXXXX
The actual delivery date was	XXXXX

Programme Issue Reports

During the programme 31 programme issue reports were received.

28 were converted into requests for change and all but three were dealt with during the programme.

Three off specification reports were raised and all were dealt with during the programme. Each of these were investigated and the reason why they occurred was that the reviewers had not applied the quality criteria with sufficient rigour. This had occurred because of their inexperience in the Quality Control Review process which was remedied by some in-house training and assistance from an external consultant with the reviews for the remainder of the project.

The programme issue reports were received as follows

Tranche 1   9   (7-RFC 2-OSR)
Tranche 2   7   (6-RFC 1-OSR)
Tranche 3   15   (15-RFC)

The three outstanding RFCs will be considered at the next meeting of the Board for consideration in future programmes.

Quality Control Reviews

37 quality control reviews were held of which 24 were informal and 13 formal.

The following is an analysis of the faults found

Informal

Total number of faults	385
Serious errors	17
Minor errors	368

Formal	
Total number of faults	174
Serious faults	26
Minor faults	48

Rework required

Max 6 Days   Min 1day   Av 1.5days

SECTION TWO   LESSONS LEARNT THAT ARE PERTINENT TO THIS PROGRAMME ONLY

There are only two Lessons Learnt pertinent to this programme that need to be recorded.

The first of these relate to use of the user liaison group that was established during tranche two – the use of an independent chairman.

The independent chairman although effective during the meetings did not provide the drive that was needed between the meetings to take things forward.

The second issue is the use of the programme and project office. The PPO were not used in the risk identification and assessment process as it was felt that these workshops should be driven by the programme management team. This resulted in the programe team not being consistent in the use of the checklist and failing to ensure that new risks were added to the checklist.

SECTION THREE LESSONS LEARNT THAT ARE PERTINENT TO ALL PROGRAMMES

There are three Lessons Learnt should passed onto future programmes.

The first of these are that the benefits realisation and sustainability plan should used as the basis of a project – The benefits realisation and sustainability project. This would ensure that all the activities need are recorded and planned.

The other two problems involve the delays encountered by the projects in the programme. The major causes of which were an inability to obtain specific staff and problems synchronising the production of major deliverables from the programme and Board meetings (resulting in progress held up whilst awaiting Board approval).

It is recommended that in future programmes that Board responsibility for approving such documents should be delegated to the finance and general purposes sub committee which meets every fortnight.

Secondly that the programme board are given the authority to utilise external resources - up to a limit of £X K per month to meet any shortfall in internal resources that emerges.

SECTION FOUR: THE ARRANGEMENTS TO REALISE AND SUSTAIN THE BENEFITS

The Benefits Realisation Plan has been updated to reflect the arrangements that have already been completed and also to include the latest action plans.

In order that this plan is continues to be monitored and the need for control action identified it has been agreed that Mr XXXX (the programe Director will ensure that the

Board is kept up to date with the further fulfilment of the benefits realisation plan and the operation of the arrangements for sustaining them. (see appendix 1 for the latest Benefits Realisation and Sustainability Plan).

SECTION FIVE: THE ARRANGEMENTS AND ACTIONS FOR THE PROJECTS NOT FINALISED.
There are three projects that were not finalized when the programme was closed:

Project Three   Management of Change
Project Eleven   Library Relocation Designs
Project Twelve   Library Relocations and Up Grades

The following arrangements have been made for these projects

Project Three is to continue until XXX and will be subsumed into the proposed programme on adult literacy

Project Eleven is to continue to the end of its stage three – this is when the draft designs will be completed under the contract – the project will then be closed. Until that point this project will be transferred to the Business As Usual Programme under the Mr XXXX the Programme Manager. Arrangements have been made for this transfer to take place this week together with the transfer of responsibility for the financial aspect of that project.

Project Twelve has been closed – The project has started its Project Initiation Stage. The relevant resource and budget managers have been informed of the closure and the resources and budgets reallocated.

EXAMPLE 21B PROJECT CLOSURE REPORT

To: **The Masterplan Committee**
                    SK Motorised Diggers Plc

From: **The Project Manager and Project Sponsor.**

INTRODUCTION

The stock and sales administration project has now been completed and this report has been prepared for the masterplan committee by the project manager and project sponsor to provide a summary of the lessons learnt during this project which can then be incorporated by the masterplan committee into future projects.

This report is divided into 6 sections:

Section One   Selection and appointment of the project team.

Section Two   The involvement of the project team in planning and controlling the project.

Section Three   The operation of the product quality review process.

Section Four   The operation of the project issue report process.

Section Five   Observations on the project management standards and procedures used.

Section Six   Recommendations for consideration for adoption in future projects.

SECTION ONE   Selection and Appointment of the Project Team.

This was rather an unusual project in that it was the first major IT project in this company and the use of a structured approach was new to all of the members of SK Motorised Diggers who took roles in this project.

The project sponsor was selected by the members of the masterplan committee. The sponsor and project requester executive and senior user attended an on site 1 day seminar which was presented by the external consultant.

This provided a good basis for their role but the lack of experience showed on two occasions when they accepted a major change to the project by approving requests for changes that took the project outside of the project initiation document. Once this had been pointed out took immediate steps to rectify the situation.

The project team also required training and it was found that they required supplementary help during the project. The role of configuration librarian was split between the project manager and the team leader from IT - this worked well except for a small problem when several pirate copies of a document were made for a cascade briefing and were inadvertently used as the basis of another product. The problem arose because the version used was out of date.

SECTION TWO.   The Involvement of the Project Team in the Planning and Control Process.

The majority of the planning effort came from the development company who did ensure that project team were fully involved in the process of developing and agreeing the deliverable descriptions and in providing input to the weekly and monthly progress reports.

The quality of the involvement and advice given by the project team improved as their experience in grew. The coaching provided for the members of the project team as part of the ongoing consultancy support from the project support office helped this confidence to grow.

The only real problem came from the user department X in Stages 4 and 5 where the volume of work initially overwhelmed the user community until they were allowed to spend additional time on the project.

The estimates provided by the user member of the project team were proved to be extremely accurate this we believe was due to the long experience of the person selected for this role.

SECTION THREE   The Operation of the Product Quality Review Process.

In stage 1 and 2 of the project the project team tended to prefer formal quality reviews. This was caused by their inexperience, the lack of guidance in when to use what form of review. To counter this problem two actions were taken.

The first was to produce a checklist of the considerations that should be made when deciding between formal and informal reviews.

The second was some additional training and coaching in the product quality review process and conduct of the review meeting.

All scheduled product quality reviews were held. The quality of the deliverable descriptions improved during the later stages of the project as the quality criteria became both realistic and useful to the producer of the product. This again was due to the inexperience of the project management team but this time we believe it was due to not having used the XXXX structured project management method previously.

SECTION FOUR   Involvement of the Project Team in the Project Issue Reporting Process

There were 31 project issue reports submitted during this project. The majority of these came in the early Stages of the project. The introduction of project information into the regular cascade briefings did reduce the flow of the reports. The only concern that the procedure gave was that twice the scope of the project seemed to be expanding out of control and the freezing of the user requirements did help considerably.

SECTION FIVE.   Observations on the Project Management Standards and Procedures Used.

The major success in this project was the use of the planning and control software. This provided all of the planning diagrams and the turnaround document system used for telling team members what is to be done and then for submitting actuals saved a considerable amount of effort. The standard proforma for all of the reports proved to be useful and they were only modified so they could be used in the cascade briefings.

The configuration management system worked effectively and apart from two isolated incidents involving users making pirate copies of documents there were no problems. The allocation of the roles to the individuals was successful although the majority of the appointees had no experience of projects and had not had any training when the job descriptions were agreed.

SECTION SIX.   Recommendations for Future Projects.

The recommendations are:

1.   Training in the XXXX project management lifecycle should be undertaken at the outset of the project prior to the discussions about the job descriptions.
2.   When team members are inexperienced then the services of an independent coach/mentor should be employed to help them come to terms with the role and the tasks and activities.
4.   A revised standard for plans should be developed which uses the deliverable flow diagram as the main document rather than the Gantt chart.

EXAMPLE 22 END OF PROGRAMME TRANCHE REPORT

To: The Programme Board

From: Jan McClelland

Subject: End-Tranche Report

Introduction
This paper summarises the reports, presentations and agreements made at the end-tranche meeting held at the office of Philip Henry 12 February 2000.

Programme Managers Report
The programme is running approximately 3 weeks later. This is due to delays experienced on project two earlier in the tranche when resources were not available and we had to recruit and train new staff to carry out part of the business process re-engineering. This had a knock on effect on projects 3,4,6 and ultimately the whole programme.

This has delayed the benefits that were planned for this tranche and as a consequence special funding arrangement were needed to match the shortfall of funds the delay caused.

In addition the communication and attitudinal change plan had not proved to be substantial enough in that several cases of actual sabotage had occurred which were traced back to disaffected staff. This had caused minor problems but were indicative that more work was needed in this area if the second and more demanding tranche of the programme was to be successful.

Benefits Realisation/Sustainability Plan
The plan has been updated to reflect the agreement and plans that that have been agreed during this tranche and the benefits that are planned to be raised when we complete this tranche.

The report will be updated once these benefits have been obtained.

At present the programme has not realised any benefits.

(see appendix 1)

Programme Plan

The programme plan has been updated and is now as follows:

Tranche Two

Project 6   Completion of project.
Project 10   Commenced.

Year Three of the Programme

Project 7   Completion of project.

End of Tranche Two
Implementation of cross charging administrative processes for government information systems service.
Benefits realised £ 261,000K

Tranche Three

Project 8   Completion of project.
Project 9   Completion of project.

Year Four of the Programme

Project 11   Commenced.
Project 12   Commenced.

End of Tranche Three
Operation of administrative processes to support cross charging for government information systems (reduction in staff in government departments) implementation of business process re-engineering - Part One - Purchasing of books and new operational processes.
Benefits realised £11,025 K (part)

Tranche Four

Project 10   Completion of project.
Project 11   Completion of project.
Project 12   Completion of project.
Project 3   Completion of project.

End of Tranche Four
Implementation of business process re-engineering - Part Two - Relocation aspects.
Benefits realised £11,025 K (part)

EXAMPLE 23 PROFORMA EXCEPTION REPORT AND PLAN

EXCEPTION REPORT			From:	To:
Why This Report is Needed				

PRODUCTS AFFECTED IN THIS STAGE					
Product ID	Due to Start	Due to Finish	Impact of Problem		
			Time	Cost	Comments

OTHER PRODUCTS/PROJECTS AFFECTED					
Product ID	Due to Start	Due to Finish	Impact of Problem		
			Time	Cost	Comments

OPTIONS CONSIDERED	Effect on Problem	COST		Comments
		Time	Resources	
1.				
2.				
3.				
RECOMMENDATION AND REASONS:				

EXAMPLE 24 PROJECT MANDATE

Memo to: Mr. I Balance   Finance Director

From: Mr. Michael Cumbermack   Managing Director

Subject: Strategic Planning Review

Ivor,

At the senior management retreat last month we discussed and agreed the strategic aims of the company for the forthcoming year. As you know this was documented in the policy paper XXXX.

At the strategy implementation committee we discussed the programme of work that will be needed to fulfill these aims and who should head up the three projects we decided to commission.

I have detailed below the project we would like you to undertake on behalf of the company.

Given
The Board of Ace Plumbing Supplies Ltd. have agreed that their business goal for this year will be:

> *To ensure continued customer loyalty by providing a service level better than its competitors.*

To help meet this goal a programme containing three major projects has been identified:

1) To install a new switchboard.
2) To upgrade the decoration of the customer area and the trade counter.
3) To develop a new sales and stock system.

The project we would like you to lead is number three.

The reason for the projects (as you know only too well) is that the existing sales and stock system is now overstretched to the extent that it is inhibiting the growth of sales to both the trade and the public sectors.

The current system does not identify excess or out-of-date stocks and also has caused a number of errors when goods were sold when they were not in stock.

The sales manager has identified several new sales campaigns which require a list of current customers - the present system cannot easily supply this.

What we need the project to do

To provide a new sales and stock system which will support the company's business goals.

The specific objectives are:

1) To ensure the sales section has easy access to details of the existing customers to support new sales initiatives.
2) Ensure out of date or excess stock is easily identified.
3) To eliminate selling of 'stock' that does not exist.

Please come back to me if you have any questions.

EXAMPLE 25 PROJECT BRIEF

Project Background

The Board of Ace Plumbing Supplies Ltd. have agreed that their business goal for this year will be:

> *To ensure continued customer loyalty by providing a service level better than its competitors.*

To help meet this goal a programme containing three major projects has been identified:

1) To install a new switchboard.
2) To upgrade the decoration of the customer area and the trade counter.
3) To develop a new sales and stock system.

This Project Brief is concerned with project number three.

The existing sales and stock system is now overstretched to the extent that it is inhibiting the growth of sales to both the trade and the public sectors.

The current system does not identify excess or out-of-date stocks and also has caused a number of errors when goods were sold when they were not in stock.

The sales manager has identified several new sales campaigns which require a list of current customers - the present system cannot easily supply this.

Project Aims and Objectives

The aim of the project is:

To provide a new sales and stock system which will support the company's business goals.

The specific objectives are:

1) To ensure the sales section has easy access to details of the existing user/*customers* to support new sales initiatives.
2) Ensure out of date or excess stock is easily identified.
3) To reduce existing stock levels by 5%.
4) To eliminate selling of 'stock' that does not exist.

Scope and Constraints

Scope

The project is to concentrate its efforts on the sales and stock sections and its systems. Any links with other sections must be documented and defined.

The new system is to support the sales and stock sections, any other assistance it provides to other sections is not to be regarded as having any priority.

Assumptions that have been identified and agreed

The project is to be developed by an external development team.

The system must be easy to use.

The system must be able to cope with the expected growth of 30% this year and 15% for each successive year for the next five years.

The system must be able to supply word processing facilities for the management team.

The new system must not cost any more than £10,000 to install and have a running cost less than the existing manual systems and the project is to be completed during this financial year.

Reporting

Ace Plumbing Supplies has given full responsibility for this project to a project board consisting of Mr. I Balance, Finance Manager (Executive), Mr. J Yorkshire, Sales Manager (Senior User/*Customer*) and Mr. J Kelly Senior Specialist Supplier) an external consultant engaged to advise Ace Plumbing Supplies.

The project board has full authority to proceed with this project within the limits of this document. If the project board expects to exceed this brief then it must report to the full board of Ace Plumbing Supplies within seven days.

EXAMPLE 26 CHECKPOINT RETURN

CHECKPOINT REPORT					
From: *Colin Bloggs*		**To:** *David Marsh*		**For period:** *w/c 12/7/98*	
Product ID	Product Name	Due to Start	Actual Start	Due to Cmplte	Actual Cmpltn
10.01.03.02	Draft building requirements report (1)	13/7/98	12/7/98	15/7/98	15/7/98
11.03.01	Quality review invitation	12/7/98	12/7/98	12/7/98	12/7/98
12.02.03	User/*customer* acceptance note for product 10.01.01.02	12/7/98	12/7/98	13/7/98	13/7/98
15.01.02	Training plan	14/7/98	14/7/98	15/7/98	15/7/98
16.02.01	Building permission letter	15/7/98	14/7/98	20/7/98	
10.01.03.03	User/customer approval of building requirements	16/7/98	15/7/98	21/7/98	

EXAMPLE 27 MONTHLY OR HIGHLIGHT REPORT

HIGHLIGHT REPORT				
From: David Marsh	**To:** Jan McClelland		**For period:** July 1998	
ID No	Product Name	Due to complete	Actual completion	Comments
10	Building Requirements Report	21/7/98	20/7/98	
11	Quality Review	23/7/98	22/7/98	
12	User/*Customer* Acceptance of Building requirements	26/7/98	27/7/98	Reviewer on holiday (unplanned)
13	Building Regulations application	16/7/98	15/7/98	
14	Equipment Order	9/7/98	7/7/98	Found a short cut in procedures
15	Training Courses	27/7/98	23/7/98	Able to use previous course materials
16	Data Collection	20/7/98	26/7/98	New data requirement identified

Variances Analysis		Max	Min	Av	Comments
	% Resources	+ 25% Product 16	-10% Product 15	+4%	
Product Production	% Cost	+18%	-9%	+1%	
	% Delay	+30%	-20%	+2%	

Problems/Opportunities Encountered
New data requirements identified in Product 16 - leading to a delay in product 16.

Impact on Rest of Stage/Product
Problem/extra work from Product 16 will mean that the data conversion (Product 22) will take 20% longer . Impact on project +5 days on that stage. Total tolerance now used is +21 days out of the allowed 30. No action needed as yet.

EXAMPLE 27B END OF PROJECT STAGE REPORT

To: The Masterplan Committee
                The Project Sponsor
                The Project Requester
                The Project Board
                Project Support Office

From: Mr P Farmer
                Project Manager

End-Stage Report

Project Managers Report

The project was still within the original project plan although a number of amendments have been made to the project initiation document. These have been approved by the project sponsor and the masterplan committee and are included in the current version (number 4) of the project initiation document.

The major uncertainty left in the project was the conversion of the existing stock and sales records. To reduce this uncertainty the project manager requested that some of the staff were asked to assist the team who were to key in the data into the database during September. The manager of department X agreed to arrange this and the project plan is to be amended to reflect the increase in user involvement.

Project Team Report

User Aspects

The only item raised by the user department was concerned with the number of deliverable descriptions that she had been asked to review for the next Stage. The project manager had explained that this was an exceptional Stage as it had contained a lot more user deliverables than previous phases and this had resulted in the user department- having to vet approx. 20 deliverable descriptions in the last 3 weeks. It was agreed that if the project manager felt that such a workload was likely to occur again then she would ask the manager of department x to appoint a further person to the project team role to help out.

Product Quality Reviews

The project team leader reports that all the product quality reviews scheduled for the stage had been completed and only two deliverables had remedial work still outstanding. The project team leader (who attended the review of Deliverable 3) said that he felt that it could have been reviewed informally. He had examined the records to see why it had been selected for a formal review and it appears as if the project manager had not correctly applied the checklist of the factors for selecting formal versus informal reviews. The project sponsor and project manager have discussed this and reviewed the agreed level of reviews for the next stage of the project to ensure that the checklist was being correctly applied and that it did reflect the needs of this project.

Project Issue Status
Three 3 project issue reports had been received and had all been processed. An analysis of all the project issues received to date will be prepared in the next two weeks to see if any trends were emerging. This will be presented at the next mid-stage meeting.

Standards
The use of the deliverable descriptions from the system development handbook has helped in setting the standards required in the quality criteria. In respect of the standards used for project management it had been requested by several of the users for the distribution of the monthly progress summary report to be amended to include them. The project manager and sponsor have discussed this and it has been agreed to amend the distribution list to include these people.

The Project Plan
The only changes to the project plan (version 5) from that agreed in the previous stage were that the data conversion and take on deliverables had been allocated additional user resources (see item 2).

The project sponsor has approved the new plan but pointed out that as there was only 13 days tolerance left any further time slippage would resort in them having to request additional time from the masterplan committee. The project sponsor has stressed that he is to be informed if the project manager felt that the project would go outside of the remaining tolerance.

The Business Case
The business case has been updated to reflect the costs incurred to date and also the updated benefits that were identified during the last stage. The project sponsor has asked the user department x to investigate the claimed increased benefits and report on this at the next mid-stage meeting.

Business Risk Assessment
A review of the risk assessment had been carried out. There were no new risks identified and the containment strategy has worked well. The overall level of risk for the project was still medium due to the development work being dependent on the new version of the operating system that was due for release in September.

Next Stage Plan
The plan for the next stage is attached. It is different from that in version 4 of the project plan as follows:

Deliverable 12 was no longer required due to the user specification being frozen by the project sponsor at the last end-stage report

Total duration of the stage is less 3 days and the resources required less 24-man days.

A new deliverable has been identified as being required this is shown as deliverable 97. It is a trial of the data conversion software that will be carried out in this stage to identify any problems that may arise when the full conversion takes place.

The changes in this plan from the project plan had been included in both the updated risk assessment and business case.

Approval to proceed
Formal approval of the project board, sponsor and masterplan committee is requested for the project to proceed.

EXAMPLE 28 PROJECT ISSUE LOG

Project Name					Project Ref.:			Stage Name/No.	
PI No.	Date Raised	Author	CI's Affected	Project Issue Type	Type Change Date	Allocated to:	Date Allocated		Date Closed

EXAMPLE 29 CONFIGURATION MANAGEMENT RECORD

Product Ref.		Product Name		CMR No.		
Product Location		File/Section		PC Directory/Filename		
Product Description Ref./Version		File/Section		PC Directory/Filename		
Quality Review Location		File/Section		PC Directory/Filename		
Product Type		Project Ref./Stage Created		Author/Supplier		
Release Baseline Ref.		Linked Product Refs.		Security Marking		
Status	Product Description Approved	Work in Progress	Product Draft Available	Product QR Compld	QR Result Note Number	Product Approved
Date	Rework Date					
Version No	Date	QRN/PI RFC/OSR Number				
ISSUE LOG						
Version No	Recipient	Purpose	Authority	Issue Date	ExPDate	Return Date

EXAMPLE 30 CONFIGURATION STATUS ACCOUNT

Legend

D = Draft; R = Reviewed; A = Approved

FC = Filing Cabinet

CONFIGURATION STATUS ACCOUNT					DATE	30/7/98	
Product ID	10	11	12	13	14	15	16
Product Name	Scrn Des	QR Rpt	Accept Memo	Impl Plan	Equip Ord	Trg Crs	Data Coll
Version Number	2	1	1	3	2	3	1
Author	BH	EP	SLS	BF	JK	SD	TB
Date Completed	20/7	22/7	27/7	15/7	7/7	23/7	26/7
QR Report number	10/02/1	11/01/1	12/01/1	13/03/1	14/02/1	15/03/1	16/01/1
Location	FC1	FC2	FC3	FC1	FC1	FC1	FC1
Linked Work Packages and or Products	11, 12, 15, 16	10, 12	10, 11	16, 7	4, 5	10,	10, 13
Status	A	A	A	A	A	A	A
Comments							

EXAMPLE 31 CONFIGURATION AUDIT REPORT

To: The Project Board

From   John Kelly (Internal Audit)

Subject: **Configuration Audit Report**

At your request I have carried out an audit of the configuration management system used on project xxxx and the configuration items contained in the system.

The Report is divided into three sections:

Section One   Application of the agreed configuration management method.

Section Two: Conformance of the configuration items to their records.

Section Three: Conformance of the records to the configuration items.

Section One Application of the Agreed Configuration Management Method.

The configuration management methods used in the organisation are defined in the standards published in the programme and project management handbook. The standard arrangements were modified in this project – these modifications were described in the project initiation document.

The review identified two discrepancies between these modified arrangements and those used on the project. These were:

> The storage location of the con figuration items.
> The person responsible for the safekeeping of the items.

The configuration management method states that the configuration items and records should be stored on the organisation T drive and no other copies are to be kept. The review found that the project used a Zip drive to store the end products on rather than the T drive. This had been instigated by the project manager to provide the off shore team with access to the deliverables at night when the T drive was not available to them.

Whilst this got over the problem it did cause a number of small problems over the use of out of date products. This situation should be examined by the organisation and the standards updated to address this problem where the development team is off shore.

The second problem concerns the person appointed to oversee the configuration management system. The standard approach is to appoint a member of the project support office as configuration librarian.

In this project two members of the project team were allocated to this role – one in the UK and one in the offshore team.

As in the previous concern it appears as if the standards for configuration management are not really designed for off shore projects.

Section Two: **Conformance of the Configuration Items to Their Records.**

The review examined a sample of 10% of the configuration items and their records. The following table shows the Items that were examined and the results of the audit of their conformance to their records.

CONFIGURATION STATUS ACCOUNT					DATE	9 August 1999	
Product ID	10	32	967	113	125	300	450
Product Name	Scrn Des	QR Rpt	Accept Memo	Impl Plan	Equip Ord	Trg Crs	Data Coll
Version Number	2	1	1	3	2	3	1
Author	BH	EP	SLS	BF	JK	SD	TB
Date Completed	20/7	22/7	27/7	15/7	7/7	23/7	26/7
QR Report number	10/02/1	11/01/1	12/01/1	13/03/1	14/02/1	15/03/1	16/01/1
Location	FC1 &TD	FC2	FC3 & TD	FC1	FC1&TD	FC1	FC1 &TD
Linked Work Packages and or Products	11, 12, 15,16	10, 12	10, 11	16, 7	4, 5	10,	10, 13
Status	A	A	A	A	A	A	A
Comments	All documents present and correct	All documents present – one had not been updated to reflect a small change	All documents present and correct	All documents present – one had not been updated to reflect a small change	All documents present and correct	All documents present and correct	All documents present – one had not been updated to reflect a small change

The non-conformances found were caused by the records not being updated when minor changes were made to the product descriptions by the off shore team – however these were not recorded by the in house team – these were not serious. It is recommended that the standards be modified to ensure that these problems do not arise in future projects.

Section Three: **Conformance of the Records to the Configuration Items.**

The review examined a sample of 10% of the configuration items. The following table shows the Items that were examined and the results of the audit of their conformance to their records.

Legend
D = Draft; R = Reviewed; A = Approved
ZD = Zip Drive
TD = T Drive

CONFIGURATION STATUS ACCOUNT					DATE	9 August 1999	
Product ID	10	32	967	113	125	300	450
Product Name	Scrn Des	QR Rpt	Accept Memo	Impl Plan	Equip Ord	Trg Crs	Data Coll
Version Number	2	1	1	3	2	3	1
Author	BH	EP	SLS	BF	JK	SD	TB
Date Completed	20/7	22/7	27/7	15/7	7/7	23/7	26/7
QR Report number	10/02/1	11/01/1	12/01/1	13/03/1	14/02/1	15/03/1	16/01/1
Location	FC1 &TD	FC2	FC3 & TD	FC1	FC1&TD	FC1	FC1 &TD
Linked Work Packages and or Products	11, 12, 15,16	10, 12	10, 11	16, 7	4, 5	10,	10, 13
Records Examined	Product Description Quality Review Report, Change Log	Product Description ,Acceptance Memo Change Log	Product Description Quality Review Report, Change Log	Product Description ,Quality Review Report, Change Log	Product Description ,Quality Review Report, Change Log	Product Description ,Quality Review Report, Change Log	Product Description Quality Review Report, Change Log
Comments	All documents present and correct	All documents present and correct	All documents present and correct	All documents present and correct	All documents present and correct	All documents present and correct	All documents present and correct

The review did not reveal any major problems.

Summary
It is recommended that the standard Configuration Management Method is updated to deal with those projects which involve off shore development teams

EXAMPLE 32 RISK REGISTER

This risk register is divided into five sections:

- business environment – external;
- business environment – internal;
- programme and project organisation and management;
- programme and project delivery mechanism;
- programme and project content.

Part One: **Business Environment - External**

When assessing the risks to the project there are a number of issues in respect of the business environment external to the organisation that need to be considered.

1.   Is there likely to be any major governmental or political changes that may occur during the development of the project that may effect:

- the stability of the market place;
- the reason for the project;
- the scope or content of the programme or project.

2.   Is there likely to be any major change in the economic environment that may occur during the development of the programme or project that may effect:

- the financial aspects;
- the market place the programme or project provides products or services for now;
- the market place the programme or project provides products or services for in the future.

3.   Is there likely to be any major change in other countries that may occur during the time the programme or project is being developed that may effect:

- the reason for the programme or project;
- the financial aspects of the programme or project;
- the scope or content of the programme or project;
- the stability of the market place;
- the market place the programme or project provides products or services for now;
- the market place the project provides products or services for in the future.

4.   Are there likely to be to any significant new developments in technology or other process improvements that may occur during the programme or project that may effect:

- the reason for the programme or project;
- the financial aspects of the programme or project;
- the scope or content of the programme or project;
- the stability of the market place;
- the market place the programme or project provides products or services for now;
- the market place the programme or project provides products or services for in the future.

5.   Are your competitors or other organisations, which you are compared to:

- undertaking any major new investments;
- re-organising themselves;
- undertaking similar programmes or project/s;
- carrying out any other form of competitive edge improvement activities.

Part Two: Business Environment - Internal
When assessing the risks to the project there are a number of issues that should be examined in respect of the business environment internal to the organisation that need to be considered.

1.   Is there likely to be any major internal changes e.g. re-organisation that may occur during the time that the programme or project is under development that may effect:

- the parts of the organisation the programme or project is to provided for;
- the reason for the programme or project;
- the scope or content of the programme or project.

2.   Is there likely to be any major change in the internal economic environment that may occur during the development of the programme or project that may effect:

- the financial aspects of the programme or project;
- the cost benefit analysis of the programme or project;
- the rate of return required for the investment to be considered viable.

3. Is there likely to be any major change in personnel, departmental structure, or internal procedures in the organisation that may occur during the development of the programme or project that may effect:

    - the reason for the programme or project;
    - the financial aspects of the programme or project;
    - the scope or content of the programme or project;
    - the stability of the market place;
    - the market place the programme or project provides products or services for now;
    - the market place the programme or project provides products or services for in the future.

4. Are they likely to be to any significant new developments in technology or other process improvements in other parts of the organisation that may occur during the programme or project that may effect:

    - the reason for the programme or project;
    - the financial aspects of the programme or project;
    - the scope or content of the programme or project;
    - the stability of the market place;
    - the market place the programme or project provides products or services for now;
    - the market place the programme or project provides products or services for in the future.

5. Are the technical and business aims of the programme or project.

    - compatible with existing business strategies;
    - compatible with existing IT/IS strategies;
    - compatible with any other relevant strategies.

6. Is the data that has been used in the estimation of the resources needed for the programme or project.

    - from a known -tried and trusted source;
    - included an allowance for all associated quality and management control activities;
    - relevant to the programme and or project/s;
    - include a calculated amount of tolerance.

7. Has a senior level management taken ownership of the programme or project and ensured that this is communicated to all members of the organisation.

Part Three: Programme or Project Organisation and Management.

When assessing the risks to the programme or project there are a number of issues that should be examined in respect of the programme or project organisation structure used to control the and manage the programme or project that need to be considered.

1.   Has the organisation put in place the necessary organisation and other infrastructure components to:

- produce an agreed brief or terms of reference for the programme or project;
- develop and agree a blueprint for the changes the programme or project is to achieve in the organisation;
- ensure the programme or project has the necessary finance and skilled resources;
- ensure the reasons for the programme or project are still valid and the progress made is regularly reviewed;
- resolve any priority clashes;
- monitor progress of the programme or project and the constituent projects;

2.   Is there likely to be any changes to the management environment that are responsible for the programme or project that may occur during the development of the programme or project that may effect:

- the senior managers who are sponsoring the programme or project/
- the amount of time these senior managers can devote to the programme or project;
- the launching of other projects that interface or interfere with this programme or project;
- changes in the priority given to the programme or project.

3.   Is there likely to be any major change in the organisation that may occur during the development of the programme or project that may effect:

- the sponsors of the programme or project;
- the position or place of the recipient parts of the organisation;
- changes to the investment profile/decisions of the organisation.

Part Four   Programme or Project Delivery Mechanism

When assessing the risks to the programme or project there are a number of issues that should be examined in respect of the programme or project delivery mechanism that needs to be considered.

1. Has the programme or project delivery been defined in terms of:

    - an agreed statement of the aims and objectives and costs and benefits of the project- a programme or project brief, terms of reference or blueprint;
    - supported by an agreed and documented programme or project management method;
    - a series of tranches, stages, milestones or phases;
    - the business products to be produced;
    - the other components of the programme or project such as management of change;
    - linkages and relationships with other related programmes or projects or change initiatives.

2. Is the programme or project to be:

    - controlled by a group of senior managers who are responsible for its delivery;
    - managed to a defined pr programme or project management method;
    - developed to defined programme or project brief or terms of reference;
    - to have its progress monitored by senior management;
    - use tried and trusted planning and control systems.

3. Are the technical development strategies to be used in the programme or project

    - established;
    - well known to the organisation;
    - well known generally.

4. Are the members of staff who will be responsible for delivering the programme or project .

    - experienced in such activities;
    - have the necessary span of control and authority;
    - allocated the necessary resources;
    - supported by a programme or project management office.

5. Have soft or human elements or change management elements been included in:

    - the responsibility matrix for the programme or project;
    - the definition of the programme or project;

- the list of products or deliverables that are to be developed.

6.   Has the organisation ensured that there are:

- effective communication between the programme or project manager and managers of other related programmes or projects;
- the estimating system used in the programme or project are accurate and up to date.

Part Five: Programme or Project Content

When assessing the risks to the programme or project there are a number of issues that should be examined in respect of the programme or project content that need to be considered.

1.   Have the management of change aspects been included in the programme or project in:

- the programme or project brief, blueprint or terms of reference;
- any human resource issues;
- ensuring that staff experienced in this topic are involved in the programme or project;
- ensuring that the organisation is equipped to deal with situation.

2.   Are the technical development strategies to be used in the programme or project:

- established;
- well known to the organisation;
- well known generally.

3.   Are the members of staff who will responsible for delivering the programme or project deliverables or products:

- experienced in such activities;
- have the necessary span of control and authority;
- allocated the necessary resources;
- supported by a programme or project support office;
- able to deliver "soft" programmes or projects e.g. personnel or attitude change.

4.   Are the programmes or projects interdependent with others to such an extent that:

- a failure or delay with another programme or project means this programme or project is at risk;
- a total or partial failure with one component of another programme or project means this programme or project is at risk.

EXAMPLE 33 RISK ACTION PLAN

To: The Project Board
              The Programme Manager
              Manager Department x,y,z
From: The Project Manager

Subject: Risk Action Plan

At the recent risk identification and assessment workshop a number of actions were agreed that now need to be implemented. The purpose of this memo is to ensure that we are all aware of who is to do what and also to provide the basis of the monitoring of the risks that will be carried out during the project.

Risk Action Plan

Risk No	Risk	Action	Responsible	Start	Complete
1	Delay due to inexperienced staff	Additional staff to be allocated to the nominated key products	Mr. D Purves (Project Manager)	09/08/99	16/11/99
2	Failure in quality review of key products	Use of external advisors during the development of these key products	Mr. D Purves (project manager) and also Mr. D Smith Manager Department X.	09/08/99	16/11/99
3	Lack of funds to carry out risk avoidance	Obtain additional tolerance for the project from the programme	Mr. D Marsh Executive member of the project board	15/08/99	15/08/99
4	Failure of prefabrication company to deliver on time	Weekly visits to the supplier by the procurement department to assess progress	Mr. G Strange Head of procurement	09/08/99	Delivery Date 20/11/99
5	Delays due to protesters on site	Construct 3 metre fence and employ security staff	Project manager and head of procurement	09/08/99	12/09/00
6	Possible problems with capacity of concrete plant	Set up standby arrangements with local suppliers	Head of procurement	09/08/99	31/08/99

EXAMPLE 34 A SCORED RISK ASSESSMENT

Introduction

The checklist is based on CCTA (Central Computing and Telecommunications Agency) documents placed by them in the public domain.

The factors are in four groups; project management, project staff, project description and the maturity of the developer's practices.

The risk factors are numbered for reference purposes when discussing the checklist or when documenting a proposal to address one of the factors. The list is a suggested generalised one. Any extra ones for a particular project can be listed on the blank sheet provided.

The "Low Risk" column contains a description of what would be considered a satisfactory situation for that factor. The "High Risk" column has a description of a bad situation. In the "Scale" column you should ring a number indicating your assessment of that factor. For example, if the project has a full-time Project Manager who has led many projects, that would rate a "1". A full-time manager who has only led one or two projects might merit a "2".

The "weighting" column is used to indicate the importance of the factor to the project. In brackets is the suggested range from which to select the weighting. This is only a suggestion based on a survey of many projects. You can go outside the recommendations, but you should document your reasons.

The chosen scale is multiplied by the weighting to give the "Total" figure for each factor. At the end of the checklist add up both the Total and Weighting columns. If the Total column is greater than Weighting column multiplied by 2.6 the project deemed is be a very high risk. If it is less than Weighting column multiplied by 2.0 then it is low risk. Between the two figures use your judgement to decide whether it is high or acceptable.

As a rough guide anything scoring 15 or more should be regarded as a high risk.

Even if you think that nothing can be done about a factor, this should be entered in your proposal to show that you have thought about it.

At each End-Stage Meeting the checklist should be reviewed by the Project Manager for any changes as part of the project re-assessment.

	Low Risk	Scale	High Risk	Weighting	Total
Project Management					
1	Full time, experienced project manager	1 2 3 4	Inexperienced or part time project manager	(5-7) ___	___
2	User management experienced in projects and will participate effectively	1 2 3 4	Users inexperienced in projects with little participation expected	(4-6) ___	___
Project Staff (User & Developer)					
3	Users expected to be of good quality actively involved with relevant knowledge of the system	1 2 3 4	Little user involvement and little relevant knowledge expected	(3-4) ___	___
4	High Standard of supervision and narrow span of control	1 2 3 4	Span of supervision too wide and control level inadequate	(4-6) ___	___
5	The technical team is experienced of good quality and with appropriate skills	1 2 3 4	Inexperienced team lacking the needed skills	(2-4) ___	___
6	Staff are dedicated 100% of their time to the project	1 2 3 4	Staff have other work and are not 100% dedicated to the project	(3-5) ___	___
7	Low staff turnover	1 2 3 4	High staff turnover	(2-4) ___	___
8	Staff are experienced in quality reviews and committed to their use	1 2 3 4	No quality reviews carried out in the past	(4-6) ___	___
Project Description					
9	Typical development cycle	1 2 3 4	Unaccustomed development cycle with no formal requirements definition	(2-4) ___	___

10	No unique or new hardware or software facilities	1 2 3 4	Pioneering new hardware or software features	(2-4) ___	___
11	Minimal impact on current operations	1 2 3 4	Significant impact on current operations	(3-5) ___	___
12	Hardware and software needs defined and documented to proven standards	1 2 3 4	Requirements not documented or not to proven standards; limited contingency margins	(2-4) ___	___
13	Little or no modification to existing application software	1 2 3 4	Extensive modification needed	(2-5) ___	___
14	Little or no other development work being done at the same time	1 2 3 4	Considerable other work competing for the same facilities	(2-5) ___	___
15	Little or no dependence on existing or developing systems not under the control of same staff	1 2 3 4	Dependent on systems or facilities not under the control of this projects staff	(3-6) ___	___
16	Project duration of one year or less, small number of workdays	1 2 3 4	Duration more than one; large number of work days	(2-4) ___	___
17	Little constraint on completion date apart from resource availability	1 2 3 4	Mandatory and tight completion date	(3-5) ___	___
18	Plans and estimates based on reliable data and methods	1 2 3 4	Unreliable or non-existent planning data and methods	(3-6) ___	___
19	Business case made out based on reliable data on methods	1 2 3 4	No business case or one based on unreliable data or methods	(3-5) ___	___
20	Suppliers are large, well established companies	1 2 3 4	Suppliers are untried, new or not well financed	(2-4) ___	___

21	Few user departments	1 2 3 4	Several user departments	(4-6) ___	___
22	Few sites affected, easily accessible to the team	1 2 3 4	Many or remote sites	(3-5) ___	___
23	Minor impact on user's current or future work	1 2 3 4	Significant impact on user's work and methods	(3-5) ___	___

Developer Maturity

24	Well developed set of standards	1 2 3 4	Few standards no enforcement	(2-4) ___	___
25	Well defined quality policy	1 2 3 4	Ill defined quality policy	(3-5) ___	___
26	Clear delegation of authority	1 2 3 4	Centralised management with little delegation	(2-4) ___	___
27	Good relations with staff and unions	1 2 3 4	Poor staff and union relations	(2-4) ___	___

Business Risk Management Summary Sheet

(a)   Sum of Total   _____

        Sum of Weighting column   _____

(b)   Weighting column x 2.6   _____

(c)   Weighting column x 2.0   _____

        Very high risk if (a) > (b)
        low risk if (a) < (c)

        Business Risk Assessment is:

        Very high   _____

        High   _____

        Acceptable   _____

        Low   _____

EXAMPLE 35 QUANTITIVE RISK ASSESSMENT

Project : Power Station Construction   Status : Pre-development   Issue : 3

SERIAL	RISK/OWNERSHIP	PROB/IMP		STRATEGY/FALL-BACK	STATUS
6.02 Rank: 1 Source: Interview	**Inability to meet H & S requirements in full** All Health & Safety requirements may not be met in full **Owner:** John Smith	**Prob:** MED **Time:** LO **Cost:** MED **Perf:** HI		**Strategy:** Fully investigate all current H&S regulations and keep abreast of any proposed changes in legislation. **Fall-Back:** Change system to meet any H&S requirements when they are introduced or seek a concession.	15 Jun 98 [HVR, PL] Risk reviewed at interview with Risk Owner. The station passes all current H&S regulations, so risk only remains for changes in legislation. Probability therefore reduced to VLO. 14 Mar 98 [HVR, PL] Risk identified at interview with Risk Owner.
1.03 Rank: 2 Source: ES	**Criteria for acceptance/performance not defined** Acceptance and performance criteria may not be fully defined or achievable leading to the power station not being accepted. **Owner:** John Smith	**Prob:** MED **Time:** MED **Cost:** MED **Perf:** LO		**Strategy:** Discuss with customer and obtain agreement on all acceptance and performance criteria, ensuring that the agreed criteria are achievable from the system or service. **Fall-Back:** Agree a phased development and acceptance programme.	15 Jun 98 [HVR, PL] Risk reviewed at interview with Risk Owner. Some success has been had in the meetings with the customer, therefore probability reduced to MED. 13 Mar 98 [HVR, PL] Risk reviewed at interview with Risk Owner. Probability increased to HI to reflect difficulties in the meetings held to clarify the issues. These are to continue. 25 Nov 97 [HVR, PL] Risk reviewed in detail at interview with Risk Owner. 25 Nov 97 [HVR, PL] Risk identified at brainstorm
4.02 Rank: 3 Source: Interview	**System integration problems** Delays may occur during system integration. **Owner:** Alexandra Norton	**Prob:** MED **Time:** MED **Cost:** MED **Perf:** VLO		**Strategy:** Plan to carry out testing using simulation programs as soon as possible as independent stand alone packages. Ensure adequate interface specifications and reviews of those specifications are carried out. Close control and co-ordination of planning of installation and integration programme with all parties concerned. **Fall-Back:** Allow for additional integration period, agree for some individual testing/installation to be carried out at a later stage.	14 Mar 98 [HVR, PL] Risk identified at interview with Risk Owner. 15 Jun 98 [HVR, PL] Risk reviewed at interview with Risk Owner. All integration specifications have now been reviewed, but risk remains. No change.

X-1

EXAMPLE 36 RISK LOG

Project Name				Project Ref.	Stage Name/No		
Risk No.	Description	Author	Date Raised.		STATUS		
					Awaiting assessment	Counter or containment measure	Owner of the Risk

EXAMPLE 37 HISTORY FILE OF RISK MANAGEMENT PROCESS

To: The Project Board

From: The Project Manager

Subject: **History File of Risk Management Process**

The following table describes the risk management process used on the project and the outcome of the management process.

Risk History

Risk No	Risk	Action	Responsible	Planned Start	Planned Complete	Actual Start	Actual Complete	Assessment of effectiveness	Impact on risk	Cost of action
1	Delay due to inexperienced staff	Additional staff to be allocated to the nominated key products	Mr. D Purves (Project Manager)	09/08/99	16/11/99	09/08/99	24/11/99	Approx. 75%	Reduced the impact of the problem	Increase of 30% on affected products
2	Failure in quality review of key products	Use of external advisors during the development of these key products	Mr. D Purves (Project Manager) and also Mr. D Smith Manager Department X.	09/08/99	16/11/99	09/08/99	24/11/99	100%	No problems were experienced	Increase in cost of 30% on affected products
3	Lack of funds to carry out risk avoidance	Obtain additional 3% tolerance for the project from the programme	Mr. D Marsh Executive member of the Project Board	15/08/99	15/08/99	15/08/99	15/08/99	100%	No money problems emerged	5% overall additional costs

4	Failure of prefabrication company to deliver on time	Weekly visits to the supplier by the procurement department to assess progress	Mr. G Strange Head of procurement	09/08/99	Delivery Date 20/11/99	09/08/99	20/12/99	Partially effective because failed to send a technical expert.	Did not succeed because no technical evaluation	Delay of one month – however no affect on costs due to penalty clause
5	Delays due to protesters on site	Construct 3 metre fence and employ security staff	Project manager and head of procurement	09/08/99	12/09/00	09/08/99	12/10/99	85% Affective	Only 15 days were lost due to protesters action	Cost 1% of project
6	Possible problems with capacity of concrete plant	Set up standby arrangements with local suppliers	Head of procurement	09/08/99	31/08/99	09/08/99	31/08/99	100 % Affective	The standby arrangements were used twice	No additional costs

EXAMPLE 38 COST ANALYSIS

	Project Cost Analysis				
	Year 1	Year 2	Year 3	Year 4	Total
Project Development Costs- Manpower					
Project Management					
Developer 1					
Developer 2					
Users					
External experts					
Total					
Project Development Costs- Equipment					
Buildings					
Computers					
Telecomms					
Software					
Temporary Costs					
Accommodation					
Staff					
Equipment					
Services					
Changeover costs (Stationery etc) c					
Total					
Grand Total					

EXAMPLE 39 BENEFIT ANALYSIS

Benefits Analysis					
Direct Savings	Year 1	Year 2	Year 3	Year 4	Total
Reduction in operational staff					
Reduction in indirect staff					
Reduction in maintenance charges					
Reductions in service charges					
Reduction in stock holdings					
Reduction in accommodation cost					
Total					
Indirect					
Income from the sale of assets					
Buildings					
Equipment					
Other					
Reduction in administration and other overheads					
Total					
Grand Total					

EXAMPLE 40   AGENDA FOR FORMAL QUALITY REVIEW MEETING

1. Chairman's opening remarks and introductions.

2. Author/presenters overview of the product.

3. Reviewers consent to proceed with review.

4. Walk-through of product.

5. Other errors from absent reviewers.

6. Summary of faults found.

7. Follow up action arrangements.

8. Review decision and observations on Product Description and Quality Criteria.

9. Chairman's closing remarks and thanks.

EXAMPLE 41 FORMS FOR QUALITY REVIEW PROCESS

QUALITY REVIEW INVITATION

Project Name		Project Ref	Stage Name/No	QR No
To:		From:		Tel:
Product Name			CI No.	Version No.
Venue		Date/Time		Duration
Chairman:		Tel:		
Author/Presenter:		Tel:		
Scribe:		Tel:		
Reviewers:		Tel:		
Attached Documentation:				
Please return QR Question list to: By:				

QUALITY REVIEW QUESTION LIST

Project Name		Project Ref.	Stage Name/No	QR No
Product Ref./Name		Reviewer		Tel No
Question No	Location in Document	Description		

274

QUALITY REVIEW ACTION LIST/RESULT NOTIFICATION

Project Name	Project Reef		Stage Name/No	Q/R No.
Product Ref./Name				Date
Action No	Description	Action By	Target Date	Checked By
Chairman's Sign-off				Date:

Result Notification

Approved - no action required

OK after actions completed

Re-review

Incomplete

Glossary Of Terms

Activity

The work needed to develop or procure an output, deliverable or product. An activity consists of a number of specific tasks.

Added value

The achievement of additional benefits or worth from a document or other output which is in addition to its primary purpose. (Similar to synergistic effect).

Added value areas/reports

The areas of activity or reports which are designed to achieve added value.

Amalgam plan

A plan which is derived from a collection and consolidation of the key events in other plans.

Asset register

A list of the assets of an organisation. These registers identify what equipment, buildings, machinery, etc is held by the organisation and all other details of their purchase and location.

Avoidance strategy

A set of activities that are commissioned in a programme or project which are designed to avoid the identified risk occurring.

Backward pass network analysis

Part of the project network technique that identified which activities have zero float and are therefore on the critical path. (*See also second pass network analysis*).

Baselined

The defined and agreed programme or project plan or costs.

Benchmarks

A measure of how much input is used by the organisation to produce a specific output. e.g. cost of producing an invoice.

Benefits framework

The totality of plans and arrangements that are used to enable the organisation to achieve the defined benefits from a programme or project.

Benefits management plan

The plan which defines the benefits and the way that they will be realised.

Benefits management process

The process used by the organisation to define and manage the achievement of the required benefits.

Benefits profile

A representation of when the benefits must be realised.

Benefits realisation plan

A document used by the programme board and programme manager to describe the benefits, how they will be achieved and the detailed plans for their realisation.

Blueprint

A document which defines and describes what a programme is designed to achieve in terms of the business vision (quantitative targets) and operational vision (how the process will be operated when the programme is completed).

BOSCARI

An acronym used to describe the contents of a terms of reference. (Background Objectives Scope Constraints Reporting Information)

Breakeven period

The time taken to recover the costs of a programme or project through savings or other benefits achieved by the same programme or project.

Budget holder

The accountable member of staff who has been given a defined budget of money or other resources.

Budget variances

The variance between the budget and the expenditure made or incurred.

Budgetary approval

The process used by an organisation to decide on the budgets that will be allocated to each of the budget holders and the approval to spend that sum.

Budgeting committee

The group of executive level management who decide on the amount of the budget to be allocated to each budget holder.

Budgeting review

The process which the organisation uses to review the bids for budget funds.

Burn rate

A calculation of the amount of resources or deliverables that should be used each day during the programme or project. These are compared to those achieved and what is left to do. (This comparison provides a measure of progress as compared to the plan).

Burn rate indicators

The calculations of planned, to date, and left to do, burn rates.

Business benchmarks

A measure of the performance of a whole business or a part of that business. e.g. sales and marketing costs are £x per £ of turnover *(see also benchmarks)*.

Business architectures

The structure of business processes that are used by an organisation to perform, deliver or provide its products and or services.

Business areas

A sub-division of an organisation into a recognised and self -contained unit. e.g. sales and marketing.

Business-as-usual

The non-programme or project activities that

are performed in order to operate or support the business of the organisation.

Business change management

The management of the changes to the organisation needed to achieve the defined benefits of the programme or project.

Business change programmes

Programmes which are primarily designed to change a substantial part of an organisation or the products or services it provides.

Business integrity

Ensuring that the programme or project follows that element of the business case which explains the financial or business reasons for the programme or project.

Business-led initiative

The direction of the programme, project or workpackage by the management of the relevant business areas.

Business objective

A part of the organisation's business plan or strategy which defines a specific objective.

Business operations

The operation of the activities and processes used by the organisation to deliver its products or services.

Business processes

The collection of processes used by an organisation to manage its activities.

Business risks

Those potential events which may occur and, if they do, affect the operation of the business.

Business strategy level plan

A document which describes how an organisation will deliver the defined and agreed business strategy.

Business strategy process

The process used by an organisation to define or update the business strategy.

Business system project

A project which is designed to provide a new or updated business system or processes.

Capital expenditure

Expenditure made which is not counted as a revenue item in the organisation's accounts. (The expenditure is written-off over a number of years).

Centre of excellence

A term used to describe a department or team which is regarded as the expert in a particular activity or function.

Chairman of a quality review

The senior manager who is appointed by the organisation to ensure that a quality review of an output, deliverable or product is conducted to the agreed process, methods and standards.

Change log

The document used to record details of all the changes requested to the programme or project.

Change management

The management of the receipt, evaluation, decision making and relevant action relating to changing an aspect of a programme or project.

Checkpoint report

A report prepared by a member of the programme or project team to notify the programme or project manager that an output, deliverable or product has been completed or procured.

Command type structures

A strict hierarchical management structure which has clearly defined roles and responsibilities (similar to a structure found in a military organisation).

Communications plan

A plan developed within a programme or project to ensure that the organisation's requirements or needs for information about the programme or project are defined and that activities are planned and assigned to individuals or groups to meet those needs.

Cone of uncertainty

A diagram used to describe the uncertainty that exists in a programme or project through its lifecycle, i.e. at the start of the programme or project the uncertainty is at its greatest and reduces as the programme or project nears completion.

Configuration audit report

A report which summarises the results of a review of the current state of the configuration management process and the configuration records and items.

Configuration item identification and numbering system

The system of numbering used to identify each item in the programme or project – the numbering system should enable the easy identification of the relationship of the configuration items to each other.

Configuration management

The processes used to ensure that the configuration is managed and controlled effectively.

Configuration management record

The information held about a configuration item. This record may be stored electronically or in a card index.

Configuration status account report

A report which describes the current status of each of the items in the configuration management system.

Conformance audit

An audit of the operation of the programme or project management or other processes to identify if the defined processes are being adhered to.

Constructive audit

An audit of the operation of the programme, project or other processes to identify if the defined processes are providing the required support or assistance. When they are not, what is being done and should it be adopted as the new standard?

Containment strategy

The strategy which is used by the programme or project manager to contain the impact that an identified risk may have on the programme or project. e.g. if the project is more that x months late then...

Contingency

An allowance made to the programme or project duration or cost to allow for any unplanned activities that may be required.

Contingency plan

A plan which is developed to be deployed if a specified event occurs.

Control actions

The actions commissioned by the programme or project board to rectify a deviation from the agreed plans.

Control documents

The documents which define the baseline of the programme or project which are used by the programme or project board in monitoring the progress made and identifying if any control action is needed.

Cultural change

The change in attitude and beliefs that is needed for the organisation to achieve the objectives of a programme or project (*see also attitude change plan*)

Data dictionary

A document that is used to ensure that each unique data item is identified and defined so that it can be used consistently in each of the information systems that use it.

Data dictionary of tasks/products

A document which is used to uniquely define and identify the tasks and products used in the programe and project support infrastructure.

Decision trees

A diagram which describes the logic involved in a decision – often supported by estimates of the probability and potential outcome at those decision points which can enable an expected value to calculated.

Deliverable specification

A written definition of what deliverable the programme or project team is expected to produce or deliver.

Deliverable/product or task category code

A system of categories and codes which are developed uniquely to identify that particular deliverable, product or task in the form of an abbreviation. These codes should be designed to ensure that they respect or enable "family" trees of such deliverables, products or tasks to be easily identified.

Deliverable/staff database

A database of information which identifies which deliverables or products have been developed by which members of staff. (Used to identify which staff have relevant experience of developing that deliverable or type of deliverable).

Deliverables

An output from a development or procurement process which is recognised as a discrete piece of a programme or project.

Delphi technique

A technique used to assess an unknown situation. The technique consists of asking different teams to asses the situation, collating the reports, identifying those assessments that are at variance with the norm of the others, discussion of the reasons for the variance and a second or more subsequent rounds of such assessment, until a consensus is (or not) reached.

Dependencies

A relationship that exists between two activities/tasks or deliverables or products e.g. you cannot do the second until the first has finished.

Design consultant

A member of staff who provides advice or develops the design of a whole (or part of) a business system(s).

Design management plan

The plan developed for the management of the design aspects of a programme or project.

Development approach

The method that will be used to develop the outputs, deliverables or products required from the programme or project.

Development process

The sequence of processes used by the programme or project team to develop the outputs, deliverables or products required from the programme or project.

Direct financial benefits

Those financial benefits which are generated as a direct consequence of the programme or project.

Direct review (of quality)

The review of the process or item by its direct examination and assessment.

Discounted cash flow

A method of calculating the effect of "time preference" on an investment which spans over a number of years. Time preference refers to the preference that money today is worth more than the same money tomorrow - ignoring the effects of interest payments and inflation.

Displaced cost

Costs of operating the current business process that will no longer be needed when the programme or project is completed e.g. maintenance costs on a piece of equipment that will be eliminated by the programme or project.

Drop-down code

The function available in a software package which is invoked by selecting an icon which reveals a range of codes, which if they are selected, are automatically transferred into the working space in the software package. This working space can be a blank document or a proforma such as a timesheet.

DSDM

An acronym for the Dynamic Systems Development Method. A Rapid Application Development method used on IT projects.

Duration

A expression used in the planning process to describe the calendar or total time that an activity, output, deliverable, or product will take to complete. This includes pure work effort and any other related non project work or enforced delay that is needed to complete it .

Earned value

An expression used to that part of the planning and the progress monitoring and control processes, where a monetary value is assigned to the planned and actual work to enable a calculation to be made to assist in defining the current status of the programme or project.

Economic viability

The results of an assessment of the relationship between the inputs and outputs involved in a programme or project.

Economies of scale

The concept that increasing the volume of output or services of a unit reduces the unit cost of those outputs or services because the fixed costs involved are spread over a greater number of units.

Effort

This term is used in the planning and progress monitoring processes to describe the amount of pure work time needed to complete an activity, output, deliverable or product.

Ego less development

The concept of the removal of the personalisation of the execution of an activity, output, deliverable or product. e.g. this will be developed by an analyst rather than Mary Smith.

Elapsed (time)

The total time used to complete an activity, output, deliverable or product (*See also duration*).

End of stage report

A report produced by a project manager at the end of a stage which summarises the achievements of that stage, updates the plans for the overall project and provides the basis of the decision of the project board of whether or not, the project should continue to the next stage.

End of tranche report

A report produced by a programme manager at the end of a tranche which summarises the achievements of that tranche, updates the plans for the overall programme and provides the basis of the decision of the programme board of whether or not, the programme should continue to the next tranche.

Error list

A list of the potential errors or non-conformance to the defined standards, of an output, deliverable or product.

Estimating guidelines

A document which provides advice to the project or programme manager on the pure work effort, or elapsed time and or expenditure, that is required to complete a defined output, deliverable or product.

Estimating system

A mechanism used to produce estimates for a variety of situations from the same base data. e.g. if the situation is x then the estimates are y if the situation is z then the estimates are y + ...

Euromethod

An initiative started by the EC to have a standard project and system development method for IT projects. This method had defined interfaces to each of the open or standard project and system development methods that were used in each of the members of the EC.

Exceptions report/plan

A report produced by either a programme or project manager to notify the programme or project board that a situation has raised that has or will cause the programme or project to exceed its planned costs or delivery dates. This report may be supported with plans for the options available to the programme or project board for actions they could commission to remedy or recover from this situation.

Execution options

The various methods or approaches that could be used to execute a programme or project.

Executive management

The most senior level of management in the organisation.

Executive member

An executive or senior manager who has been appointed as the member of the project board who has the overall responsibility for the project.

First level decision

A part of the decision making process used to assess such things as issues, changes. The first level relates to the decision being made at the lowest level in the decision making process.

First level evaluation

A part of the decision making process used to evaluate the impact of such things as issues, changes. The first level relates to the evaluation being made at the lowest level in the decision making process.

First pass network chart

The inclusion on a network diagram for a programme or project of the estimates of cost or duration for each component and the calculation of its total cost or duration *(See also forward pass network analysis)*.

Formal review

A system of meetings and documentation of each of the steps in the review or assessment of an output, deliverable or product to ensure that it meets or matches its defined specification.

Forward pass network analysis

See – First pass network chart.

Gantt chart

Named after its inventor Henry Gantt. A chart used in the planning process which describes what activities, outputs, deliverables or products are to be developed or procured – in what sequence – and their start and finish dates.

Generic resources

A skill group in a plan or report, rather than a specific person.

Granularity

The various levels of detail – used in plans or progress reports.

Hard deliverables

Tangible outputs (things), deliverable or products developed or procured as part of a programme or project.

Highlight report

A report produced by the project manager to summarise the progress made over a defined period – usually a month.

Incidental costs

Those costs associated with the programme or

project which are not directly caused by it.

Indirect benefits

Benefits that are included in a business case which are not directly caused by, or the primary purpose of the programme or project - e.g. the new ...Will enable the organisation to also...

Indirect financial benefits

Financial benefits that are included in a business case which are not directly caused by or the primary purpose of the programme or project - e.g. the new .... Will enable the organisation to also...

Indirect review

The review of the item or process by its indirect examination and assessment by using other measures as a guide to its current status e.g. we have received no requests for changes therefore the arrangements we have made for the agreement of the requirements are satisfactory.

Informal Review

A system of documentation of each of the steps in the review or assessment of an output, deliverable or product to ensure that it meets or matches its defined specification.

Infrastructure projects

Those projects which are designed to provide systems or facilities that will be used by other processes. These projects cannot usually be directly linked to a specific goal or business target.

Integrated framework

A system of processes and information that are integrated e.g. the same reference number for an output, deliverable or product is used in the template plans, estimating guidelines, deliverable library, etc.

Integrated personal plan

A collation of the extracts of all plans which contains the work to be performed e.g. by a specific individual or machine.

Interfaces

The points at which one method, lifecycle or process meets and joins with, another method, lifecycle or process.

Intermediate review points

Those points in a programme or project where a progress review is carried out usually monthly, or when a defined event occurs e.g. a major milestone is either achieved or planned to be achieved.

Internal rate of return

A calculation used to asses if a programme or project will produce a defined rate of return (or percentage profit).

ISEB

The Information Systems Examination Board - a part of the British Computer Society which sets up and runs examinations and awards certificates in professional IT skills – e.g. programme and project support.

Islands of stability

The points in a programme which mark the end of a tranche. These are where either a significant part of the programme is delivered or a major commitment needs to be made. These are called islands of stability to illustrate that they provide a point at which a gap in the execution process occurs which can be used to reassess the situation.

Issue log

The document used to record details of all the issues raised during the programme or project.

Issue management

The management of the receipt, evaluation, decision making and relevant action relating to issues raised during a programme or project.

IT/IS strategies

The defined strategies for the deployment and use of information technology and information systems in the organisation.

Keeper of the vision

The members of staff who have the responsibility for ensuring that the vision of the programme or project is understood and that only authorised changes in that vision occur.

Knowledge capture

The process of gathering information from existing sources.

Lessons learnt report

A report which documents the lessons learnt during a programme or project that it is felt, will be of assistance to subsequent programmes or projects.

Levels of plan

The concept of having a structure of interlinking plans for a programme or project. This typical structure has a high level plan (little detail) for the whole programme or project. This is supported by more detailed plans for each tranche or stage, these in turn are supported by more detailed plans and so on.

Lifecycles

A term used to describe a collection of processes which are used to perform a business process from start to finish.

Logical entity

The operation of a business department predominately or exclusively through processes and functions that require little or no human intervention.

Logical implementation of a PSO

The operation of a PSO predominately or exclusively through processes and functions that require little or no human intervention.

Macro tuning/tailoring

The significant amendment of a method, process or standard to reflect the specific needs of a programme or project.

Maintainability risks

Those events identified in the risk analysis which may affect the ability of the organisation to maintain the outputs, deliverables or products from a programme or project.

Major decision points

Those points in the execution of either a programme or project where significant decisions need to be made as to its continuance or otherwise.

Major deliverables

Those deliverables which are considered as having a major importance to the successful completion of either a programme or project.

Major interdependencies

The dependencies between the outputs,

deliverables or product from one project with another which have a major impact on the delivery of the programme or project.

Making the case

The completion and acceptance of the business case for a recommended course of action.

Masterplan (portfolio)

The term used in this book to describe the documents and plans which describe all the programmes, projects and other activities that are managed by the masterplan committee.

Masterplan committee

The committee which is empowered by the organisation to ensure that the programmes, project and activities (the portfolio) which are commissioned will enable the organisation to meet its business strategy and plans. In addition to monitor the progress made with their execution and commission remedial action if necessary.

Masterplan portfolios

In some organisations the number of programmes or project may be so large that the masterplan may need to be subdivided into a series of masterplan portfolios.

Maximum cumulative cost

Part of the business case which shows the maximum total cost or expenditure that a programme or project will incur.

Mentor

An experienced member of staff working with a junior or new member of staff to help them to learn a new skill or improve the performance of their role.

Method of approach

The method, or collection and sequence of processes and outputs, deliverable or products that will be used to execute a programme or project.

METHOD ONE

A project or system development method developed by Andersen Consulting.

Metrics

An expression used to describe the production of statistics from an existing programme or project that will be used in the management of a future programme or project e.g. estimating information.

Micro tuning/tailoring

The detailed amendment of a method, process or standard to reflect the specific needs of a programme or project.

Milestones

Points in a programme or project that mark the significant points in their delivery which are used to measure progress achieved to that planned and to re-assess the remainder of the programme or project.

Minor decision points

Those points in the execution of programme or project where minor decisions may need to be taken as to its direction or method of development. (Usually identified as such in the project or system development method that is being used.)

Monitor/review/control cycle

The collection of processes used to monitor progress made, compare it to that planned, identify and analyse the reasons for any differences and the identification and commissioning of any necessary control action.

Monitoring and control process
The processes used in the monitor/review/control cycle.

Monte Carlo simulations
The use of a probability-based simulation method – called Monte Carlo because it is based on selecting the potential outcomes that are examined, by random chance.

Multi-level codes
The use of a code system which is hierarchical, e.g. the multi-level code for a business-as-usual activity might use the first part of the code to indicate the department, the second the type of work, the third the task type etc.

Multi-function technology driven projects
Projects which are driven by the availability and use of, a number of technologies.

Net present value (NPV)
The figure calculated in a business case which is the result of applying the discounted cash flow formulae to the costs and or benefits of a programme or project.

Network diagrams
The construction of diagram which represents the sequence of activities, outputs, deliverables or products that are to be produced or procured by a programme or project (part of the project network technique.)

Nine box matrix
A 3 x 3 matrix used to contain related information – particularly in estimating guidelines.

Non-productive work
A generic name for sickness, authorised absence, and holidays. (An organisations total workload consists of programmes or projects, business as usual and non-productive work).

Non-proprietary software tools
Software tools that do lock the user of the tools into other tools supplied by the same manufacturer – they may be either based on open or standard databases or allow easy transfer of information to and from them.

Off-shore development
The use of a programme or project team which is not based in the same location as the main part of the programme or project – usually where that team is located in another country.

On costs
Additional costs added to the prime or base costs to cover overheads and non productive cost.

Open or national methods and standards
The methods and standards which have been published and are in the public domain – i.e. they can be used by others. These can usually can be used without charge.

OSINTOT
An acronym for OH Surprise I Never Thought Of That! This describes the reason for using methods and lifecycle to provide the

programme and project managers as guidance as to what needs to be done to execute the programme and project and thus, avoiding the realisation later on, that they have forgotten or did not know what was should have been done.

Output flow diagram

A diagram similar to a network diagram which shows the sequence of production or procurement of the outputs from a programme or project.

Output, deliverable or product quality review process

The process used to conduct a review of an output, deliverable or product to ensure it meets its specification and is therefore fit for purpose.

Output

A defined outcome of an activity that is used to execute a programme or project. (Sometimes called a deliverable or product).

Outsourced

The sub-contracting or commissioning of a business process, or producing an output or deliverable to an organisation external to the organisation which commissioned it.

Owner of the Vision

The member of the management team who has been designated as the prime mover in a programme or project (sometimes known as the champion, requester or sponsor).

Parallel running

The trial running of a new business process or system at the same time as the original. This is to confirm that the new process or system produces the same results, outputs or service level as the existing one before switching over to the new business process or system.

PERT (Project Evaluation or Review Technique)

The name given to a special type of project network technique which like a decision tree uses probabilities and a range of possible duration's or costs for each of the activities. This is used to produce an overall expected outcome for the whole programme or project.

Physical implementation of a PSO

The operation of a PSO predominately or exclusively through processes and functions that are driven by and involve, members of the PSO.

Portfolio

A collection of programmes or projects or other activities which the organisation wish to collect together and manage as a set.

Post programme or post project review

A review carried out sometime after the programme or project has been completed to identify whether the programme or project met its objectives and any lessons that were learnt.

PRINCE

The latest version which is widely used is PRINCE2.

Probability/impact grids

A matrix which is used to contain a range of information relating to the assessment of the impact of an event on the programme or project and the probability of that event occurring.

Procedures

A set of defined steps that form part of a process.

Process engineering tool

A specialist software tool that enables the organisation to develop a new process and to provide support for the use of that process, in the form of example deliverables, estimates template plans etc.

Process maps

A diagram which describes all the processes in a specific method or lifecycle.

Processes

A series of steps that are followed to perform a specific activity or achieve a defined output.

Product breakdown structure

A hierarchical chart which describes all the products in the programme or project and their sub-components.

Product descriptions

A document used to define the product given to its developer or procurer, to ensure they provide what is wanted by the programme or project.

Product flow diagram

A chart similar to a network diagram but using products rather than activities.

Products

An output or deliverable generated from an activity in a programme or project.

Programme

A number of projects, workpackages and initiatives which need to be managed as a composite set.

Programme (management) documentation

The documents used by the programme manager to manage and control the programme.

Programme and project lifecycles

A series of processes with agreed roles and responsibilities, standards and techniques that are used to decide whether a programme or project should be commissioned, to ensure it is feasible, and that it is executed and completed according to the agreed resources and costs.

Programme and project management methods

A series of processes with agreed roles and responsibilities, standards and techniques that are used to manage a programme or project.

Programme and project team leaders

The members of staff who are responsible to the programme or project manager for the delivery of a part of the programme or project.

Programme and/or project contribution matrix

A document used to record the details of the projects which have been commissioned in order to complete the programme and the agreed level of contribution, that each of the projects make to the attainment of the programmes aims and objectives.

Programme and/or project management processes

The processes used by the programme and project managers to manage the programme and projects (part of the programme and project management methods).

Programme and/or project management support processes

The supporting processes used to assist the programme and project manager when using the programme or project management method. For example, template documents and reports, systems that collect or provide information used by the programme and project managers.

Programme and/or project planning software

Specialist software designed to support the programme and project manager in planning and monitoring of the activities and resources needed to execute the programme or project.

Programme and/or project support infrastructure

The collection of supporting processes, standards, information systems and other services provides to support the operation of programme and project management.

Programme benefits realisation

The activities that are performed to enable the programme to realise the benefits. The programme only provides the basic ingredients - the new processes, attitudes and products and services. The benefits are realised by the use or exploitation, of these new processes, attitudes and products and services. The realisation process is the arrangements made by the organisation to action the exploitation.

Programme board or executive

The members of executive level management who provide strategic guidance and assistance to the programme manager in achieving the programmes aims and objectives.

Programme brief

A small document usually produced as part of the programme commissioning process to initially define what the programme is to provide and its budget.

Programme closure and benefits sustainability

The fourth and final phase in a programme where the development activities have been completed – or the programme has been closed by the programme executive or board, and plans agreed for how the planned benefits will be realised and sustained.

Programme closure report

A report produced by the programme manager at the completion of the programme to measure the success of the programme in meeting its aims and objectives and the budgets set for it. It also includes a summary of the lessons learnt during the programme.

Programme definition

The second phase in a programme which leads to the production and agreement of the programme definition statement.

Programme definition statement (PDS)

A collection of documents including the programme plan and all the other documents which describe the arrangements made to manage the programme. This document is used as the basis of the monitoring and control of the execution of the programme.

Programme director

The member of executive level management who is responsible for the successful completion of the programme.

Programme execution

The third phase in a programme where the projects have been commissioned and are delivering the required outputs, deliverables and products.

Programme identification

The first phase in a programme where the blueprint for the programme is developed and agreed and the attitude change and communication plans are prepared.

Programme initiation

The formal initiation of the programme by the programme executive or board once they are assured that the programme, (as defined in the programme definition statement) will meet the requirements of the organisation.

Programme management

The processes, standards outputs and techniques used to manage a programme.

Programme management framework

The framework of processes, organisation structure, techniques and documents which can be deployed by the organisation to manage a programme.

Programme management method

The conversion of the programme management framework into a defined structure of processes, outputs and standards which is used when managing a programme.

Programme management process

The processes used to complete the four phases in a programme and to develop the prescribed outputs.

Programme manager

The manager responsible for the day-to-day management of the programme.

Programme or project code

The identification code allocated to a programme or project as part of the commissioning process to ensure that it can be uniquely identified.

Programme or project commissioning process/procedure

The process used in the programme or project lifecycle to commission a new programme or project.

Programme or project feasibility study report

The report which summarises the findings of the investigation carried out to determine the programme is economically or technically feasible and has a sound business case.

Programme or project idea form

A form containing an overview of the programme or project which is used during the programme and project lifecycle to start the process of that programme or project being considered for inclusion in the masterplan.

Programme or project liaison group

A group of relevant experts or interested parties that are used to provide the programme or project board with information, advice and other services to assist with the management of the programme or project.

Programme or project monitoring and control

The processes used to monitor the progress made with the programme or project to date and to assess whether control action is required. If control action is needed then these processes should provide sufficient information to the programme executive/board or project board to identify what action is needed.

Programme or project requestor

The member of the organisation who has requested the programme or project and will usually complete the programme or project idea form.

Programme or project risks

Events that may occur which will affect (positively or negatively) the programme or project.

Programme or project team costs

The costs of the programme or project team including prime and on costs.

Programme organisation structure

The structure of managers that is implemented to ensure the programme is managed efficiently and effectively.

Programme phases

The four phases that a programme is usually divided into - programme identification; programme definition; programme execution, monitoring and control; and programme closure, benefits realisation and sustainability.

Programme plan

A document which contains a description of the activities, resources and timescales need to complete the programme.

Programme progress reports

Reports produced by the programme manager about the progress made to date and an analysis of any variances that have occurred and the projected impact of those variances on the remainder of the programme.

Programme support office (PSO)

A department that is established to provide support to the organisation's programmes.

Programme tranche plan

A part of the programme plan which relates to one of the tranches. (This plan is usually in greater detail than that at programme level).

Project

A temporary structure of activities which are designed to produce a defined output to meet defined aims and objectives.

Project (management) documents

The documents used by the project manager to manage and control the project.

Project and system development methods documents

The documents used by the project manager to manage and control the project or system development processes.

Project assurance

The provision of assurance to the project board that the project's business integrity (business case) and technical integrity, (method of approach) is being maintained.

Project board

The group of senior managers who are responsible for the strategic direction and successful completion of it.

Project brief

A document developed as part of the project initiation process which provides the basis of the project initiation document.

Project champion

A senior manager who is the driving force behind the project and acts as an ambassador for the project.

Project closure report

A report produced by the project manager at the completion of the project to measure the success of the project in meeting its aims and objectives and the budgets set for it. It also includes a summary of the lessons learnt during the project.

Project filing and document management systems

The system of filing and management of the documents developed during the project. The system must interface with the other processes used by the project such as configuration management, issue and change management.

Project initiation

The formal initiation of the project by the project board having satisfied themselves that the project initiation document indicates that the project will meet its defined requirements.

Project initiation document (PID)

The document produced at the end of the project initiation process by the project manager to summarise the arrangements, plans and estimated budgeted resources needed to fulfil the projects aims and objectives.

Project management board

Another name for the *project board*.

Project management framework

The framework of processes, organisation structure, techniques and documents which can be deployed by the organisation to manage a project.

Project management method

The conversion of the project management framework into a defined structure of processes, outputs and standards which is used when managing a project

Project management process

The processes used to complete the phases in a project and to develop the prescribed outputs.

Project manager

The manager responsible for the day-to-day management of the project.

Project mandate

The initial terms of reference for the project - in some instances this is the project idea form – this is document is used to develop the project brief.

Project network technique

A technique defined as a British Standard which is used in the programme and project planning process to identify the sequence that the activities or outputs, deliverables or products should be developed and the resources (timescales, and costs) needed to complete the project. This information is then further refined before being translated into a Gantt chart and resource spreadsheet.

Project or system development methods

A defined set of processes, outputs, standards and techniques which is used as the basis of the project execution.

Project organisation structure

The structure of managers and their roles and responsibilities that is implemented to ensure the project is managed efficiently and effectively.

Project plans

A document which contains a description of the activities, resources and timescales need to complete the project.

Project progress reports

Reports produced by the project manager about the progress made to date and an analysis of any variances that have occurred and the projected impact of those variances on the remainder of the project.

Project status report

Reports produced by the project manager about the progress made to date and an analysis of any variances that have occurred and the projected impact of those variances on the remainder of the project.

Project steering committee

Similar to a project board but with no specific responsibility for the project.

Project Support Office (PSO)

A department that is established to provide support to the organisations projects.

Project team (members)

The members of the organisation and others allocated to the execution of the project.

Project/programme – strategy contribution matrix

A document used to record the details of the projects/programmes which have been commissioned in order to deliver the required business strategy and the agreed level of contribution, that each of the projects/programmes make to the attainment of the strategy.

Proprietary software tools

Those tools which use propriety databases or where the information contained in the tools cannot be easily transferred to other tools.

Pseudo project plans

Plans developed for business-as-usual and non-productive work which are used primarily for assessing how much effort is required and when it will be required and collecting actual expenditure, to ensure that all of the effort expended by the organisations staff is accounted for.

PSO implementation project

A project commissioned to design and implement a PSO.

PSO programme and project support infrastructure

The infrastructure of processes, standards, information systems and other method used by the PSO to support its operation.

'Pull then push' timesheets

A timesheet system which sends each member of staff a blank timesheet. Each person completes that timesheet by accessing the relevant programme or project or other plan and transferring those details to the timesheet. The timesheet is then sent to a central point where it is compared to the planned activities for that person and if any discrepancies are identified then the timesheet is returned to its author for amendment or confirmation.

'Pull' timesheets

A timesheet system which sends each member of staff a blank timesheet. Each person completes that timesheet which is then sent to a central point where it is compared to the planned activities for that person and if any discrepancies are identified then the timesheet is returned to its author for amendments or confirmation.

Pure work effort

The amount of effort needed to complete an activity, output, deliverable or product.

'Push then pull' timesheets

A timesheet system which sends to each member of staff a timesheet which is pre loaded with the work allocated to them in the programme, project or other plans.

Qualitative benefits

Benefits defined in the business case which relate to changes or improvement in quality.

Qualitative risk assessment

A method of risk assessment that results in an assessment of the impact on those risks in qualitative terms, such as it will be difficult to maintain or enhance.

Quality control review

A review of an output, deliverable or product to ensure that it conforms to its defined and agreed specification and is fir for purpose.

Quality management

A system of defined and agreed process and standards used to perform or deliver a defined service or product.

Quality plan

The arrangements made in a programme or project to ensure that it follows the agreed quality management system.

Quality review

A review of the quality management arrangements deployed in a programme or project to ensure that adequate and that they are being adhered to.

Quality review meeting

A meeting to review an output, deliverable or product and to identify any non conformance to its agreed specification.

Quality standards

The standards or criteria that will be used to assess if the output, deliverable or product is fit for purpose.

Quantitative benefits

Benefits identified in a business case which are quantified e.g. will save £X per year, increase sales to...

Quantitative risk assessment

A method of risk assessment that results in an assessment of the impact on those risks in quantitative terms such as it will be late by x weeks, or will cost £x less.

RAD

Rapid Application Development method of approach. This refers to the use of techniques which minimise the time needed to complete a programme or project.

Radar charts

A graphical representation of the current status of the programme or project which looks like a radar screen.

Realisation of business benefits

The process of exploiting the changes provided by the programme or project to provide the organisation with the defined benefits.

Recharge basis

A method of operating a PSO where the programme or project manager is charged for the services provided to them by the PSO.

Recurring costs

Those costs identified in a business case which recur each year - for example the cost of maintenance of a new item of machinery.

Re-inventing the wheel syndrome

A phrase used to describe rediscovering knowledge that has already been gained, or repeating mistakes.

Repository

A database (either manual or computer based) which is used to store all relevant information about the organisation's programmes and projects.

Residual value

The written down value of a capital item at the end of the period, used in the business case to assess the financial integrity of the programme or project.

Resource category/code

A system of codes used to uniquely identify a resource.

Resource management system

A "use booking" system used by a resource or line manager to ensure the effective deployment and allocation of the available resources.

Resource manager

The manager responsible for the resources. (Human or machinery or…)

Resource register

A record of all the resources of the organisation. This should interface other related processes and information systems.

Resource usage

The planned use of resources in a project or programme.

Resources usage spreadsheet

A summary of all the resources required by the programme or project which is displayed in a format similar to that of a spreadsheet.

Resourcing plan

A document which describes the resources required by the programme or project.

'Responsibility flip over'

A description of the situation that the use of a programme or project organisation structure is designed to prevent, in that the senior management are not aware of their responsibilities as a member of the programme or project board and concentrate on tactical matters rather than the strategic direction.

Results management

A phrase used to describe the overall collection of information about all the activities of an organisation in order to assess whether the organisation is deploying its resources effectively.

Review error list

The list of potential errors identified by the reviewers which are discussed with the producer or developer of the product either at a formal review meeting or an informal review discussion.

Reviewer (quality review)

A defined role in the quality control review process which is responsible for identifying any discrepancies between the output, deliverable or product and its specification.

Risk

An event (positive or negative) that may occur and effect the programme or project.

Risk analysis

The process used to identify the potential risks to the programme or project and their impact.

Risk checklist

A list of the risks identified in previous programmes and projects which are used in the risk analysis process.

Risk identification workshop

The workshop used to identify the risks and assess their impact on the programme or project.

Risk library

A list of both the risks identified in previous programmes and projects and the risk management, containment or assurance measures that were used and their success or failure.

Risk log

A list of the risks identified as relevant to this programme or project and the measures or actions deployed to manage them.

Risk management

The generic name given to the risk identification, impact assessment and management, containment, avoidance, or insurance strategy, action plan and review of the effectiveness processes.

Risk management history file

A file which provides a complete history of each risk - from their initial identification through to their removal from the risk log.

Risk management monitoring sheet

A document which contains details of all the active risks and the measures being used to manage them.

Risk management plan

A plan which describes the way that the risk

management processes will be operated and monitored in a specific programme or project.

Risk management strategy

The strategy applied to each risk i.e. whether it will be managed, contained, avoided, or insured.

Risk Register

A list of the risks that need to be considered by each programme or project. OR The term is also often used to also describe the list of risks that were identified for a specific programme or project.

RISKMAN

A risk management method which was developed by the EC as part of the EUREKA initiative.

'Rule of nine'

This rule refers to the number of discussions needed to arrive at a decision, if the programme or project does not have a defined organisation structure and roles and responsibilities.

'Rule of seven'

This rule refers to the size of the increase in detail or complexity that is needed when a plan is decomposed to a lower level.

'Rule of six'

This rule refers to the number of codes that should be used at each level in a multi level code system.

Runaway programme or project

An expression used to describe a programme or project in which the programme or project board and or the programe or project manager, have lost control and it has taken on a life of its own.

Schedule variance(s)

The difference between the planned or baselined dates for the delivery of the outputs, deliverables and products and that actually achieved. (How late or early is the programme or project.)

Scribe (quality review)

The member of the quality review team that is responsible for ensuring that the decisions made at the review meeting are recorded.

Second level decision

A part of the decision making process used to assess such things as issues, changes. The second level relates to the decision being made at the highest level in the decision making process.

Second level evaluation

A part of the decision making process used to evaluate the impact of such things as issues, changes. The second level relates to the evaluation being made at the highest level in the decision making process.

Second pass network chart

The inclusion in a network diagram for a programme or project of the calculation of the float available for each of the activities (and thereby the programme's or project's critical path).

Security risks

Those risks which affect the security of the new

business system, or by implication, the security of the other business systems affected by the introduction of the new business system.

Senior management

Those managers which are not executive level and not first line managers.

Senior supplier

A member of a project board who is responsible for providing the resources required to execute the project.

Senior user

A member of the project board who is to represent the end users or customer of the output, deliverables or products from the project.

Sign-off

The acceptance by the customer or user or reviewer that the output, deliverable or product is fit for purpose or use.

Simulation tools

The software and other tools used to simulate the operation of business or other process, so that its effectiveness or efficiency can be assessed.

Single function projects

Those projects which are commissioned to provide a single new business function.

Skeleton project plans

A project plan which has the minimum amount of information e.g. a list of tasks, dates, estimates and allocated generic resources.

Skills database

A database which contains a list of the skills of the members of staff who are available to be used in the execution of the programmes and projects.

'So what?' test

This term relates to a method which can be used on intangible or qualitative benefits to identify any partial quantitative measures of the benefits that may apply.

Soft deliverables

Those deliverables which improve the quality of the service and which do not produce easily recognised benefits.

Soft or people-driven projects

Those projects which predominately involve changes in attitude or working practices and are primarily involve the staff of an organisation. (Soft here is used to describe that these projects involve people, not things (hard deliverables).

Soft systems analysis

An analysis method which identifies various views of the components of a business or other system.

Sponsor

The member of executive or senior management who has agreed to act as the ambassador or champion for the programme or project. This person usually has a vested interest in the programe or project.

SSADM

An acronym for Structured Systems Analysis and Design Method. The UK Government's standard project or systems development for IT projects.

Stage plan

A plan which describes only one specific stage of a project.

Strategic and business planning functions

The functions in an organisation which are responsible for the development, updating and review of the strategic and business plans.

Strategic and business risk analysis

The application of the risk analysis process to the strategic and business areas that may affect either a programe or project.

Strategic decision making process

The process used by the organisation to decide its business strategy.

Strategic guidance

The guidance provided by the programme or project board as to what the course of action the programme or project should follow.

Strategic plan

The plan which describes how the business strategy will be delivered.

Supporting software tools

Those software tools which support the operation of the PSO, or a programme or project manager.

Supporting tools

Those other tools which support the operation of the PSO, or a programme or project manager.

Task

A part of an activity – the lowest unit of work in a plan.

Team managers

The manager of the team allocated to execute part of a programme or project.

Team plan

A plan of the work to be performed by a specific team in a programme or project.

Technical assurance

The vetting of the technical matters of the programme or project by an independent expert, to assure the programme or project board that the technical issues are being dealt with appropriately.

Technical design integrity

The assurance that the technical design of the programme or project conforms to relevant independent standards.

Technical design manager

The manager appointed to the programme executive or board to oversee the technical design aspects of the programme and to provide assurance to the organisation of the integrity of the technical design.

Technical development stage

A part of a project or system development method which represents a complete output, deliverable or product, that its completion marks a significant part of that method.

Technical infrastructure

The equipment and machinery installed by the

organisation to support its operations e.g. the computer network.

Technical integrity

The assurance that the technical aspects of the programme or project conforms to relevant standards.

Technical viability

The ability of the proposed technical solution to be developed and perform to, agreed budgets and requirements.

Techniques

Methods used to perform specific tasks e.g. planning a programme or project

Technology driven projects

Those projects which are driven by the availability of a specific technology.

Template deliverables

Those deliverables from previous programmes and projects that have been converted to "shell" documents (any programme or project specific details have been removed) so that they can be used on subsequent programmes or projects.

Template plans

Those plans from previous programmes or projects or plans, which conform to the organisation's standard methods, (e.g. project or systems development methods) which are provided to programme and project managers as a start point for the programme or project plan.

Templates

A generic term to describe any template document or plan that is provided.

Terms of reference

A definition of what either the programme or project should provide or what role or function an individual should perform.

The 'M's'

An expression used in this book to describe the resources used in a programe or project – Manpower, Money, Minutes (time), Materials, Machinery, Mortar (Bricks and mortar – buildings)

Timesheet system

A manual or software driven process which distributes and collects timesheets.

Timesheets

A document that that is used to record details of the activities performed by a member of the organisation.

Tolerance

An allowance made in addition to the agreed budget in respect of time and other resources to the programme and project manager within which they are allowed to operate or use before they notify the programme or project board. This tolerance is given to cover the impact of the inaccuracy of the estimates and unexpected events. (See also contingency which is apart of tolerance).

Traffic light reports

A type of progress reports which explains the current status of an aspect of the programe or project in the form of a traffic light colour – red problems; amber some concerns; green no problems.

Tranche

A discrete part of a programme that represents a significant part of, or the delivery of parts of the benefits, of the programme.

Transition management

The management plan used to describe how the programme or project will manage the implementation of the changes between the old methods of working and the new one, provided by the programme or project.

Trend analysis

An analysis of the trends that may be occurring for example in the patterns of programmes or project undertaken by the organisation or in the methods of approach used in their execution.

Understood standards

Those standards which are regarded by the member's of the organisation as being relevant to a particular situation, but are not documented or formally agreed.

User Costs

The cost of the users involvement in the design, development and implementation of the programe or project.

Vision statement

That part of the programme blueprint or the project documentation that describes the vision of what the programe or project is to provide.

Walkthrough

The process used in a quality control review where the output, deliverable or product is examined systematically - line by line or demonstrated step by step.

'What if?' analysis

The analysis carried out to examine the consequences of a specific action or event.

Work breakdown structure

The decomposition of the activities used to execute a programe or project into its component tasks.

Work flow

The construction of a business process that uses technology to move the document or other piece of work between the various procedures or steps.

Work packages

A collection of products into a discrete group.

Working practices

The methods and rules used to perform a task or activity.

Worksheet

A list of the tasks, activities, outputs, deliverables or products that must be produced e.g. by an individual or a machine.